Focus on GRAMMAR **1**

THIRD EDITION

Irene E. Schoenberg

Jay Maurer

ALWAYS LEARNING

PEARSON

Focus on Grammar 1: An Integrated Skills Approach, Third Edition

Pearson Education, 10 Bank Street, White Plains, NY 10606

Staff credits: The people who made up the *Focus on Grammar 1, Third Edition* team,
representing editorial, production, design, and manufacturing, are John Barnes, Andrea Bryant,
Elizabeth Carlson, Tracey Cataldo, Aerin Csigay, Dave Dickey, Christine Edmonds,
Nancy Flaggman, Ann France, Lise Minovitz, Barbara Perez, Robert Ruvo, and Debbie Sistino.

Cover image: Shutterstock.com
Text composition: ElectraGraphics, Inc.
Text font: New Aster

Library of Congress Cataloging-in-Publication Data

Schoenberg, Irene, 1946–
   Focus on grammar. 1: an integrated skills approach / Irene E. Schoenberg, Jay Maurer. -- 3rd ed.
      p. cm.
   Includes index.
   ISBN 0-13-245591-9 — ISBN 0-13-254647-7 — ISBN 0-13-254648-5 — ISBN 0-13-254649-3 —
ISBN 0-13-254650-7 1. English language—Textbooks for foreign speakers. 2. English language—
Grammar—Problems, exercises, etc. I. Maurer, Jay. II. Title.
   PE1128.S3456824 2011
   428.2'4—dc22
                                                                                              2011014126

PEARSON LONGMAN ON THE **WEB**

Pearsonlongman.com offers online
resources for teachers and students. Access
our Companion Websites, our online catalog,
and our local offices around the world.

Visit us at **pearsonlongman.com**.

Printed in the United States of America

ISBN 10: 0-13-245591-9
ISBN 13: 978-0-13-245591-6

4 5 6 7 8 9 10—V082—16 15 14

ISBN 10: 0-13-248412-9 (with MyLab)
ISBN 13: 978-0-13-248412-1 (with MyLab)

1 2 3 4 5 6 7 8 9 10—V082—16 15 14 13 12 11

Contents

WELCOME TO FOCUS ON GRAMMAR

Now in a new edition, the popular five-level *Focus on Grammar* course continues to provide an integrated-skills approach to help students understand and practice English grammar. Centered on thematic instruction, *Focus on Grammar* combines controlled and communicative practice with critical thinking skills and ongoing assessment. Students gain the confidence they need to speak and write English accurately and fluently.

NEW for THIS EDITION

VOCABULARY

Key vocabulary is highlighted, practiced, and recycled throughout the unit.

PRONUNCIATION

Now, in every unit, pronunciation points and activities help students improve spoken accuracy and fluency.

LISTENING

Expanded listening tasks allow students to develop a range of listening skills.

UPDATED CHARTS and NOTES

Target structures are presented in a clear, easy-to-read format.

NEW READINGS

High-interest readings, updated or completely new, in a variety of genres integrate grammar and vocabulary in natural contexts.

NEW UNIT REVIEWS

Students can check their understanding and monitor their progress after completing each unit.

MyFocusOnGrammarLab

An easy-to-use online learning and assessment program offers online homework and individualized instruction anywhere, anytime.

Teacher's Resource Pack   One compact resource includes:

THE TEACHER'S MANUAL: General Teaching Notes, Unit Teaching Notes, the Student Book Audioscript, and the Student Book Answer Key.

TEACHER'S RESOURCE DISC: Bound into the Resource Pack, this CD-ROM contains reproducible Placement, Part, and Unit Tests, as well as customizable Test-Generating Software. It also includes reproducible Internet Activities and PowerPoint® Grammar Presentations.

THE *FOCUS ON GRAMMAR* APPROACH

The new edition follows the same successful four-step approach of previous editions. The books provide an abundance of both controlled and communicative exercises so that students can bridge the gap between identifying grammatical structures and using them. The many communicative activities in each Student Book provide opportunities for critical thinking while enabling students to personalize what they have learned.

- **STEP 1: GRAMMAR IN CONTEXT** highlights the target structures in realistic contexts, such as conversations, magazine articles, and blog posts.

- **STEP 2: GRAMMAR PRESENTATION** presents the structures in clear and accessible grammar charts and notes with multiple examples of form and usage.

- **STEP 3: FOCUSED PRACTICE** provides numerous and varied controlled exercises for both the form and meaning of the new structures.

- **STEP 4: COMMUNICATION PRACTICE** includes listening and pronunciation and allows students to use the new structures freely and creatively in motivating, open-ended speaking and writing activities.

Recycling

Underpinning the scope and sequence of the *Focus on Grammar* series is the belief that students need to use target structures and vocabulary many times, in different contexts. New grammar and vocabulary are recycled throughout the book. Students have maximum exposure and become confident using the language in speech and in writing.

Assessment

Extensive testing informs instruction and allows teachers and students to measure progress.

- **Unit Reviews** at the end of every Student Book unit assess students' understanding of the grammar and allow students to monitor their own progress.

- Easy to administer and score, **Part and Unit Tests** provide teachers with a valid and reliable means to determine how well students know the material they are about to study and to assess students' mastery after they complete the material. These tests can be found on MyFocusOnGrammarLab, where they include immediate feedback and remediation, and as reproducible tests on the Teacher's Resource Disc.

- **Test-Generating Software** on the Teacher's Resource Disc includes a bank of *additional* test items teachers can use to create customized tests.

- A reproducible **Placement Test** on the Teacher's Resource Disc is designed to help teachers place students into one of the five levels of the *Focus on Grammar* course.

COMPONENTS

In addition to the Student Books, Teacher's Resource Packs, and MyLabs, the complete *Focus on Grammar* course includes:

Workbooks Contain additional contextualized exercises appropriate for self-study.

Audio Program Includes all of the listening and pronunciation exercises and opening passages from the Student Book. Some Student Books are packaged with the complete audio program (mp3 files). Alternatively, the audio program is available on a classroom set of CDs and on the MyLab.

THE *FOCUS ON GRAMMAR* UNIT

Focus on Grammar introduces grammar structures in the context of unified themes. All units follow a **four-step approach**, taking learners from grammar in context to communicative practice.

STEP 1 GRAMMAR IN CONTEXT

This section presents the target structure(s) in a natural context. As students read the **high-interest texts**, they encounter the form, meaning, and use of the grammar. **Before You Read** activities create interest and elicit students' knowledge about the topic. **After You Read** activities build students' reading vocabulary and comprehension.

Vocabulary exercises improve students' command of English. Vocabulary is **recycled** throughout the unit.

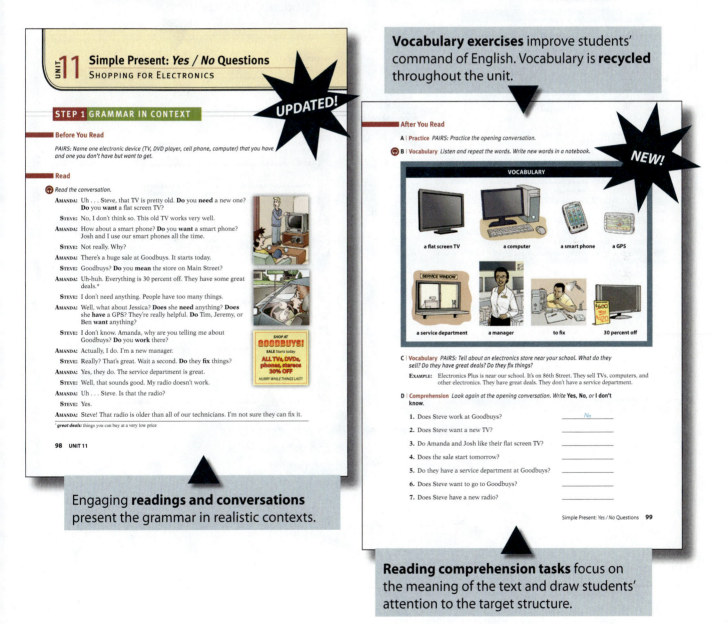

Engaging **readings and conversations** present the grammar in realistic contexts.

Reading **comprehension tasks** focus on the meaning of the text and draw students' attention to the target structure.

STEP 2 GRAMMAR PRESENTATION

This section gives students a comprehensive and explicit overview of the grammar with detailed **Grammar Charts** and **Grammar Notes** that present the form, meaning, and use of the structure(s).

Grammar Charts present the structure in a clear, easy-to-read format.

Grammar Notes give concise, simple **explanations** and **examples** to ensure students' understanding.

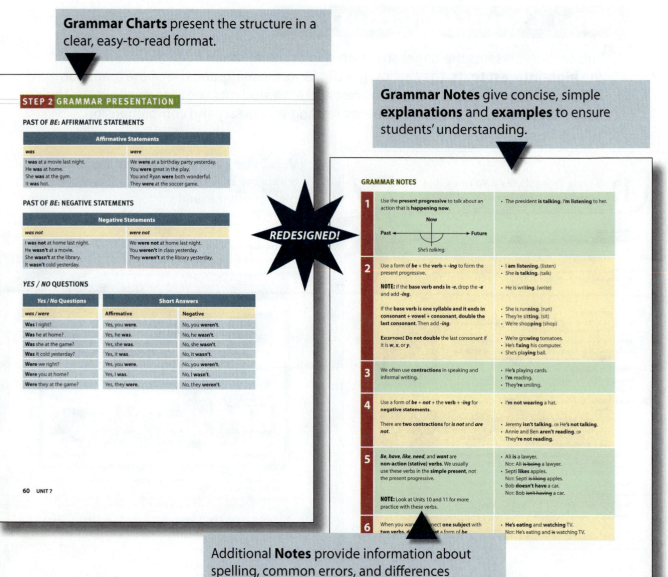

REDESIGNED!

Additional **Notes** provide information about spelling, common errors, and differences between spoken and written English.

Controlled practice activities in this section lead students to master form, meaning, and use of the target grammar.

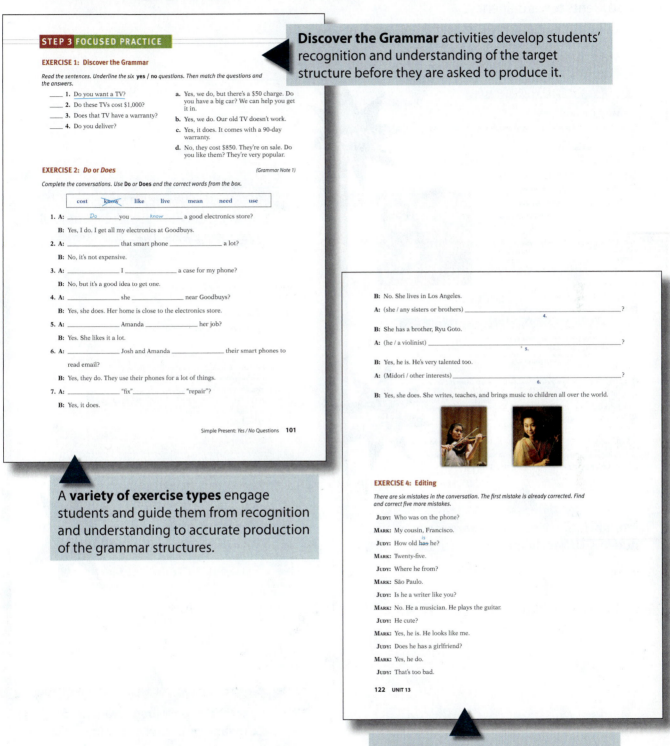

STEP 3 FOCUSED PRACTICE

EXERCISE 1: Discover the Grammar

Read the sentences. Underline the six **yes** / **no** *questions. Then match the questions and the answers.*

_____ **1.** Do you want a TV?

_____ **2.** Do these TVs cost $1,000?

_____ **3.** Does that TV have a warranty?

_____ **4.** Do you deliver?

a. Yes, we do, but there's a $50 charge. Do you have a big car? We can help you get it in.

b. Yes, we do. Our old TV doesn't work.

c. Yes, it does. It comes with a 90-day warranty.

d. No, they cost $850. They're on sale. Do you like them? They're very popular.

EXERCISE 2: Do or Does   *(Grammar Note 1)*

Complete the conversations. Use **Do** *or* **Does** *and the correct words from the box.*

cost	~~know~~	like	live	mean	need	use

1. A: _____Do_____ you _____know_____ a good electronics store?

B: Yes, I do. I get all my electronics at Goodbuys.

2. A: _____ that smart phone _____ a lot?

B: No, it's not expensive.

3. A: _____ I _____ a case for my phone?

B: No, but it's a good idea to get one.

4. A: _____ she _____ near Goodbuys?

B: Yes, she does. Her home is close to the electronics store.

5. A: _____ Amanda _____ her job?

B: Yes. She likes it a lot.

6. A: _____ Josh and Amanda _____ their smart phones to read email?

B: Yes, they do. They use their phones for a lot of things.

7. A: _____ "fix" _____ "repair"?

B: Yes, it does.

Simple Present: Yes / No Questions   **101**

Discover the Grammar activities develop students' recognition and understanding of the target structure before they are asked to produce it.

A **variety of exercise types** engage students and guide them from recognition and understanding to accurate production of the grammar structures.

B: No. She lives in Los Angeles.

A: (she / any sisters or brothers) _____?

4.

B: She has a brother, Ryu Goto.

A: (he / a violinist) _____?

5.

B: Yes, he is. He's very talented too.

A: (Midori / other interests) _____?

6.

B: Yes, she does. She writes, teaches, and brings music to children all over the world.

EXERCISE 4: Editing

There are six mistakes in the conversation. The first mistake is already corrected. Find and correct five more mistakes.

JUDY: Who was on the phone?

MARK: My cousin, Francisco.

JUDY: How old ~~has~~ *is* he?

MARK: Twenty-five.

JUDY: Where he from?

MARK: São Paulo.

JUDY: Is he a writer like you?

MARK: No. He a musician. He plays the guitar.

JUDY: He cute?

MARK: Yes, he is. He looks like me.

JUDY: Does he has a girlfriend?

MARK: Yes, he do.

JUDY: That's too bad.

122   UNIT 13

An **Editing** exercise ends every Focused Practice section and teaches students to find and correct typical mistakes.

STEP 4 COMMUNICATION PRACTICE

This section provides practice with the structure in **listening** and **pronunciation** exercises as well as in communicative, open-ended **speaking** and **writing** activities that move students toward fluency.

Listening activities allow students to hear the grammar in natural contexts and to practice a range of listening skills.

STEP 4 COMMUNICATION PRACTICE

EXERCISE 5: Listening

A | *Judy is telling Mark about a new friend. Listen and answer the questions about Judy's friend Olivia.*

1. What does Olivia do? _____

2. Where is she from? _____

B | *Listen again. Complete the paragraph about Olivia. Then circle her in the picture.*

She's _____average_____ height and

_____ weight. She has _____

_____ hair. It's very _____.

She's a _____ saxophone

_____.

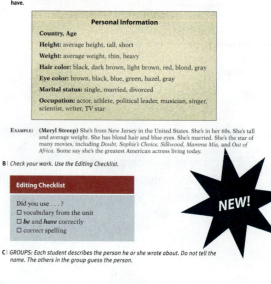

EXERCISE 6: Pronunciation

A | *Read and listen to the Pronunciation Note.*

> **Pronunciation Note**
>
> **The /h/ sound: /h/ is a breathing sound.**
>
> The **/h/** sound is sometimes dropped in the words *he, his, her, have,* and *has* when they are unstressed inside a sentence. The **/h/** sound is not dropped when those words start a sentence or are in short answers.

B | *Listen to the /h/ sound in the underlined words. Then listen again and repeat.*

His hair is black.
Last week his hair was gray.
He's a happy man.

I think he's sad.
Her husband is 40 years old.
I don't know her husband.

C | *Listen and repeat. Practice with a partner.*

A: Is he tall?
B: Yes, he is.

A: When does her concert start?
B: Her concert starts at 9:00.

A: What's his last name?
B: His last name is Kim.

A: Give him the tickets.
B: Where is he?

Simple Present: *Be and Have* **123**

Pronunciation Notes and **exercises** improve students' spoken fluency and accuracy.

Speaking activities help students synthesize the grammar through discussions, debates, games, and problem-solving tasks, developing their fluency.

EXERCISE 7: Describe People

Work with a partner. Describe one of the people in Exercise 5 to your partner. Your partner points to the person. Take turns.

EXERCISE 8: Writing

A | *Write a description of a famous person. Use the vocabulary from the unit. Use **be** and **have**.*

> **Personal Information**
>
> **Country, Age**
>
> **Height:** average height, tall, short
>
> **Weight:** average weight, thin, heavy
>
> **Hair color:** black, dark brown, light brown, red, blond, gray
>
> **Eye color:** brown, black, blue, green, hazel, gray
>
> **Marital status:** single, married, divorced
>
> **Occupation:** actor, athlete, political leader, musician, singer, scientist, writer, TV star

EXAMPLE: **(Meryl Streep)** She's from New Jersey in the United States. She's in her 60s. She's tall and average weight. She has blond hair and blue eyes. She's married. She's the star of many movies, including *Doubt, Sophie's Choice, Silkwood, Mamma Mia,* and *Out of Africa.* Some say she's the greatest American actress living today.

B | *Check your work. Use the Editing Checklist.*

> **Editing Checklist**
>
> Did you use . . . ?
> ☐ vocabulary from the unit
> ☐ *be* and *have* correctly
> ☐ correct spelling

C | *GROUPS: Each student describes the person he or she wrote about. Do not tell the name. The others in the group guess the person.*

124 UNIT 13

Writing activities encourage students to produce meaningful writing that integrates the grammar structure.

An **Editing Checklist** teaches students to correct their mistakes and revise their work.

Unit Reviews give students the opportunity to check their understanding of the target structure. **Answers** at the back of the book allow students to monitor their own progress.

UNIT 11 Review

Check your answers on page UR-1.
Do you need to review anything?

NEW!

EXERCISE A

Match the questions and answers.

_____ 1. Do you have a flat screen TV?   a. Yes, they do.

_____ 2. Do they fix radios?   b. No, I don't.

_____ 3. Does Josh have a smart phone?   c. Yes, he does.

_____ 4. Does this car have a GPS?   d. No, it doesn't.

EXERCISE B

Write **yes** / **no** *questions. Use* **do** *or* **does** *and the words in parentheses. Then answer the questions.*

1. (Steve's radio / work)

   A: _____?

   B: No, _____.

2. (the store / have radios)

   A: _____?

   B: Yes, _____.

3. (Tim and Jeremy / work at Goodbuys)

   A: _____?

   B: No, _____.

EXERCISE C

Correct the conversation. There are five mistakes.

A: Does you want to go to the park today?

B: Sorry. I need to get a gift for my sister. Do you

A: Sure. Does she likes music? CDs are a good gi

B: No, she don't.

A: Well, does she like books?

B: Yes, she is. Thanks. That's a great idea!

A section at the back of the book contains writing tasks for each part. Students are guided to practice the grammar in a piece of **extended writing**.

FROM GRAMMAR TO WRITING

PART I   USING *This is / These are*; SINGULAR AND PLURAL NOUNS

Write a Description

1 | *Take a photograph or draw a picture of your favorite room in your home. Write about five things. Say something about each thing. Use* **this is** / **these are** *with singular and plural nouns. Follow the model.*

MODEL

> This is an armchair. It's soft. It's my favorite chair. It's in my living room. These are my lamps. They're from my parents. They're beautiful.

2 | *Exchange papers with a partner. Did your partner follow directions and the model? Correct any mistakes in grammar and spelling.*

3 | *Talk to your partner. Discuss the mistakes you made. Then rewrite your own paper and make any necessary changes.*

PART II   USING THE PRESENT OF *Be*: QUESTIONS

Write Questions

1 | *Email a friend. Ask your friend four questions about his or her English class. Choose from the question words in the box. Follow the model.*

| Are | Is | What | Where | Who |

MODEL

> Hi Françoise,
>
> I hope your classes are good.
>
> Who's your new teacher? Where is your class? Are your classmates friendly? Are your classes interesting?
>
> I'm at work now, but I finish soon. Are you free for coffee at five o'clock?
>
> Abby

FG-1

SCOPE AND SEQUENCE

UNIT	READING	WRITING	LISTENING
1 page 2 **Grammar:** *This is / These are*; Subject Pronouns **Theme:** An Apartment	A monologue: Self-Introduction	Sentences about people in photos	A conversation about students and a teacher
2 page 10 **Grammar:** Singular and Plural Nouns; Proper Nouns; *A* and *An* **Theme:** Things in the Kitchen	A conversation: Things in the kitchen	Sentences about things in a classroom	A conversation about a restaurant
3 page 20 **Grammar:** Present of *Be*: Statements **Theme:** Meeting People	A conversation: Meeting visitors to a city	Sentences about your city	A meeting between a chef and a student
4 page 30 **Grammar:** *That is / Those are*; Possessive Adjectives **Theme:** Sightseeing in Seattle	A conversation: Sightseeing	Sentences about a photo of a place in your town	A conversation about children
5 page 38 **Grammar:** Present of *Be*: *Yes / No* Questions; Questions with *Who* and *What* **Theme:** A Wedding	A conversation: People at a wedding	*Yes / no* questions and *who* and *what* questions for an interview	A conversation about family and friends
6 page 48 **Grammar:** Present of *Be*: *Where* Questions; Prepositions of Place **Theme:** Giving Addresses	Emails: The address of a party	Sentences about the locations of places in your neighborhood	A conversation about directions and locations
7 page 58 **Grammar:** Past of *Be*: Statements, *Yes / No* Questions **Theme:** Movies and Other Pastimes	A conversation: An evening at the movies	Sentences about a movie, a play, a concert, or a game	Messages on a telephone answering machine
8 page 68 **Grammar:** Past of *Be*: *Wh-* Questions **Theme:** Travel and Leisure Activities	A conversation: A vacation	Sentences about your last vacation	A conversation about two friends' weekends

SPEAKING	PRONUNCIATION	VOCABULARY
Pair / Group Activity: Introductions *Class Discussion:* Photos of family or friends	*This* or *these*	a family, parents, father, mother, children, son, daughter, husband, wife, brother, sister, big, small, on the left, in the middle, on the right
Group Activity: Things in the home from A to Z *Memory Game:* Naming and remembering things in the home	Syllables and stress	a refrigerator, an egg, an apple, an orange, a pineapple, a knife, a fork, a spoon, a glass, an oven, a chicken, a stove, a pot, a counter, a muffin, a banana
Class Discussion: Your classroom *Pair Discussion:* The city you are in	Full forms and contractions	clean, dirty, delicious, awful, friendly, unfriendly, popular, unpopular, great, good, bad, terrible, expensive, reasonable, cheap
Pair Activity: Suggestions about leisure activities *Game:* Identifying students' possessions	*Your / you're; its / it's; their / they're*	a building, a camera, a park, a movie theater, a concert hall, a coffee shop, shapes
Pair Discussion: Occupations *Pair Activity:* Questions about classmates *Game:* Identifying famous people	Intonation in *yes / no* questions and questions with *who* and *what*	married, single, a writer, a travel agent, a nurse, a dentist, a teacher, a student, a clerk, a police officer, a mechanic, a cashier
Group Activity: Locations in a building *Pair Activity:* Locations in a neighborhood	Syllable stress in *-teen* and *-ty* numbers	a supermarket, a gym, a library, an apartment building, first, second, third, fourth, fifth, sixth, seventh, eighth, ninth, tenth
Pair Activity: Questions about past activities *Pair Discussion:* Leisure activities	*Was* or *wasn't; were* or *weren't*	alone, asleep, awake, funny, scary, interesting, boring, exciting
Pair Activity: Clarifying unclear statements *Group / Class Activity:* Asking where students have visited	*Wh-* question words	a vacation, a tour, a guide, the weather, sunny, windy, cloudy, rainy, hot, warm, cool, cold, freezing

UNIT	READING	WRITING	LISTENING
9 page 78 **Grammar:** Imperatives **Theme:** Giving Directions	A conversation: Finding a restaurant	Directions to a place near your school	A conversation between students about places in a building
10 page 87 **Grammar:** Simple Present: Statements **Theme:** Likes and Dislikes	A conversation: A brother	True statements about yourself	A conversation between strangers on a train
11 page 98 **Grammar:** Simple Present: *Yes / No* Questions **Theme:** Shopping for Electronics	A conversation: Electronic devices	Questions about electronic devices	A conversation about a gift for a grandmother
12 page 107 **Grammar:** Simple Present: *Wh-* Questions **Theme:** Cross-Cultural Differences	A conversation: Cross-cultural differences	Questions for a visitor from another country	A conversation about getting to work
13 page 117 **Grammar:** Simple Present: *Be* and *Have* **Theme:** Describing People	A conversation: A student's appearance	A description of a famous person	A conversation describing a musician
14 page 126 **Grammar:** Simple Present with Adverbs of Frequency **Theme:** Habits	A conversation: Habits and health	*Yes / no* questions about habits	A conversation between a grandmother and her grandson
15 page 136 **Grammar:** Present Progressive: Statements **Theme:** A Friend from Long Ago	An email: To an old friend	Present progressive sentences about photos	A conversation about photos
16 page 147 **Grammar:** Present Progressive: *Yes / No* Questions **Theme:** Babysitting	A conversation: Babysitting	Present progressive *yes / no* questions about a cartoon	A conversation about what children are doing

SPEAKING	PRONUNCIATION	VOCABULARY
Group Activity: Making requests *Pair Activity:* Giving directions using a map	/ɪ/ (*bit, hit*) or /i/ (*beat, heat*)	a gas station, a restaurant, a bus stop, a truck, a sign, empty, turn left, turn right, walk, drive, park, at the corner
True or False: Deciding whether sentences are true or false	Third-person singular present verb endings	look like, surf the Internet, a magazine, a novel, a newspaper, a blog, Arabic, Chinese, English, French, Portuguese, Russian, Spanish, Swahili
Pair Activity: Yes / no questions *Group Discussion:* Classmates' answers to questions	Stress on important words	a flat screen TV, a computer, a smart phone, a GPS, a service department, a manager, fix, 30 percent off
Pair Activity: Wh- questions *Information Gap:* Meanings of words	Sentence stress	go to bed early, stay up late, get up, take off your shoes, have breakfast, start work, have lunch, have dinner
Pair Activity: Describing people from a picture	The /h/ sound	tall, average height, short, thin, average weight, heavy, pregnant, wavy black hair, curly red hair, straight blond hair, dark brown hair, light brown hair
Pair Discussion: Your habits	The /r/ sound	fast food, broccoli, carrots, vegetables, green beans, fish, rice, donuts, meat, sweets, potatoes
Pair Activity: Comparing statements about yourselves	The /l/ sound	wear, sit, watch, smile, text, play cards, stand
Class Game: Pantomiming activities	The /tʃ/ and /ʃ/ sounds	babysit, help someone with homework, get a haircut, cut someone's hair, make a mess, worry, celebrate an anniversary, around five o'clock

UNIT	READING	WRITING	LISTENING
17 page 156 **Grammar:** Present Progressive: *Wh-* Questions **Theme:** Ways of Traveling	A conversation: A brother	An email to ask about a friend's visit to a foreign country	A conversation about present activities
18 page166 **Grammar:** Possessive Nouns; *This / That / These / Those* **Theme:** Clothing	A conversation: Looking good for an important event	A paragraph about birthday celebrations	A conversation about a dinner
19 page 176 **Grammar:** Count and Non-count Nouns; *Some* and *Any* **Theme:** Food	Interviews: Eating habits	A short composition about your favorite food or favorite dish	A conversation in a restaurant
20 page 187 **Grammar:** *A / An* and *The*; *One / Ones* **Theme:** Shopping for Clothes	A conversation: Shopping for clothing	Sentences about what is wrong in a picture	A conversation about going to a concert
21 page 196 **Grammar:** *Can / Can't* **Theme:** Abilities	A conversation: Students' problems in school	Sentences about special abilities of someone you know well	A conversation about dealing with school problems
22 page 208 **Grammar:** Simple Past: Regular Verbs (Statements) **Theme:** Business Trips	Email messages: A business trip	Sentences about yourself as a child	Phone messages
23 page 218 **Grammar:** Simple Past: Regular and Irregular Verbs; *Yes / No* Questions **Theme:** A Biography	A conversation: A student composition	A short biography about a famous person	A school interview with a foreign student
24 page 228 **Grammar:** Simple Past: *Wh-* Questions **Theme:** A Car Accident	Conversations: A car accident	A conversation about something that happened on the way to school	A conversation about paying for damage to a car

SPEAKING	PRONUNCIATION	VOCABULARY
Picture Discussion: Describing famous places	Intonation in *yes / no* and *wh-* questions	by car, by bus, by train, by subway, by metro, by plane, by bicycle, by boat
Picture Differences: Two pictures of students *Class Game:* Identifying owners of various items	The pronunciation of the *'s* in possessive nouns	a tie, a sports jacket, slacks, dress shoes, go well with
Pair Discussion: Food likes and dislikes *Class Discussion:* Favorite foods	Plural noun endings	a bagel, a cup of coffee, fruit, cereal, candy, yogurt, a sandwich, salad, a slice of toast
Picture Discussion: Clothing likes and dislikes	*A* and *an*	fit, a sale, try on, two sizes, bright, dull, formal, casual
Find Someone Who: Classmates able to do activities from a list *Find Someone Who:* Classmates able to do pictured activities	*Can* and *can't*: reductions and full forms	a team, a coach, a star, an idea, pass, fluent, sounds like a plan
True or False: Guessing which sentences are false	Regular simple past verb endings	a hotel, check in, check out, a convention, a presentation, arrive, stay, enjoy, miss
Class Activity: Past *yes / no* questions *Class Activity:* Reporting interesting answers to the *yes / no* questions	Reduction of *did* + /y/	be born, pick, act, move, give up, injure, die
Pair Activity: Interviewing each other about your past	Contracting *did* after *wh-* questions	an accident, headlights, a bumper, an auto repair shop, a dent, slippery

UNIT	READING	WRITING	LISTENING
25 page 238 **Grammar:** Subject and Object Pronouns **Theme:** Gifts and Favors	A conversation: A gift for a boss	Sentences about a time you gave a gift that made someone happy	A conversation about gifts for family members
26 page 247 **Grammar:** *How much / How many*; Quantity Expressions **Theme:** A trip to the Galápagos Islands	A conversation: A trip to Ecuador	Sentences about a trip to an interesting place	A news broadcast
27 page 257 **Grammar:** *There is / There are* **Theme:** Describing Places	A conversation: A visit to Mt. Rushmore	Sentences about a favorite place	A conversation between travelers
28 page 268 **Grammar:** Noun and Adjective Modifiers **Theme:** Personal Characteristics	Personal ads	An answer to a personal ad	A conversation describing a classmate
29 page 278 **Grammar:** Comparative Adjectives **Theme:** Planning a Get-Together	A conversation: Planning a party	A paragraph comparing two people	A conversation between a grandmother and grandson about his classes
30 page 288 **Grammar:** Prepositions of Time: *In, On, At* **Theme:** Leisure Activities	A conversation: Inviting someone to a party	A short letter describing a party	A telephone conversation about a trip
31 page 298 **Grammar:** Future with *Be going to*: Statements **Theme:** Sporting events	A conversation: A soccer game	A paragraph about something you are going to do in the future	A conversation at a soccer game
32 page 307 **Grammar:** Future with *Be going to*: Questions **Theme:** Career Plans and Goals	A conversation: A career change	An email about a friend's new job	Two conversations about someone who is going to have a baby

SPEAKING	PRONUNCIATION	VOCABULARY
Pair Discussion: Gifts for family and friends	Stress to clarify corrections	flowers, chocolates, a ride, tickets, a DVD, a gift certificate
Group Activity: Questions about spending habits	/dʒ/ and /y/ sounds	an island, the capital, an animal, a plant, a flight, only
Group Game: Remembering what people are packing for a trip	*There are / they are*; *there aren't / they aren't*	a drugstore, a bed-and-breakfast, a national park, a snack bar, a monument, a waterfall, an amusement park, a traffic jam
Group Activity: Describing people with adjectives from a list of opposites *Pair Activity:* Describing materials and fabrics of classroom items	Reduction of *and*	fun-loving man, honest man, artistic woman, personal ads, spy movies, chemistry professor, computer science major
Group Activity: Comparing people and things	The *th* sounds /ð/ and /θ/	a list, an invitation, entertainment, a game, snacks, pop music, beverages, desserts
Group Activity: Questions about activities using frequency abverbs	/æ/ and /ɑ/	have a barbecue, play volleyball, go shopping, go to a play, a two-story house, be free, of course, look forward to
Memory Game: What students are going to take on a trip to the Olympics	*Going to:* reductions and full form	basketball, baseball, football, soccer, hockey, swimming, skiing, gymnastics, running
Pair / Class Activity: Questions about what people in a picture are going to do	/b/ and /v/	a producer, national TV, a big part, awesome, a program, the news

ABOUT THE AUTHORS

Irene E. Schoenberg has taught ESL for more than two decades at Hunter College's International English Language Institute and at Columbia University's American Language Program. Ms. Schoenberg holds a master's degree in TESOL from Columbia University. She has trained ESL and EFL teachers at Columbia University's Teachers College and at the New School University. She has given workshops and academic presentations at conferences, English language schools, and universities in Brazil, Chile, Dubai, El Salvador, Guatemala, Japan, Mexico, Nicaragua, Peru, Taiwan, Thailand, Vietnam, and throughout the United States.

Ms. Schoenberg is the author of *Talk about Trivia*; *Talk about Values*; *Speaking of Values 1: Conversation and Listening*; *Topics from A to Z*, Books 1 and 2; and *Focus on Grammar 2: An Integrated Skills Approach*. She is the co-author with Jay Maurer of the *True Colors* series and *Focus on Grammar 1: An Integrated Skills Approach*. She is one of the authors of *Future 1: English for Results* and *Future 3: English for Results*.

Jay Maurer has taught English in binational centers, colleges, and universities in Spain, Portugal, Mexico, the Somali Republic, and the United States; and intensive English at Columbia University's American Language Program. In addition, he has been a teacher of college composition, technical writing, literature and speech at Santa Fe Community College and Northern New Mexico Community College. Mr. Maurer holds an MA and an MEd in applied linguistics and a PhD in the teaching of English, all from Columbia University.

Mr. Maurer is the co-author with Penny LaPorte of the three-level *Structure Practice in Context* series and author of *Focus on Grammar 5: An Integrated Skills Approach*. He is the co-author with Irene Schoenberg of the five-level *True Colors* series; the *True Voices* video series; and *Focus on Grammar 1: An Integrated Skills Approach*. Currently he lives and writes in Arizona and Washington state.

ACKNOWLEDGMENTS

The challenge of writing a new edition of **Focus On Grammar 1** has been above all one of keeping the materials that were the most simple, natural, and interesting; and one of deciding what to change. It was a task we could not do alone. We extend our thanks to our students, who helped us realize what made their eyes light up.

We are also grateful to the wonderful people at Pearson for their support and devotion to this project. In particular, we wish to thank the following:

- The people in design and production who helped carry the project through: **Rhea Banker, Ann France, Robert Ruvo**, and **Shelley Gazes**
- **Aerin Csigay**, who researched and found great photos to make the pages come alive
- **Lise Minovitz**, supervising editor, for her expert guidance and unflagging energy in keeping a very complex project on target
- **Joanne Dresner** for her original vision and guidance of the **Focus on Grammar** series
- **Debbie Sistino**, editorial manager, who, in addition to managing the entire series, was able to integrate the language skills more effectively by adding a pronunciation and vocabulary thread
- Finally, **John Barnes**, our development editor, who offered many thoughtful and perceptive comments and suggestions. We thank him for his dedication to the project, for being available to answer any and all of our questions, and for turning over material so quickly.
- As always, our thanks to our families for their love and support: **Harris, Dan, Dahlia, Jonathan, Olivia**, and **Priscilla**

I. E. S. and J. K. M.

REVIEWERS

We are grateful to the following reviewers for their many helpful comments:

Aida Aganagic, Seneca College, Toronto, Canada; **Aftab Ahmed**, American University of Sharjah, Sharjah, United Arab Emirates; **Todd Allen**, English Language Institute, Gainesville, FL; **Anthony Anderson**, University of Texas, Austin, TX; **Anna K. Andrade**, ASA Institute, New York, NY; **Bayda Asbridge**, Worcester State College, Worcester, MA; **Raquel Ashkenasi**, American Language Institute, La Jolla, CA; **James Bakker**, Mt. San Antonio College, Walnut, CA; **Kate Baldrige-Hale**, Harper College, Palatine, IL; **Leticia S. Banks**, ALCI-SDUSM, San Marcos, CA; **Aegina Barnes**, York College CUNY, Forest Hills, NY; **Sarah Barnhardt**, Community College of Baltimore County, Reisterstown, MD; **Kimberly Becker**, Nashville State Community College, Nashville, TN; **Holly Bell**, California State University, San Marcos, CA; **Anne Bliss**, University of Colorado, Boulder, CO; **Diana Booth**, Elgin Community College, Elgin, IL; **Barbara Boyer**, South Plainfield High School, South Plainfield, NJ; **Janna Brink**, Mt. San Antonio College, Walnut, CA; **AJ Brown**, Portland State University, Portland, OR; **Amanda Burgoyne**, Worcester State College, Worcester, MA; **Brenda Burlingame**, Independence High School, Charlotte, NC; **Sandra Byrd**, Shelby County High School and Kentucky State University, Shelbyville, KY; **Edward Carlstedt**, American University of Sharjah, Sharjah, United Arab Emirates; **Sean Cochran**, American Language Institute, Fullerton, CA; **Yanely Cordero**, Miami Dade College, Miami, FL; **Lin Cui**, William Rainey Harper College, Palatine, IL; **Sheila Detweiler**, College Lake County, Libertyville, IL; **Ann Duncan**, University of Texas, Austin, TX; **Debra Edell**, Merrill Middle School, Denver, CO; **Virginia Edwards**, Chandler-Gilbert Community College, Chandler, AZ; **Kenneth Fackler**, University of Tennessee, Martin, TN; **Jennifer Farnell**, American Language Program, Stamford, CT; **Allen P. Feiste**, Suwon University, Hwaseong, South Korea; **Mina Fowler**, Mt. San Antonio Community College, Rancho Cucamonga, CA; **Rosemary Franklin**, University of Cincinnati, Cincinnati, OH; **Christiane Galvani**, Texas Southern University, Sugar Land, TX; **Chester Gates**, Community College of Baltimore County, Baltimore, MD; **Luka Gavrilovic**, Quest Language Studies, Toronto, Canada; **Sally Gearhart**, Santa Rosa Community College, Santa Rosa, CA; **Shannon Gerrity**, James Lick Middle School, San Francisco, CA; **Jeanette Gerrity Gomez**, Prince George's Community College, Largo, MD; **Carlos Gonzalez**, Miami Dade College, Miami, FL; **Therese Gormley Hirmer**, University of Guelph, Guelph, Canada; **Sudeepa Gulati**, Long Beach City College, Long Beach, CA; **Anthony Halderman**, Cuesta College, San Luis Obispo, CA; **Ann A. Hall**, University of Texas, Austin, TX; **Cora Higgins**, Boston Academy of English, Boston, MA; **Michelle Hilton**, South Lane School District, Cottage Grove, OR; **Nicole Hines**, Troy University, Atlanta, GA; **Rosemary Hiruma**, American Language Institute, Long Beach, CA; **Harriet Hoffman**, University of Texas, Austin, TX; **Leah Holck**, Michigan State University, East Lansing, MI; **Christy Hunt**, English for Internationals, Roswell, GA; **Osmany Hurtado**, Miami Dade College, Miami, FL; **Isabel Innocenti**, Miami Dade College, Miami, FL; **Donna Janian**, Oxford Intensive School of English, Medford, MA; **Scott Jenison**, Antelope Valley College, Lancaster, CA; **Grace Kim**, Mt. San Antonio College, Diamond Bar, CA; **Brian King**, ELS Language Center, Chicago, IL; **Pam Kopitzke**, Modesto Junior College, Modesto, CA; **Elena Lattarulo**, American Language Institute, San Diego, CA; **Karen Lavaty**, Mt. San Antonio College, Glendora, CA; **JJ Lee-Gilbert**, Menlo-Atherton High School, Foster City, CA; **Ruth Luman**, Modesto Junior College, Modesto, CA; **Yvette Lyons**, Tarrant County College, Fort Worth, TX; **Janet Magnoni**, Diablo Valley College, Pleasant Hill, CA; **Meg Maher**, YWCA Princeton, Princeton, NJ; **Carmen Marquez-Rivera**, Curie Metropolitan High School, Chicago, IL; **Meredith Massey**, Prince George's Community College, Hyattsville, MD; **Linda Maynard**, Coastline Community College, Westminster, CA; **Eve Mazereeuw**, University of Guelph, Guelph, Canada; **Susanne McLaughlin**, Roosevelt University, Chicago, IL; **Madeline Medeiros**, Cuesta College, San Luis Obispo, CA; **Gioconda Melendez**, Miami Dade College, Miami, FL; **Marcia Menaker**, Passaic County Community College, Morris Plains, NJ; **Seabrook Mendoza**, Cal State San Marcos University, Wildomar, CA; **Anadalia Mendoza**, Felix Varela Senior High School, Miami, FL; **Charmaine Mergulhao**, Quest Language Studies, Toronto, Canada; **Dana Miho**, Mt. San Antonio College, San Jacinto, CA; **Sonia Nelson**, Centennial Middle School, Portland, OR; **Manuel Niebla**, Miami Dade College, Miami, FL; **Alice Nitta**, Leeward Community College, Pearl City, HI; **Gabriela Oliva**, Quest Language Studies, Toronto, Canada; **Sara Packer**, Portland State University, Portland, OR; **Lesley Painter**, New School, New York, NY; **Carlos Paz-Perez**, Miami Dade College, Miami, FL; **Ileana Perez**, Miami Dade College, Miami, FL; **Barbara Pogue**, Essex County College, Newark, NJ; **Phillips Potash**, University of Texas, Austin, TX; **Jada Pothina**, University of Texas, Austin, TX; **Ewa Pratt**, Des Moines Area Community College, Des Moines, IA; **Pedro Prentt**, Hudson County Community College, Jersey City, NJ; **Maida Purdy**, Miami Dade College, Miami, FL; **Dolores Quiles**, SUNY Ulster, Stone Ridge, NY; **Mark Rau**, American River College, Sacramento, CA; **Lynne Raxlen**, Seneca College, Toronto, Canada; **Lauren Rein**, English for Internationals, Sandy Springs, GA; **Diana Rivers**, NOCCCD, Cypress, CA; **Silvia Rodriguez**, Santa Ana College, Mission Viejo, CA; **Rolando Romero**, Miami Dade College, Miami, FL; **Pedro Rosabal**, Miami Dade College, Miami, FL; **Natalie Rublik**, University of Quebec, Chicoutimi, Quebec, Canada; **Matilde Sanchez**, Oxnard College, Oxnard, CA; **Therese Sarkis-Kruse**, Wilson Commencement, Rochester, NY; **Mike Sfiropoulos**, Palm Beach Community College, Boynton Beach, FL; **Amy Shearon**, Rice University, Houston, TX; **Sara Shore**, Modesto Junior College, Modesto, CA; **Patricia Silva**, Richard Daley College, Chicago, IL; **Stephanie Solomon**, Seattle Central Community College, Vashon, WA; **Roberta Steinberg**, Mount Ida College, Newton, MA; **Teresa Szymula**, Curie Metropolitan High School, Chicago, IL; **Hui-Lien Tang**, Jasper High School, Plano, TX; **Christine Tierney**, Houston Community College, Sugar Land, TX; **Ileana Torres**, Miami Dade College, Miami, FL; **Michelle Van Slyke**, Western Washington University, Bellingham, WA; **Melissa Villamil**, Houston Community College, Sugar Land, TX; **Elizabeth Wagenheim**, Prince George's Community College, Lago, MD; **Mark Wagner**, Worcester State College, Worcester, MA; **Angela Waigand**, American University of Sharjah, Sharjah, United Arab Emirates; **Merari Weber**, Metropolitan Skills Center, Los Angeles, CA; **Sonia Wei**, Seneca College, Toronto, Canada; and **Vicki Woodward**, Indiana University, Bloomington, IN.

Getting Started

CLASSROOM INSTRUCTIONS

EXERCISE 1: In Class

 Listen and read. Listen again and repeat.

Look at page 1.

Listen to the CD.

Read the sentence.

Write the word *English*.

Circle the word *English*.

Underline the word *English*.

Ask a question.

Answer the question.

EXERCISE 2: Working Together

PAIRS: Student A, read a sentence from Exercise 1. Student B, point to the sentence.
Take turns.

THIS IS / THESE ARE; SUBJECT PRONOUNS; NOUNS

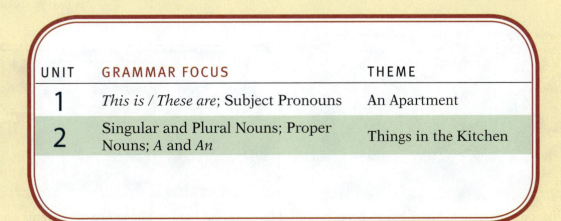

UNIT	GRAMMAR FOCUS	THEME
1	*This is / These are*; Subject Pronouns	An Apartment
2	Singular and Plural Nouns; Proper Nouns; *A* and *An*	Things in the Kitchen

This is / These are; Subject Pronouns
An Apartment

Before You Read

PAIRS: Look at the pictures. Point and name things you see.

Read

Read about Steve Beck.

Hi. **I**'m Steve Beck. **This is** my apartment in Seattle. **It**'s small but comfortable.

These are my CDs. **They**'re classical and jazz. **This is** my guitar.

These are my pets, Pam and Kip. **They**'re wonderful. Pam is eight years old and can talk. Kip is two years old.

We like our apartment. **We**'re happy here.

I have a great family. **These are** my parents on the left. **This is** my sister Jessica in the middle, with her husband and children.

After You Read

A | Practice *PAIRS: Practice the opening reading. Each person reads about one picture.*

B | Vocabulary *Listen and repeat the words. Write new words in a notebook.*

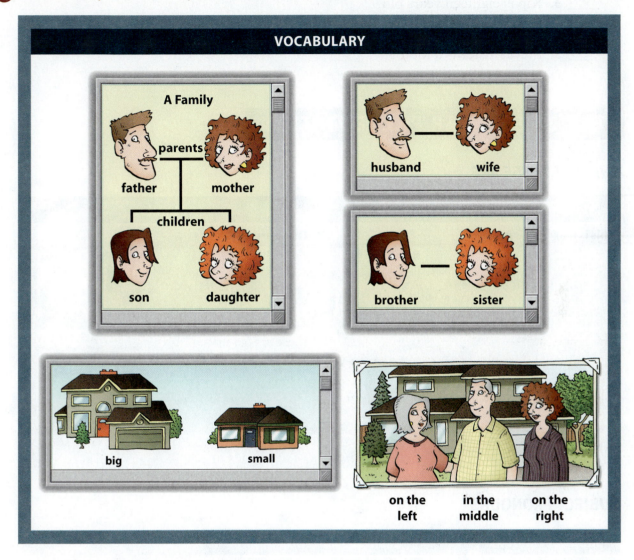

VOCABULARY

C | Vocabulary *Match the words and meanings.*

_e_ 1. **children**   **a.** in the center

____ 2. **father and mother**   **b.** a place to live

____ 3. **an apartment**   **c.** types of music

____ 4. **pets**   **d.** parents

____ 5. **classical and jazz**   **e.** son and daughter

____ 6. **in the middle**   **f.** animals in the home

D | Comprehension *Look again at the opening reading. Write* **T (True)** *or* **F (False).**

   F   **1.** Steve Beck's apartment is big.

   ____   **2.** Steve's CDs are classical and rock.

   ____   **3.** Kip is eighteen years old.

   ____   **4.** Steve is happy.

   ____   **5.** Steve's sister is a mother.

STEP 2 GRAMMAR PRESENTATION

THIS IS / THESE ARE

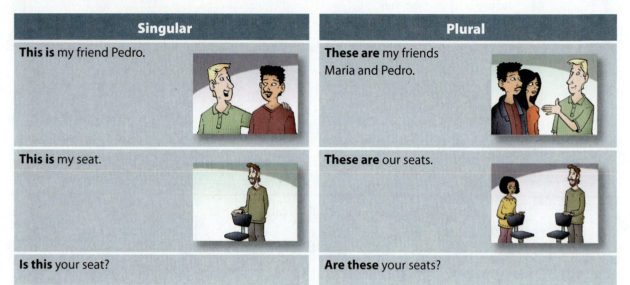

Singular	Plural
This is my friend Pedro.	**These are** my friends Maria and Pedro.
This is my seat.	**These are** our seats.
Is this your seat?	**Are these** your seats?

SUBJECT PRONOUNS

Subject Pronouns	Example Sentences
I	**I**'m Steve Beck.
you	Hi, Maria. How are **you**?
he	**He**'s a teacher.
she	**She**'s a reporter.
it	This is my apartment. **It**'s in Seattle.
we	The apartment is small, but **we**'re happy here.
you	Hi, Mom and Dad. How are **you**?
they	**They**'re wonderful.

GRAMMAR NOTES

1	Use **this is** to introduce or talk about **one** person or thing **near** you.	• **This is** my friend Pedro. • **This is** my seat.
2	Use **these are** to introduce or talk about **two or more** people or things **near** you.	• **These are** my friends Maria and Pedro. • **These are** our seats.
3	Use **Is this** and **Are these** to ask questions.	**Is this** your cat? Yes, it is. **Are these** your books? No, they aren't.
4	**I**, **you**, **he**, **she**, **it**, **we**, **you**, and **they** are **subject pronouns**. They replace a subject noun.	• **Pam and Kip** are my pets. **They**'re wonderful. • **Kip** is my cat. **He**'s smart.
	Use **contractions** (short forms) with pronouns in speaking and informal writing.	• I am = **I'm** • you are = **you're** • he is = **he's** • she is = **she's** • it is = **it's** • we are = **we're** • they are = **they're**
	NOTE: Use **it** or **he** or **she** to talk about an animal.	• **It**'s a big cat! OR **He**'s a big cat! OR **She**'s a big cat!

STEP 3 FOCUSED PRACTICE

EXERCISE 1: Discover the Grammar

Match the sentences.

___b___ **1.** These are my parents.

_____ **2.** These are my pets.

_____ **3.** This is my apartment.

_____ **4.** This is Jessica.

_____ **5.** This is Kip.

_____ **6.** These are my CDs.

a. He's my cat.

b. They're on the left.

c. She's my sister.

d. They're smart and wonderful.

e. They're classical and jazz.

f. It's in Seattle.

EXERCISE 2: *This* and *These*

Complete the sentences. Circle the correct answer. Use **this** *or* **these**.

1. **This /(These)** are my photos.

2. **This / These** is my mother.

3. **This / These** are my sisters.

4. **This / These** is my father.

5. **This / These** is my apartment.

6. **This / These** are my friends

7. **Is this / these** your cat?

8. **Are this / these** your keys?

EXERCISE 3: Subject Pronouns

(Grammar Note 4)

Complete the passage with **I, you, he, she, it, we,** *or* **they.**

This is Judy Johnson. ____*She*____'s a student at the
                              1.
University of Washington. Judy and her roommate,

Elena, live in an apartment. _____ like it.
                              2.
_____'s small but nice.
3.

Judy's parents telephone her sometimes: "Are

_____ OK?"
4.

"Yes, _____ am."
        5.

"How are your classes?"

"_____'re good, and _____ like Seattle a lot."
  6.   **7.**

Judy is in Steve Beck's journalism class at the university. Everyone likes Steve. "_____
                                                                                        8.
all think _____'s a very good teacher," Judy says.
          9.

EXERCISE 4: Editing

*There are five mistakes in the conversations. The first mistake is already corrected. Find
and correct four more mistakes.*

1. **A:** ~~These~~ is my friend Pedro.
   This

   B: Hi, Pedro.

2. **A:** This are my brothers.

   B: Hello. Nice to meet you.

3. **A:** This my partner, Ahmed.

   B: Hi, Ahmed.

4. **A:** Is these your books?

   B: No, they not.

EXERCISE 5: Listening

A | *Listen to the conversation. Write the names **Mr. Singer, Hai,** and **Yuan** under the people in the picture.*

_____   _____   _____

B | *Listen again. Complete the sentences. Circle the correct letter.*

1. Mr. Singer is a _____.
   a. teacher
   b. student

2. Mr. Singer is from _____.
   a. the United States
   b. Canada

3. Hai and Yuan are _____.
   a. friends
   b. brothers

4. Hai and Yuan are from _____.
   a. Canada
   b. China

EXERCISE 6: Pronunciation

A | *Listen to the sentences. Then listen again. Check (✔) **This** or **These**.*

	This	These			This	These			This	These
1.	✔	☐		**3.**	☐	☐		**5.**	☐	☐
2.	☐	☐		**4.**	☐	☐				

B | *PAIRS: Say a sentence, **a** or **b**. Your partner points to the correct sentence.*

1. a. This is my friend.   **b.** These are my friends.

2. a. These are my photos.   **b.** This is my photo.

3. a. These are our tickets.   **b.** This is our ticket.

4. a. This is my sister.   **b.** These are my sisters.

5. a. Is this your key?   **b.** Are these your keys?

EXERCISE 7: Introduce Yourself

A | *PAIRS: Read the conversation. Take turns.*

> **A:** I'm Steve Beck.
>
> **B:** Nice to meet you, Steve. I'm Sally Johnson.
>
> **A:** Nice to meet you too.

B | *Walk around the classroom. Meet four classmates. Introduce one classmate to the class.*

> **EXAMPLE:** This is my classmate, Eun Young.

EXERCISE 8: Talk about Photos

GROUPS: Bring photos of your family or friends to class. Talk about the photos.

> **EXAMPLE:** **A:** Is this your mother?
> **B:** Yes. She's in Lima right now.
> **C:** This is my boyfriend. He's in Tokyo.
> **D:** These are my friends. So-Young is on the right, and Ho-Jin is on the left.

EXERCISE 9: Writing

A | *Write four sentences about the people in the photos from Exercise 8. Use* **This is** *or* **These are** *and subject pronouns.*

> **EXAMPLE:** This is my friend Miryam. She's from Istanbul. She's 21 years old. She's a student at Istanbul University

B | *Check your work. Use the Editing Checklist.*

Editing Checklist
Did you use . . . ? ☐ *This is* or *These are* and subject pronouns correctly ☐ correct spelling

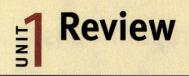

UNIT 1 Review

Check your answers on page UR-0.

Do you need to review anything?

EXERCISE A

*Complete the sentences with **This is** or **These are**.*

1. _____ my daughter.

2. _____ my sons.

3. _____ my classmate.

4. _____ my apartment.

5. _____ good photos.

EXERCISE B

*Complete the sentences with **He, She, It, We,** or **They**.*

1. My daughter is a student. _____ is smart.

2. My son is in Seattle. _____ is a reporter.

3. My apartment is small. _____ is near the university.

4. My photos are in my book. _____ are family photos.

5. My father and I are in Seattle. _____ are happy.

EXERCISE C

Complete the sentences. Circle the correct words.

1. **This is / These are** my parents.

2. **This is / Is this** your cat?

3. **We / We're** reporters.

4. **Is / Are** these your CDs?

5. **I / I'm** happy to be in this class.

Unit 1 Review: *This is / These are*; Subject Pronouns   **9**

UNIT 2

Singular and Plural Nouns; Proper Nouns; *A* and *An*

THINGS IN THE KITCHEN

STEP 1 GRAMMAR IN CONTEXT

Before You Read

A | *Make a list of seven things in a kitchen. Use your dictionary or ask your teacher for help.*

   EXAMPLES: a refrigerator, an oven, an apple . . .

B | *GROUPS: Compare your lists.*

Read

Judy and Elena are roommates. Elena is an English language student from Brazil. They're in the kitchen. Read the conversation.

ELENA: Judy, what's this called in English?

JUDY: It's **a toaster**.

ELENA: **A toaster**? T-O-A-S-T-E-R?

JUDY: That's right.

ELENA: And this?

JUDY: It's **an oven**. O-V-E-N.

ELENA: And what's this called?

JUDY: It's **a spoon**. S-P-O-O-N.

ELENA: **Spoon**.

Elena: Is this **a knife**?

Judy: Yes. These are **knives**, and these are **forks**. **Knives**—K-N-I-V-E-S. **Forks**—F-O-R-K-S.

Elena: **Knives**, **forks**.

Judy: Yes.

Elena: What are these?

Judy: They're **glasses**. G-L-A-S-S-E-S.

Elena: Thank you. You're **a** good **teacher**. Let's go out.

Judy: Not so fast. Now in **Portuguese**. This time I'm **a student**, and you're **a teacher**.

After You Read

A | Practice *PAIRS: Practice the opening conversation.*

B | **Vocabulary** *Listen and repeat the words. Write new words in a notebook.*

VOCABULARY

a refrigerator

a knife

a fork

a spoon

a glass

an egg

an oven

a chicken

an apple

an orange

a pineapple

a stove

a pot

a counter

a muffin

a banana

C | **Vocabulary** *PAIRS: Ask which things are in your partner's kitchen.*

D | **Comprehension** *Look again at the opening conversation. Complete the sentences. Circle the correct letter.*

1. Elena and Judy are _____.

    a. roommates   **b.** cousins

2. Elena is learning words in _____.

    a. English   **b.** Portuguese

3. They are in the _____.

    a. kitchen   **b.** bathroom

4. Elena learns _____ new words.

    a. five   **b.** six

NOUNS AND ARTICLES

Singular and Plural Nouns		Articles: *A* and *An*	
Singular Noun	**Plural Noun**	*a*	*an*
This is a **toaster**.	These are **toasters**.	This is **a** fork.	This is **an** egg.
This is a **glass**.	These are **glasses**.		

PROPER NOUNS

Proper Noun
My roommate is **Elena Gomes**. She is from **Brazil**.

GRAMMAR NOTES

1	A **noun** is a word that refers to a person, animal, place, thing, or idea.	• Elena, Kip, Seattle, oven, friendship
	Singular means "one." **Plural** means "more than one."	• This is a **spoon**. (singular) • These are **spoons**. (plural)
	Add *-s* to most nouns to make them **plural**. Add *-es* to nouns that end in *s, ss, z, ch, sh,* and *x*. Say an extra syllable.	• This is a **glass**. (singular) • These are **glasses**. (plural)
2	*A* and *an* come before singular nouns.	
	Use *a* before a word that begins with a consonant sound. Use *an* before a word that begins with a vowel sound (usually *a, e, i, o, u*).	**a** spoon **an** apple **a** fork **an** egg **a** kitchen **an** idea **a** roommate **an** oven **a** toaster **an** umbrella
	NOTE: Do not put *a* or *an* before plural nouns.	Not: ~~a spoons~~
3	Some nouns have special plural forms.	• one man, two **men** • one woman, two **women** • one knife, two **knives** • one child, two **children** • one person, two **people**
4	**Proper nouns** are the names of people and of places on a map. They start with a capital letter. All other nouns are *common* nouns.	• My roommate **Elena** is from **São Paulo, Brazil**.
	NOTE: Do not put *a* or *an* before proper nouns.	Not: ~~a Judy~~

STEP 3 FOCUSED PRACTICE

EXERCISE 1: Discover the Grammar

A | *Circle the **singular** words.*

apples   forks   knife   kitchen

B | *Circle the words that begin with **a vowel sound**.*

apple   egg   knife   oven   spoon   toaster

C | *Circle the **proper nouns**.*

Brazil   country   Elena   Johnson   Judy   student

EXERCISE 2: Singular and Plural Nouns

(Grammar Note 1)

Complete the conversation. Use the singular or plural form of the words in parentheses.

ELENA: Excuse me. This is my shopping cart.

MAN: Really?

ELENA: Yes. This is my (pineapple)

_____*pineapple*_____, and these are my
           1.

(egg) _____.
       2.

MAN: Well, this is my (chicken) _____, and these are my (apple)
                            3.

_____.
    4.

ELENA: But these are my (muffin) _____.
                       5.

MAN: No, they're my (muffin) _____.
                    6.

ELENA: Oh, there are two (package) _____ of muffins.
                           7.

MAN: So, where's my shopping cart?

EXERCISE 3: Articles

(Grammar Note 2)

Look at Elena's shopping list. Complete the sentence. Use **a, an,** *or* **no article** *with the things.*

TO BUY

~~1 eraser~~

~~2 pens~~

3 notebooks

1 dictionary

3 apples

1 orange

1 banana

Elena needs _____*an eraser*_____, _____*pens*_____,
               1.   **2.**

_____, _____, _____,
    3.   **4.**   **5.**

_____, and _____.
    6.   **7.**

EXERCISE 4: Editing

There are five mistakes in the sentences. The first mistake is already corrected. Find and correct four more mistakes.

1. These are ~~a~~ apples.

2. Elena is from brazil.

3. She wants a orange.

4. These banana are good.

5. This is toaster.

EXERCISE 5: Pronunciation

 A | *Read and listen to the Pronunciation Note.*

Pronunciation Note
English words have one or more than one syllable. A syllable is like a beat. Each syllable has one vowel sound. In words of more than one syllable, one syllable gets primary stress.

B | *Listen and repeat the words.*

One Syllable	Two Syllables	Three Syllables	Four Syllables
egg pen pot stove	apple orange toaster	banana umbrella	dictionary

C | *Listen and mark the stressed syllable in each word.*

   •
ap ple   or ange   toast er   ba na na   um brel la   dic tion ar y

EXERCISE 6: Listening

A | *Listen to the conversation between Judy and Elena. Read the sentence. Then listen again. Complete the sentence. Circle the correct letter.*

Judy and Elena are _____.

a. in their apartment

b. at school

c. at a restaurant

B | *Listen again. Check (✔) the things that are dirty.*

____ classes   ____ glasses   ____ forks   ____ spoons

____ knives   ____ restaurant   ____ apartment

EXERCISE 7: Name Things from A to Z

*GROUPS: Name things in a home. Try to name one for each letter of the alphabet. Include **a** or **an** with each thing. The group with the most correct words wins.*

    EXAMPLES: **1.** an apple
               2. a bed

EXERCISE 8: Memory Game

*GROUPS OF SEVEN: Student 1 names one thing in a home. Student 2 names the first thing and a new thing. Student 7 names all seven things. Include **a** or **an**.*

EXAMPLE: **Student 1:** A spoon.
   Student 2: A spoon and a fork.

EXERCISE 9: Writing

A | *Look around your classroom. Learn the names of six new things. Write a sentence for each thing. Use a dictionary for help. Use **a**, **an**, or no article before nouns.*

EXAMPLES: These are windows.
   This is an eraser.

B | *Check your work. Use the Editing Checklist.*

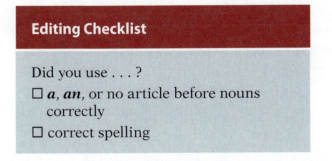

Editing Checklist

Did you use . . . ?
☐ *a*, *an*, or no article before nouns
   correctly
☐ correct spelling

C | *Draw a picture near each sentence from Part A.*

EXAMPLES: These are windows.

This is an eraser.

EXERCISE A

Write the plural form of the singular nouns.

Plural Form   **Plural Form**

1. spoon _____   **4.** knife _____

2. glass _____   **5.** pot _____

3. fork _____

EXERCISE B

*Look at Judy's shopping list. Complete the sentence. Use **a, an,** or no article with the things on the list.*

Shopping List

1 chicken

5 bananas

10 apples

1 umbrella

1 notebook

Judy needs _____, _____, _____, _____,
              1.   2.   3.   4.
and _____.
        5.

EXERCISE C

Correct the sentences. There are five mistakes.

1. These are good muffin.

2. I have a idea.

3. My sister has two child.

4. My roommate is from canada.

5. I need fork.

II

Be: Present; *That is / Those are*; Possessive Adjectives

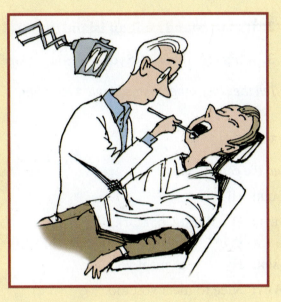

UNIT	GRAMMAR FOCUS	THEME
3	Present of *Be*: Statements	Meeting People
4	*That is / Those are*; Possessive Adjectives	Sightseeing in Seattle
5	Present of *Be*: *Yes / No* Questions, Questions with *Who* and *What*	A Wedding
6	Present of *Be*: *Where* Questions; Prepositions of Place	Giving Addresses

Present of *Be*: Statements

MEETING PEOPLE

STEP 1 GRAMMAR IN CONTEXT

Before You Read

A | *PAIRS: Complete the statements about Australia. Choose the correct words in parentheses.*

1. It's (**big / small**)

2. It's (**an island / not an island**)

3. A big city there is (**Sydney / Singapore**)

B | *Tell the class other things about Australia.*

Read

Read the conversation.

MARK: Hi, Steve.

STEVE: Hi, Mark. Uh, Mark . . . This **is** my cousin Amy, and this **is** her friend Jenny. They**'re** here on vacation.

MARK: Hi. Nice to meet you.

AMY: Nice to meet you too.

MARK: So you**'re** not from around here?

AMY: No. We**'re** from Australia.

MARK: Australia? That**'s** pretty far away. Are you from Melbourne?

AMY: No. We**'re** from Sydney. How about you? Are you from Seattle?

MARK: Yes, I **am**.

AMY: Jenny and I love Seattle. It**'s** a beautiful and clean city. The people **are** friendly. And the coffee **is** delicious.

MARK: How's Sydney?

AMY: It**'s** a great city too—and not because I live there!

A | Practice *GROUPS OF THREE: Practice the opening conversation.*

B | Vocabulary *Listen and repeat the words. Write new words in a notebook.*

VOCABULARY

clean   dirty   delicious   awful

friendly   unfriendly   popular   unpopular

great — good — bad — terrible   expensive — reasonable — cheap

C | Vocabulary *Complete the passage. Choose the correct words.*

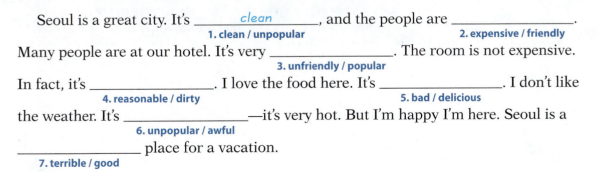

Seoul is a great city. It's _____*clean*_____, and the people are _____.
        1. clean / unpopular   **2. expensive / friendly**
Many people are at our hotel. It's very _____. The room is not expensive.
                              3. unfriendly / popular
In fact, it's _____. I love the food here. It's _____. I don't like
        4. reasonable / dirty   **5. bad / delicious**
the weather. It's _____—it's very hot. But I'm happy I'm here. Seoul is a
            6. unpopular / awful
_____ place for a vacation.
7. terrible / good

D | Comprehension *Look again at the opening conversation. Correct the underlined words if they are incorrect.*

Seattle

Jenny and Amy are in ~~Sydney~~ on business. Steve is Amy's uncle. Mark introduces

                 1.   **2.**   **3.**   **4.**

Jenny and Amy to Steve. Mark and Amy talk about their families. Amy says Seattle is a

               5.   **6.**

beautiful and dirty city. Amy says Sydney is an awful city.

 7.   **8.**   **9.**

STEP 2 GRAMMAR PRESENTATION

PRESENT OF *BE*

Affirmative Statements		
am	*is*	*are*
I **am** from Seattle.	He **is** from Seattle. She **is** from Sydney. It **is** clean. Seattle **is** clean.	We **are** from Sydney You **are** cousins. They **are** friends. Jenny and I **are** from Sydney. Jenny and Amy **are** friends.
Contractions		
I am = I**'m**	he is = he**'s** she is = she**'s** it is = it**'s**	we are = we**'re** you are = you**'re** they are = they**'re**

Negative Statements		
am not	*is not*	*are not*
I **am not** from Sydney.	He **is not** from Sydney. She **is not** from Seattle. It **is not** dirty.	We **are not** from Seattle. You **are not** from here. They **are not** from here.
Contractions		
I am not = I**'m not**	he is not = he**'s not** OR he **isn't** she is not = she**'s not** OR she **isn't** it is not = it**'s not** OR it **isn't**	we are not = we**'re not** OR we **aren't** you are not = you**'re not** OR you **aren't** they are not = they**'re not** OR they **aren't**

GRAMMAR NOTES

1	The **present** of **be** has three forms: **am**, **is**, **are**.	• I **am** from Seattle. • It **is** clean. • They **are** friendly.
2	Use the correct form of **be + not** to make a **negative statement**.	• I **am not** from Sydney. • It **is not** dirty. • We **are not** cold.
3	**Sentences** have a subject and a verb. The **subject** is a noun or a pronoun.	SUBJECT NOUN · **Amy** VERB **is** my cousin. SUBJECT PRONOUN · **She** VERB **is** from Australia.
4	We often use **contractions** (short forms) in speaking and informal writing. **NOTE:** There are two negative contractions for **is not** and **are not**. We often use **isn't** or **aren't** after subject nouns. We often use **'s not** or **'re not** after **subject pronouns**.	• I**'m** from Seattle. I**'m** not from Sydney. • Sydney **isn't** cold. OR It**'s not** cold. • Jenny and Amy **aren't** cousins. OR They**'re not** cousins.

STEP 3 FOCUSED PRACTICE

EXERCISE 1: Discover the Grammar

Read the sentences. Write **A (Affirmative)** *or* **N (Negative).**

___N___ **1.** She's not from around here.

_____ **2.** She's here with a friend.

_____ **3.** They're here on vacation.

_____ **4.** They aren't here on business.

_____ **5.** I'm not from Melbourne.

_____ **6.** It's not a popular place.

EXERCISE 2: Affirmative Statements

(Grammar Note 1)

A | *Complete the sentences with* **She is, He is, It is, We are,** *or* **They are.**

1. Amy is a student. _____*She is*_____ from Australia.

2. Amy and Jenny are students. _____ in Seattle on vacation.

3. Sydney is a great city. _____ in Australia.

4. My friends and I are in school. _____ in room 2.

5. Mark is a student. _____ in Seattle.

B | *On a separate piece of paper, rewrite the sentences using contractions. Then say each sentence aloud.*

EXERCISE 3: *Be*: Negatives and Contractions

(Grammar Notes 1–2, 4)

A | *Check (✔) the true sentences. Change the false sentences to the negative. Write the full form.*

_____ **1.** I am a teacher. _____ *I am not a teacher.* _____

_____ **2.** I am a new student. _____

_____ **3.** My parents are in Australia. _____

_____ **4.** The Sydney Opera House is in Canberra. _____

_____ **5.** We are in room 2. _____

_____ **6.** Our school is in Australia. _____

_____ **7.** Koala bears are from Australia. _____

_____ **8.** My parents are from around here. _____

B | *Write each negative sentence using contractions. Say each sentence aloud.*

EXERCISE 4: Present of *Be*

(Grammar Notes 1–4)

Complete the letter. Choose the correct words in parentheses.

Dear Mum and Dad,   Sept. 15

   Amy and I _____are_____ in Seattle. We _____ at the Western Hotel now.
              1. (am / are)   2. (not / 're not)

It was expensive and far from everything. We _____ at a youth hostel on
                                              3. ('re / be)

Second Avenue. It _____ clean. It _____ expensive. And all the
                   4. ('s / 're)   5. (no is / 's not)

people here _____ friendly.
            6. (are / aren't)

   We love Seattle! It _____ a beautiful city, and the food _____
                       7. ('s / 's not)   8. (is / are)

delicious, especially the Asian dishes. It _____ cool at night, and you often
                                            9. (be / 's)

need an umbrella. But we _____ happy to be here.
                         10. ('s / 're)

   I hope you _____ fine. Send my love to Aunt Kitty.
              11. (is / are)

                              Love,

                              Jenny

EXERCISE 5: Editing

There are seven mistakes in the conversations. The first mistake is already corrected.
Find and correct six more mistakes. Use contractions.

1. **A:** The coffee _{is} expensive.

    B: You're right.

2. **A:** My cousin from Tokyo. She's a student.

    B: I'm from Tokyo. I no am a student.

3. **A:** Seattle is a big city in California.

    B: No, it's isn't. Seattle is in Washington.

4. **A:** The people is friendly here.

    B: I know. They're great.

5. **A:** I be from a big city.

    B: I'm not. I from a small town.

STEP 4 COMMUNICATION PRACTICE

EXERCISE 6: Pronunciation

A | *Listen to the underlined words in each sentence.*

Full Form	Contractions
They are from Italy.	**They're** from Italy.
He is a chef.	**He's** a chef.
I am a student.	**I'm** a student.

The full form has two syllables (sounds). The contraction (short form) has one syllable.

B | *Listen again and repeat.*

C | *Listen to the sentences. Check (✓)* **Full Form** *or* **Contraction**.

	Full Form	Contraction
1.		✓
2.		
3.		
4.		
5.		
6.		

EXERCISE 7: Listening

A | *Listen to the conversation. Check (✓) the one true sentence.*

_____ **1.** The woman is a student, and the man is a chef.

_____ **2.** The woman and the man are chefs.

_____ **3.** The woman is a chef, and the man is a student.

B | *Listen again. Check (✓)* **T (True), F (False),** *or* **NI (No Information)**.

	T	F	NI
1. The woman is from Australia.	☑	☐	☐
2. The woman's parents are from Australia.	☐	☐	☐
3. The man is from Italy.	☐	☐	☐
4. They are at a hotel.	☐	☐	☐
5. The woman thinks Italian food is delicious.	☐	☐	☐

EXERCISE 8: True Sentences about You

A | *PAIRS: Write true sentences about you. Then read your sentence aloud. Check (✓) sentences that are the same for you and your partner. The first sentence is written for you.*

Same

1. I / here on business. *I'm not here on business.* _____ ☐

2. I / here on vacation. _____ ☐

3. It / hot in class. _____ ☐

4. I / from Italy. _____ ☐

5. My teacher / from Australia. _____ ☐

6. I / happy to be here. _____ ☐

7. I / cold. _____ ☐

8. My parents / from Seattle. _____ ☐

9. It / noisy in class. _____ ☐

10. Italian food / popular in our city. _____ ☐

B | *Write two true sentences and one false sentence about people or things in the classroom. Read your sentences to the class. The class says "True" or "False" after each sentence.*

EXAMPLE: **Marie:** My teacher is from Australia.
           Class: False.

1. _____

2. _____

3. _____

EXERCISE 9: Talk about a City

PAIRS: Tell about the city you are in. Use words from the Vocabulary section. Use "I agree" or "I disagree" in your answer.

EXAMPLE: **A:** The people are friendly here.
          B: Yes, I agree. And the city is clean.
          A: Well, some places are dirty.
          B: That's true. But the coffee is delicious.
          A: I agree.

EXERCISE 10: Writing

A | *Write four sentences about your city. Use the present of* **be**. *Use vocabulary from the unit.*

EXAMPLE: Seoul is a great city.

1. _____

2. _____

3. _____

4. _____

B | *Check your work. Use the Editing Checklist.*

Editing Checklist

Did you use . . . ?
- ☐ the present of *be* correctly
- ☐ vocabulary from the unit
- ☐ correct spelling

EXERCISE A

Complete the sentences with **She is, He is, It is, We are,** *or* **They are.**

1. I don't like this coffee. _____ terrible.

2. John is not a student. _____ a teacher.

3. Amy is from Australia. _____ friendly.

4. Michelle and Lisa are not sisters. _____ cousins.

5. My friends and I are in Italy. _____ on vacation.

EXERCISE B

Rewrite the sentences using contractions.

1. It is expensive. _____

2. They are not on vacation. _____

3. I am not a chef. _____

4. He is not in Australia. _____

5. We are in the class. _____

EXERCISE C

Correct the conversations. There are five mistakes.

1. **A:** The hotels is cheap here.

   B: You right. They great.

2. **A:** Machiko from Seattle. She's a student.

   B: No, she not. She's a chef.

That is / Those are; Possessive Adjectives
SIGHTSEEING IN SEATTLE

Before You Read

PAIRS: Name three places for visitors to your city. Then compare your answers with those of other pairs.

> EXAMPLES: the park
> the art museum
> the sports stadium

Read

Read the conversation.

STEVE: Well, here we are. **That's** the Space Needle. How about a picture?

AMY: Sure. Too bad Jenny isn't here, but I have **her** camera.

STEVE: Come on. Let's go up.

* * * * *

AMY: Wow! Look at those buildings.

STEVE: They're the stadiums. Here, take a look.

AMY: They're big! **Are those** people next to them? They look so small.

STEVE: Yep. Now look over there. **That's** the University of Washington.

AMY: **That's your** university, right?

STEVE: Yes. OK, now look down. Look at that colored building.

AMY: The colors are beautiful, but **its** shape is really unusual.

STEVE: **That's** the EMP. It's a music museum. It belongs to Paul Allen. It's **his** "baby."

AMY: Let's go see it.

STEVE: **That's** a great idea.

After You Read

A | **Practice** *PAIRS: Practice the opening conversation.*

B | **Vocabulary** *Listen and repeat the words. Write new words in a notebook.*

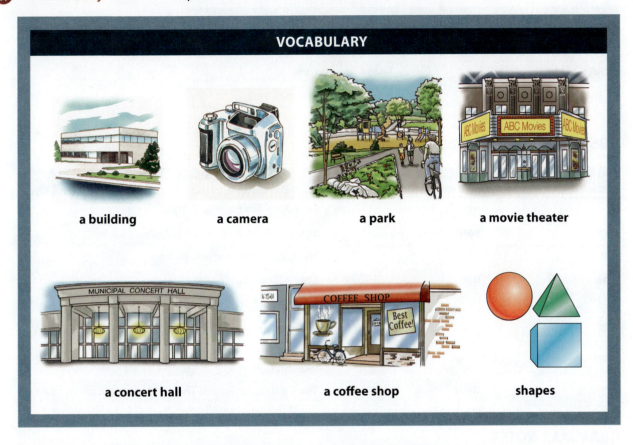

VOCABULARY

a building a camera a park a movie theater

a concert hall a coffee shop shapes

C | **Vocabulary** *PAIRS: Which of these things are in your town or city?*

big buildings a concert hall a movie theater a museum a stadium

D | **Comprehension** *Look again at the opening conversation. Write* **T (True)** *or* **F (False)**.

_____ **1.** Jenny is with Amy and Steve.

_____ **2.** Amy has a camera with her.

_____ **3.** The stadiums are very big.

_____ **4.** You can learn about music at the EMP.

E | *PAIRS: Read the text and complete the last sentence. Then check your answer on page P-1.*

Name Me

I am famous in Seattle and in the world. I am very tall—my height is about 600 feet, or 200 meters. My top has a very good restaurant. I have elevators. My initials are S. N.

My name is the _____.

THAT IS / THOSE ARE

Singular	Plural
That is the stadium.	**Those are** the stadiums.
That's his car.	**Those are** his cars.
Is that your key?	**Are those** your keys?

POSSESSIVE ADJECTIVES

Subject Pronouns	Possessive Adjectives	Example Sentences
I	my	**I** am Amy. **My** name is Amy.
you	your	**You** are Judy. **Your** name is Judy.
he	his	**He** is Steve. **His** name is Steve.
she	her	**She** is Jenny. **Her** name is Jenny.
it	its	**It** is the EMP. **Its** shape is unusual.
we	our	**We** have one daughter. **Our** daughter is Judy.
you	your	**You** are Steve and Mark, right? **Your** city is very beautiful.
they	their	**They** are our children. **Their** names are Judy and Ken.

GRAMMAR NOTES

1	Use *that is* to talk about one person or thing **away from** you. We often contract *that is* to *that's* in informal speaking and writing.	• **That is** the University of Washington. • **That's** the Space Needle.
2	Use *those are* to talk about two or more people or things **away from** you.	• **Those are** our stadiums. • **Those are** my pets.
3	Use *Is that* and *Are those* to ask questions. Answers usually take a **subject pronoun**.	• **Is that** your dictionary? Yes, **it** is. • **Are those** your keys? No, **they** aren't.
4	Possessive adjectives are *my*, *your*, *his*, *her*, *its*, *our*, and *their*. They tell who someone or something belongs to.	• That's **my** daughter. • Those are **her** friends. • The car belongs to Steve. It's **his** car.

REFERENCE NOTE
For more about *this*, *that*, *these*, and *those*, see Units 1 and 18.

EXERCISE 1: Discover the Grammar

Read the questions and answers. Underline the possessive adjectives. Then match the questions and answers.

___d___ 1. Are those <u>your</u> books?

_____ 2. Is that his camera?

_____ 3. Are those your children?

_____ 4. Is that the EMP?

_____ 5. Is that your college?

_____ 6. Are those sports stadiums?

a. Yes. One is our football stadium. The other is our baseball stadium.

b. Yes. Their names are Judy and Ken.

c. Yes. Its shape is unusual, right?

d. No, they're <u>her</u> books.

e. No, it's my camera.

f. No, I go to Boston College.

EXERCISE 2: *That* and *Those*

(Grammar Notes 1–3)

Complete the sentences with **that** *or* **those.**

1. _____*That*_____'s my favorite coffee shop.

2. Are _____ your children?

3. Is _____ Jenny's camera?

4. _____ are my friends.

5. Is _____ a park?

6. Are _____ your pets?

That is / Those are; Possessive Adjectives **33**

EXERCISE 3: Possessive Adjectives

(Grammar Note 4)

Circle the correct possessive adjective to complete the sentences.

1. Kip and Pam are (**my** / **our**) pets.

2. Jeremy, Annie, and Ben are (**my** / **our**) children.

3. Annie has (**her** / **their**) books with her.

4. Ben is riding (**her** / **his**) bicycle.

5. I like (**my** / **our**) car, but (**its** / **his**) tires are flat.

6. Judy and Ken Johnson love (**their** / **your**) parents.

EXERCISE 4: Possessive Adjectives

(Grammar Note 4)

Judy is showing a DVD about her visit home. Complete the passage with **my, his, her, its, our,** *or* **their.**

That's me and _____**my**_____ brother, Ken, with
                    1.
_____ parents in front of _____ house. See
       2.   **3.**
those cars? The old one belongs to Ken—it's _____
                                                       4.
first car. _____ battery is dead, so it doesn't
             5.
run. But he loves it. The new car belongs to Dad. It's
_____ favorite thing. And the garden belongs to
      6.
Mom. It's _____ favorite place.
               7.

EXERCISE 5: Editing

There are six mistakes in the conversations. The first mistake is already corrected. Find and correct five more mistakes.

1. **A:** Are ~~that~~ *those* your keys?

   B: No, they her keys.

2. **A:** Those is my daughter.

   B: She's a beautiful woman.

3. **A:** Are that your child?

   B: Yes. That's our son.

4. **A:** Those cat is very cute.

   B: It name is "Tiger."

EXERCISE 6: Pronunciation

A | *Read and listen to the Pronunciation Note.*

Pronunciation Note

Some words sound the same, but they are different in meaning and spelling:

your = possessive adjective   • **Your** name is Maria.

you're = *you are*   • **You're** a student.

its = possessive adjective   • **Its** name is the Space Needle.

it's = *it is*   • **It's** 600 feet high.

their = possessive adjective   • **Their** children are happy.

they're = *they are*   • **They're** happy.

B | *Listen to the sentences. Which word is used? Circle the correct letter.*

1. **a.** their   (**b.**) they're   4. **a.** your   **b.** you're
2. **a.** their   **b.** they're   5. **a.** its   **b.** it's
3. **a.** your   **b.** you're   6. **a.** its   **b.** it's

EXERCISE 7: Listening

Listen to the conversation. Then listen again. Complete the sentences. Circle the correct letter.

1. Jessica has _____ children.   4. Fluffy is _____.
   a. two   (**b.**) three   **a.** a cat   **b.** a dog

2. Ben is her _____.   5. The other kids are from _____.
   a. dog   **b.** son   **a.** their class   **b.** their school

3. Annie is Jessica's _____.
   a. son   **b.** daughter

EXERCISE 8: Suggestions and Information

A | *PAIRS: Listen and repeat the conversation.*

A: Let's go to the park.   **B:** That's a great idea.

B | *Make a new suggestion. Use the words from the box.*

go to a concert	go to the coffee shop	have lunch
go to a movie	go to the Space Needle	see the art museum

That is / Those are; Possessive Adjectives   **35**

C | *Listen and repeat the conversation.*

A: That's your university, right?

B: Yes, it is.

D | *Follow the conversation in Part C. Name a new place or thing. Use the words from the box.*

| building | camera | car | school | university |

EXERCISE 9: Game

A | *Play the game with the class. Each student puts an item on the teacher's table. For example:*

a backpack	a jacket	an earring
a camera	a notebook	keys
a CD player	a watch	sunglasses

B | *The teacher picks up one thing. A student points to the owner and says, "That's his / her _____."*

EXAMPLE:
(Teacher points to a backpack)
Student A: *(pointing to Student B)* That's her backpack.
Student B: Right. It's my backpack. OR
(pointing to Student C) No, that's his backpack.

EXERCISE 10: Writing

A | *Bring a photograph of a place in your town or city. Write five sentences about things in the photograph. Use **that** or **those**. Then tape the picture to the board. Tell the class about the picture.*

EXAMPLE: That's our stadium. It's for football.

B | *Check your work. Use the Editing Checklist.*

Editing Checklist
Did you use . . . ? □ *that* or *those* correctly □ correct spelling

UNIT 4 Review

Check your answers on page UR-0.

Do you need to review anything?

EXERCISE A

*Complete the sentences with **that** or **those**.*

1. _____'s an expensive car.

2. Are _____ Steve's CDs?

3. Is _____ your brother?

4. _____'s Judy's camera.

5. _____ aren't my keys!

EXERCISE B

Circle the correct words to complete the sentences.

1. **He / His** is my friend.

2. That's my sister. **She / Her** name is Lynn.

3. What are **you / your** names?

4. Those are good cameras. **Their / They** are very popular.

5. I really like this coffee shop. **It's / Its** my favorite place.

EXERCISE C

Correct the conversation. There are five mistakes.

A: Is that you family in the photo?

B: Yes. That's me brother and sister.

A: What are they're names?

B: He's name is Robert, and her name is Tammy.

A: And is that you're dog?

B: Yes. Its name is "Spot."

UNIT 5

Present of *Be*: *Yes / No* Questions, Questions with *Who* and *What*

A WEDDING

STEP 1 GRAMMAR IN CONTEXT

Before You Read

Check (✔) the sentences that are true for you. Then compare your answers with two other students' answers.

_____ **1.** I'm single.

_____ **2.** Weddings are fun.

_____ **3.** I like small weddings.

_____ **4.** Most of my friends are married.

Read

Mark, Steve, and Kathy are at a wedding reception for Amanda and Josh. Read the conversations.

STEVE: Mark?

MARK: Steve! **Are you** here for the wedding?

STEVE: **Yes, I am.** Amanda is my cousin. What about you?

MARK: Josh and I are friends from school. Boy, this is a great wedding.

STEVE: Yes, it is.

KATHY: **Who's** that man with Steve?

AMANDA: His name is Mark. He and Josh are friends.

KATHY: Hmm. **Is he** single?

AMANDA: **Yes, he is.**

KATHY: What does he do?

AMANDA: He's a student and a writer.

KATHY: What kind of writer?

AMANDA: He writes travel books.

38 UNIT 5

MARK: **Who's** that woman with Amanda?

STEVE: Her name is Kathy.

MARK: **Is she** married?

STEVE: **No, she's not.**

MARK: Hmm . . . What does she do?

STEVE: She's a travel agent.

After You Read

A | Practice *PAIRS: Practice the opening conversations.*

B | Vocabulary *Listen and repeat the words. Write new words in a notebook.*

VOCABULARY

married   single   a writer   a travel agent

a nurse   a dentist   a teacher   a student

a clerk   a police officer   a mechanic   a cashier

C | Vocabulary *GROUPS: List words that go with each occupation:*

EXAMPLES: a writer—paper   a cashier—money

Each student says a word that goes with an occupation. Another group calls out the occupation.

D | Comprehension *Look again at the opening conversations. Complete the sentences. Circle the correct letter.*

1. Steve and Amanda are ____.
   a. brother and sister
   (b.) cousins

2. Mark and Josh are ____.
   a. brothers
   b. friends

3. Kathy is ____.
   a. single
   b. married

4. Who is a writer?
   a. Kathy
   b. Mark

5. Who is a travel agent?
   a. Amanda
   b. Kathy

STEP 2 GRAMMAR PRESENTATION

PRESENT OF *BE*: *YES / NO* QUESTIONS

Yes / No Questions	Short Answers	
Singular	**Affirmative**	**Negative**
Am I right?	Yes, **you are.**	No, **you're not.** OR No, **you aren't.**
Are you a writer?	Yes, **I am.**	No, **I'm not.**
Is he a student?	Yes, **he is.**	No, **he's not.** OR No, **he isn't.**
Is she single?	Yes, **she is.**	No, **she's not.** OR No, **she isn't.**
Is your car new?	Yes, **it is.**	No, **it's not.** OR No, **it isn't.**
Plural	**Affirmative**	**Negative**
Are we late?	Yes, **we are.**	No, **we're not.** OR No, **we aren't.**
Are you happy?	Yes, **you are.**	No, **you're not.** OR No, **you aren't.**
Are they brothers?	Yes, **they are.**	No, **they're not.** OR No, **they aren't.**

PRESENT OF *BE*: QUESTIONS WITH *WHO* AND *WHAT*

Questions with *Who / What*	Short Answers	Long Answers
Who is that woman?	Kathy.	That's Kathy.
What's her name?	Kathy.	It's Kathy.

GRAMMAR NOTES

1	In a **yes/no question** with **be**, put **am**, **is**, or **are** before the subject.	SUBJECT • Statement: **He is** at a wedding. SUBJECT • Question: **Is he** at a wedding?
2	We often use contractions in **negative short answers**. **BE CAREFUL!** Don't use contractions in **affirmative short answers**.	A: Is she married? B: No, she**'s not**. OR No, she **isn't**. A: Are they brothers? B: No, they**'re not**. OR No, they **aren't**. A: Am I right? B: Yes, **you are**. NOT: Yes, ~~you're~~. A: Is she single? B: Yes, **she is**. NOT: Yes, ~~she's~~.
3	Use **who** to ask for information about **people**. Use **what** to ask for information about **things** or **ideas**. We often use the contractions **who's** and **what's** in speaking and informal writing.	• **Who** is that woman with Amanda? • **What** is her name? • **Who's** that woman? • **What's** her name?

STEP 3 FOCUSED PRACTICE

EXERCISE 1: Discover the Grammar

Match the questions and answers.

___c___ 1. Is Amanda your sister?

_____ 2. Are Mark and Helen teachers?

_____ 3. Am I right?

_____ 4. Are you and Josh friends?

_____ 5. Is Mark married?

_____ 6. Are you and Tim from Seattle?

a. No, he isn't.

b. No, we're from Redmond.

c. No, she isn't. She's my cousin.

d. No, they aren't. They're writers.

e. Yes, you are.

f. Yes, we are.

EXERCISE 2: *Who* and *What*

(Grammar Note 3)

Complete the conversations with **Who** or **What**.

1. **A:** _____Who_____'s that woman with Mark?

   B: That's my mother.

2. **A:** _____'s her name?

   B: Mary.

3. **A:** _____'s that man with Judy?

   B: That's Mark.

4. **A:** _____'s the teacher for this class?

   B: Professor Beck. Steve Beck.

5. **A:** _____'s a big city in Australia?

   B: Sydney.

6. **A:** _____'s a big country in South America?

   B: Brazil.

EXERCISE 3: *Yes / No* Questions and Answers

(Grammar Notes 1–3)

Put the words in the correct order. Make conversations.

1. **A:** Steve / Portland / Is / from /

   B: not / No, / he's /

   A: _Is Steve from Portland_____?

   B: _No, he's not_____.

2. **A:** today / the game / Is /

   B: Yes, / is / it /

   A: _____?

   B: _____.

3. **A:** cousins / Are / they /

   B: aren't / No, / they / . / brothers / They're /

   A: _____?

   B: _____.

4. **A:** man / that / Who / is /

   B: my / 's / teacher / He /

   A: _____?

   B: _____.

5. **A:** Seattle / hot / Is /

   B: isn't / No, / it /

   A: _____?

   B: _____.

EXERCISE 4: *Yes / No* Questions and Answers

(Grammar Notes 1–3)

Complete the conversations with words from the boxes.

is	not	she	she's	~~who's~~	woman

1. **A:** ____Who's____ that _____ with Amanda?

   B: That's Kathy.

   A: _____ _____ married?

   B: No, _____ _____.

he	he's	is	is	not	writer	yes

2. **A:** _____ _____ your brother?

   B: _____, he _____.

   A: Is he a _____?

   B: No, he's _____. _____ a doctor.

EXERCISE 5: Editing

There are eight mistakes in the conversations. The first mistake is already corrected.
Find and correct seven more mistakes.

1. **A:** ~~Is~~ *Are* you a nurse?

   B: Yes, I'm.

2. **A:** Is she single?

   B: No, she not.

3. **A:** They students?

   B: No, they are.

4. **A:** Is he a mechanic?

   B: No, he's.

5. **A:** Is your car new?

   B: No, it old.

6. **A:** Is he a dentist?

   B: No, he's not. He a writer.

EXERCISE 6: Pronunciation

A | *Read and listen to the Pronunciation Note.*

> **Pronunciation Note**
>
> In *yes / no* questions, your voice goes up at the end of the sentence:
>
> **EXAMPLES:**
>
> Are you married?   Are you here for the wedding?
>
> In questions with *who* and *what*, your voice goes down at the end of the sentence.
>
> **EXAMPLES:**
>
> Who's that woman with Josh?   What do you do?

B | *Listen to the questions. Does the speaker's voice go up or down at the end of the sentence? Write* **Up** *or* **Down**.

1. ___Up___   5. _____

2. _____   6. _____

3. _____   7. _____

4. _____   8. _____

C | *Listen again and repeat the questions.*

EXERCISE 7: Listening

A | *Listen to the conversation. Then listen again. Answer each question with a short answer.*

1. Is Mai a doctor? _____

2. Is she married? _____

3. Are Jaime and Diego brothers? _____

4. Is Alicia single? _____

B | *Listen again. Answer the questions.*

1. Who is Ahmed's friend? _____

2. Who are Diego's cousins? _____

3. What's the name of Diego's wife? _____

EXERCISE 8: Talk about Occupations

A | *PAIRS: Read the conversation aloud.*

> **A:** What do you do?
>
> **B:** I'm a writer. What about you?
>
> **A:** I'm a student.

B | *Go around the room. Practice the conversation with different classmates. Give yourself a new occupation. Use the words from the box or your dictionary.*

a cashier	a dentist	a nurse	a student	a travel agent
a clerk	a mechanic	a police officer	a teacher	a writer

C | *PAIRS: Ask your partner about other people in the class.*

> **EXAMPLE:** **A:** Who's the man / woman near _____?
>
> **B:** That's _____.
>
> **A:** What does he / she do?
>
> **B:** He's / She's _____.

EXERCISE 9: Game

A | *CLASS: On the board, write the names of five famous people:*

writers   actors   singers

B | *Your classmates choose the name of one of the people. They write it on a piece of paper and put it on your back. You don't see the name.*

C | *Ask your classmates a maximum of 10* **yes** / **no** *questions about the person. Your classmates answer with short answers.*

EXAMPLES: **A:** Is it a man?
            B: No, it isn't.

            A: Is she a writer?
            C: No, she isn't.

D | *Guess who the person is.*

EXAMPLE: **A:** Is she Angelina Jolie?
          B: Yes, she is.

EXERCISE 10: Writing

A | *Prepare to interview a classmate. Write three* **yes** / **no** *questions, a question with* **who,** *and a question with* **what.** *Use the words from the box.*

happy to be here	name	you do	your favorite writer
married	new student	your favorite actor	

EXAMPLES: What's your name? / What do you do? / Are you married? / Who's your favorite writer?

B | *Check your work. Use the Editing Checklist.*

Editing Checklist

Did you use . . . ?
☐ questions correctly
☐ correct spelling

C | *Ask your classmate the questions you wrote.*

5 Review

Check your answers on page UR-0.

Do you need to review anything?

EXERCISE A

Match the questions and answers.

_____ 1. Are you actors?

_____ 2. Am I late?

_____ 3. Is John married?

_____ 4. Are your parents teachers?

_____ 5. Is your sister a dentist?

a. No, they aren't.

b. No, she isn't.

c. Yes, you are.

d. Yes, we are.

e. No, he isn't.

EXERCISE B

*Complete the conversation with **Who** or **What**.*

A: That's a great photo. _____'s that woman on the right?

B: That's my cousin.

A: Oh, really? _____'s her name?

B: Rosa.

A: And _____'s that man on her left?

B: That's her husband, Carlos.

A: I see. _____'s his occupation?

B: He's a police officer.

A: And _____'s that in the middle? Is that their son?

B: No, that's their daughter!

EXERCISE C

Correct the conversations. There are five mistakes.

1. **A:** Is he a dentist?

   B: No, he's not. He a writer.

2. **A:** Is your sister single?

   B: No, she not.

3. **A:** Is your mother a travel agent?

   B: No, she no is.

4. **A:** Is you from Brazil?

   B: Yes, I'm.

6 Present of *Be*: *Where* Questions; Prepositions of Place

GIVING ADDRESSES

STEP 1 GRAMMAR IN CONTEXT

Before You Read

PAIRS: What is the address of your school? Give the street and building number. Then give the address of another place you know.

> **EXAMPLES:** Our school is at 270 First Avenue.
> The library is at 1140 Elm Street.

Read

Read the email messages.

Subj: Yuko's birthday
Date: Wednesday, November 3
From: judyjohnson@uw.edu
To: mm@uw.edu

a birthday cake

Hi Mark,

I want to go to Yuko's party, but I don't have her address. **Where's** her new apartment?

Judy

Subj: Yuko's birthday
Date: Wednesday, November 3
From: mm@uw.edu
To: judyjohnson@uw.edu

a gift

Hi Judy,

Her apartment is **on** First Avenue **between** Jackson and Main. (I think it's **at** 10 First Avenue, but I'm not sure.) It's **across from** a library and **next to** a gym. She's **on** the second floor, Apartment 2A. Take the number 4 bus. It stops **on the corner of** First and Jackson. (Her phone number is 206-555-2343.)

See you Saturday.

Mark

After You Read

A | **Practice** *PAIRS: Practice the opening readings. Each person reads an email.*

B | **Vocabulary** *Listen and repeat the words. Write new words in a notebook.*

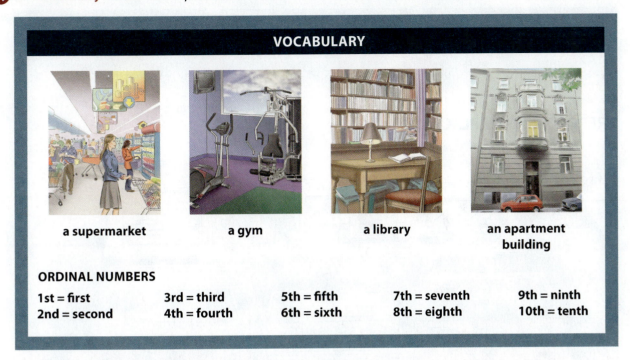

VOCABULARY

a supermarket   a gym   a library   an apartment building

ORDINAL NUMBERS

1st = first	3rd = third	5th = fifth	7th = seventh	9th = ninth
2nd = second	4th = fourth	6th = sixth	8th = eighth	10th = tenth

C | **Vocabulary** *PAIRS: Give the location of a supermarket, a gym, and a library near your school.*

> **EXAMPLE:** Don's Supermarket is on Second Avenue. It's across from an apartment building and next to a library.

D | **Comprehension** *Look again at the opening email messages. Then look at the map. What's Yuko's address? Complete the sentence.*

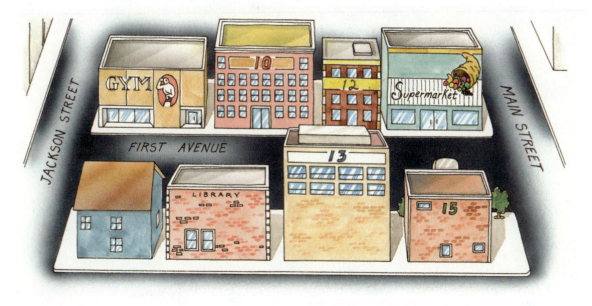

She lives at _____.

PRESENT OF *BE*: QUESTIONS WITH *WHERE*

Questions with *Where*	Short Answers	Long Answers
Where is the art museum?	On First Avenue.	It's on First Avenue.
Where are Bruno and Elaine from?	Haiti.	They're from Haiti.

PREPOSITIONS OF PLACE

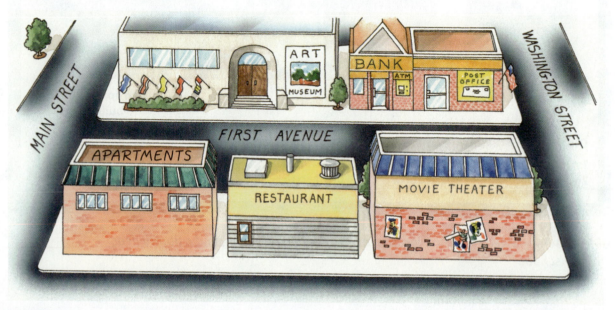

The art museum is **on** First Avenue. It's **across from** an apartment building and a restaurant. The bank is **between** the art museum and the post office. The restaurant is **next to** the movie theater.

GRAMMAR NOTES

1	Use **where** to ask questions about location.	**A: Where is** the restaurant? **B:** It's on First Avenue.
	Where's is the short form for **where is**.	**A: Where's** the bank? **B:** It's next to the museum.
2	**In**, **on**, **at**, **next to**, **between**, and **across from** are prepositions of place. They tell the location of places and things.	• My school is **in** Seattle. • It's **on** Main Street. • It's **next to** a bank.
3	**at** + street address **on** + street name **on the** + floor **in** + city, state, country, or continent **NOTE:** We don't always say "street" or "avenue" in informal speaking or writing.	• My school is **at** 15 Main Street. • It is **on** Main Street. • My English class is **on the** second floor. • It is **in** Seattle. **A:** Where's your school? **B:** It's on **Main**. OR It's on **Main Street**.
4	Use ordinal numbers for streets and floors.	• It's on **Tenth** Street. • She's on the **second** floor.

STEP 3 FOCUSED PRACTICE

EXERCISE 1: Discover the Grammar

Look at the map on page 50. Match the places and locations.

_____ **1.** It's on First Avenue between Washington and Main. It's between a movie theater and an apartment building.

_____ **2.** It's on the corner of First Avenue and Washington Street. It's next to a bank.

_____ **3.** It's on the corner of First and Washington. It's next to a restaurant.

a. the post office

b. the movie theater

c. the restaurant

EXERCISE 2: Prepositions of Place

(Grammar Note 3)

Look at Yuko's business card. Complete the sentences.

1. Yuko lives (city, state) _____.

2. She lives on _____ Avenue.

3. Her building is at _____.

4. Her apartment is _____ floor.

Yuko Shinohara
10 First Avenue, Apt. 2A
Seattle, Washington 98104

EXERCISE 3: Using a Map

(Grammar Notes 1–2)

Look at the map. The letters **N, S, E,** and **W** *stand for* north, south, east, *and* west. *Match the questions and answers.*

_____ 1. Where's the art museum?

_____ 2. Where's the hospital?

_____ 3. Where's the bank?

_____ 4. Where's the park?

a. It's across from the hospital.

b. It's next to the bank.

c. It's between the art museum and the post office.

d. It's on the northeast corner of Second and Washington.

EXERCISE 4: Questions about Location

(Grammar Notes 1–3)

A | *Complete the conversation. Write the correct sentences from the box.*

Is it on Main Street?	Turn right at the corner.
Is this Main Street?	Where's First Avenue?

MAN: Excuse me. _____

1.

WOMAN: Yes, it is. We're on Main Street near Second Avenue.

MAN: I'm looking for the post office. _____

2.

WOMAN: No, it's not. It's on First Avenue.

MAN: Oh. _____

3.

WOMAN: Walk to the corner of this street. _____ The post

4.

office is next to the bank. It's on the corner of First and Washington.

B | *Look at the map in Exercise 3. Where are the man and woman now? Put an **X** on the street.*

EXERCISE 5: Editing

There are seven mistakes in the conversations. The first mistake is already corrected.
Find and correct six more mistakes.

1. **A:** ~~Where's~~ *Where* are you from?

   B: I'm from Bogotá.

   A: Where is Bogotá?

   B: It's on Colombia.

2. **A:** Is your apartment in this floor?

   B: No, it's on the eight floor.

3. **A:** Where's the bookstore?

   B: It's First Avenue.

   A: Is it next the museum?

   B: Yes, it is.

4. **A:** Is the supermarket on First in Main and Washington?

   B: No, it's between Main and Jackson.

EXERCISE 6: Listening

 A | *Look at the map on page 52. Listen to the conversation. Then complete the sentence. Circle the correct letter.*

The man and the woman are on _____.

    a. Main Street   **b.** Washington Street

B | *Look at the map. Listen again. Write* **supermarket** *and* **flower shop** *on the correct buildings.*

EXERCISE 7: Pronunciation

A | *Read and listen to the Pronunciation Note.*

Pronunciation Note
Stress the first syllable of 30, 40, 50, 60, 70, 80, and 90. Stress the first or last syllable of 13, 14, 15, 16, 17, 18, and 19.

B | *Listen to the numbers.*

thirteen—thirty

fourteen—forty

fifteen—fifty

sixteen—sixty

seventeen—seventy

eighteen—eighty

C | *Listen to the conversations. Circle the correct letter.*

    1. a. 15   **b.** 50

    2. a. 14   **b.** 40

    3. a. 15   **b.** 50

    4. a. 16   **b.** 60

EXERCISE 8: Locations in a Building

GROUPS OF THREE: Student A, ask where the places in the building are. Student B, give the floor and room number. Student C, close your book, listen to your partners, and write the information. Your partners check your information. Then change roles.

EXAMPLE: **Student A:** Where's Dr. Tran's office?
Student B: It's on the first floor, in room 115.
Student C: (Writes: Dr. Tran, 1st floor, room 115.)

1st Floor
Dr. Jazmin Tran — Dentist   115
Dr. Suzanna Lim — Family Medicine   150

2nd Floor
Nonna's Nail Salon   213
Ria's Spa   230

3rd Floor
Passport Office   315
Phil's Photos   350

EXERCISE 9: Locations in a Neighborhood

*PAIRS: Take turns. Ask for the location of these places in your area: a park, a gym, an Italian restaurant, a hospital, a bank, a post office. Use **in, on, at, next to, between,** or **across from** in your answer.*

EXAMPLE: **A:** Where's the nearest park?
B: It's on Elm Street. It's across from Sinai Hospital. It's next to a big bank.

EXERCISE 10: Writing

A | *Make a class directory of places you like in your neighborhood. Each student gives the location for three places. Use prepositions of place. Add information about each place.*

EXAMPLE: PIERRE'S CAFÉ—Pierre's Café is at 40 River Street. It's next to West Park. It's across from the library. It's open 7 days a week. The food is great.

B | *Check your work. Use the Editing Checklist.*

Editing Checklist

Did you use . . . ?
☐ prepositions of place correctly
☐ correct spelling

Check your answers on page UR-0.

Do you need to review anything?

EXERCISE A

Complete the passage. Choose the correct words in parentheses.

I live _____ Denver. Denver is a big city _____
        1. (in / at)   **2. (in / on)**

Colorado. My apartment is _____ 143 Oak Street. It's
                          3. (at / on)

_____ 141 Oak Street and 145 Oak Street. I live _____
4. (across from / between)   **5. (on / on the)**

fourth floor.

EXERCISE B

Look at the map on page 52. Complete the sentences with **across from, between, next to, on,** *or* **on the corner of.**

1. The movie theater is _____ First Avenue.

2. The restaurant is _____ the apartment and the movie theater.

3. The bank is _____ the movie theater.

4. The art museum is _____ the bank.

5. The park is _____ Second Avenue and Washington Street.

EXERCISE C

Correct the conversations. There are five mistakes.

1. **A:** Is your apartment in the second floor?

   B: No, it's on the three floor.

2. **A:** Where the bookstore?

   B: It's First Avenue.

   A: Is it next the museum?

   B: Yes, it is.

Be: Past

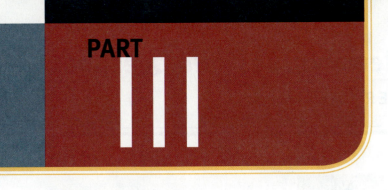

UNIT	GRAMMAR FOCUS	THEME
7	Past of *Be*: Statements, *Yes / No* Questions	Movies and Other Pastimes
8	Past of *Be*: *Wh-* Questions	Travel and Leisure Activities

Past of *Be*: Statements, *Yes / No* Questions
MOVIES AND OTHER PASTIMES

STEP 1 GRAMMAR IN CONTEXT

Before You Read

Check (✔) the sentences that are true for you. Then compare your answers with two other students' answers.

_____ **1.** I was asleep at 2 A.M. last night.   _____ **3.** I like movies.

_____ **2.** I was awake at 6 A.M. this morning.   _____ **4.** I was at a movie last night.

Read

Read the conversation.

KATHY: Hello?

AMANDA: Hi, Kathy. This is Amanda.

KATHY: Hi, Amanda. How's it going?

AMANDA: Fine. Hey, Josh and I stopped by your house last night, but you **weren't** there. Or **were you** asleep? I guess we **were** there about 9:00.

KATHY: Actually, I **wasn't** at home last night. I **was** at the movies.

AMANDA: **Were you** with Olivia?

KATHY: No, I **wasn't**.

AMANDA: With Sally?

KATHY: No.

AMANDA: **Were you** alone?

KATHY: Uh, no. I **was** with . . . someone. The movie **was** great. Really exciting. And funny too.

AMANDA: Really! What movie **was** it?

KATHY: *Frankenstein's Uncle.*

After You Read

A | **Practice** *PAIRS: Practice the opening conversation.*

B | **Vocabulary** *Listen and repeat the words. Write new words in a notebook.*

VOCABULARY

| alone | asleep | awake | funny |

| scary | interesting | boring | exciting |

C | **Vocabulary** *PAIRS: List a movie for each of the adjectives:* funny, scary, interesting, boring, exciting.

EXAMPLE: exciting: *Harry Potter and the Half-Blood Prince*

D | **Comprehension** *Look again at the opening conversation. Write* **T (True)** *or* **F (False)**.

__T__ **1.** Kathy is at home tonight.

_____ **2.** Kathy was at home last night at 9:00.

_____ **3.** Amanda and Josh were at Kathy's house last night.

_____ **4.** Kathy was alone at the movies last night.

_____ **5.** The movie was *Young Frankenstein*.

PAST OF *BE*: AFFIRMATIVE STATEMENTS

Affirmative Statements	
was	**were**
I **was** at a movie last night. He **was** at home. She **was** at the gym. It **was** hot.	We **were** at a birthday party yesterday. You **were** great in the play. You and Ryan **were** both wonderful. They **were** at the soccer game.

PAST OF *BE*: NEGATIVE STATEMENTS

Negative Statements	
was not	**were not**
I **was not** at home last night. He **wasn't** at a movie. She **wasn't** at the library. It **wasn't** cold yesterday.	We **were not** at home last night. You **weren't** in class yesterday. They **weren't** at the library yesterday.

YES / NO QUESTIONS

Yes / No Questions	Short Answers	
was / were	**Affirmative**	**Negative**
Was I right?	Yes, you **were**.	No, you **weren't**.
Was he at home?	Yes, he **was**.	No, he **wasn't**.
Was she at the game?	Yes, she **was**.	No, she **wasn't**.
Was it cold yesterday?	Yes, it **was**.	No, it **wasn't**.
Were we right?	Yes, you **were**.	No, you **weren't**.
Were you at home?	Yes, I **was**.	No, I **wasn't**.
Were they at the game?	Yes, they **were**.	No, they **weren't**.

GRAMMAR NOTES

1	The past of *be* has two forms: *was* and *were*. Use *was* with these subject pronouns: *I, he, she,* and *it.* Use *were* with these subject pronouns: *you, we,* and *they.*	• I **was** at a movie last night. • The girls **were** at the library yesterday. • They **were** at the library yesterday.
2	Use **was** or **were** + **not** to make negative statements. We often use the contractions **wasn't** and **weren't** in speaking and informal writing.	• I **was not** alone. • You **were not** at home. • I **wasn't** alone. • You **weren't** at home.
3	To ask a *yes / no* question, put **was** or **were** before the subject.	**SUBJECT** • **Was** the movie interesting? **SUBJECT** • **Were** you alone at the movie?
4	You can use a subject pronoun and **was**, **wasn't**, **were**, or **weren't** in short answers. You can also just answer *yes* or *no,* then give more information.	**A:** Was Mary at the library yesterday? **B:** Yes, **she was**. **A:** Were your friends at home last night? **B:** No, **they were at a concert**.

STEP 3 FOCUSED PRACTICE

EXERCISE 1: Discover the Grammar

A | *Circle the subjects and underline the past forms of* **be.** *Then match the questions and answers.*

   d   **1.** Were (you) at home yesterday?

_____ **2.** Was he in class yesterday?

_____ **3.** Was the concert good?

_____ **4.** Was the movie interesting?

_____ **5.** Was Susan at the library yesterday?

_____ **6.** Were you at the ball game last night?

a. No, it wasn't. The music was pretty bad.

b. Yes, she was. We were both there.

c. Yes, I was. It was a really exciting game.

d. No, (I) wasn't. (I) was at a concert.

e. No, he wasn't. He was sick.

f. Yes, it was. Johnny Depp is a great actor.

B | *Read the email. Underline the past forms of* be *and circle their subjects.*

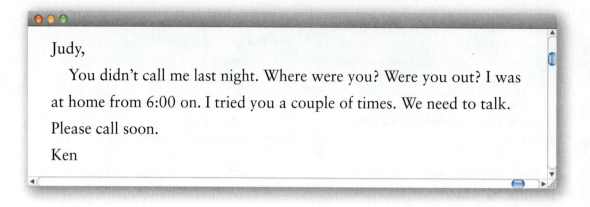

Judy,

You didn't call me last night. Where were you? Were you out? I was at home from 6:00 on. I tried you a couple of times. We need to talk. Please call soon.

Ken

EXERCISE 2: *Was* and *Were*

(Grammar Note 1)

Look at the pictures. Where were the people last night? Complete the sentences. Use **was** *or* **were** *and a phrase.*

at a concert   at the movies   at a play

at a party   at a soccer game   at home

1. Last night, Tim and Jessica _were at the movies_____.

2. Mary, Annie, and Ben _____.

3. Jeremy _____.

4. Mark _____.

5. Steve and his father _____.

6. Judy _____.

EXERCISE 3: Affirmative and Negative

(Grammar Notes 3–4)

Complete the conversation with **was**, **wasn't**, **were**, *or* **weren't**.

A: _____*Was*_____ Joan in class yesterday morning?
       1.

B: Yes, she _____.
             2.

A: _____ you at home last night?
   3.

B: No, I _____. I _____ at the movies.
       4.   **5.**

A: _____ the kids with you?
     6.

B: No, they _____. They _____ at a concert.
          7.   **8.**

EXERCISE 4: Questions and Answers

(Grammar Notes 1–4)

Answer the questions. Use short answers with **was** *or* **were**. *Then provide more information.*

1. Were you late to class yesterday morning?

   Yes, __*I was*__. __*The bus was late.*__
                      (The bus / late)

2. Were you at a concert yesterday evening?

   No, _____. _____
                 (I / at home)

3. Were you and Jessica at home last night?

   No, _____. _____
                 (We / at a play)

4. Was Annie with you at the library yesterday afternoon?

   No, _____. _____
                 (She / at a soccer game)

5. Were you and Tim at the movies last night?

   Yes, _____, but _____
                     (the film / boring)

6. Was Jeremy at school yesterday?

   Yes, _____, but _____ only in the morning.
                     (he / there)

EXERCISE 5: Editing

There are seven mistakes in the note. The first mistake is already corrected. Find and correct six more mistakes.

Mark,

               wasn't
   Sorry I ~~was~~ home last night. I were at a basketball game.

Amanda and Josh was with me. It were really exciting.

   Where were you on Tuesday afternoon? Susan and Brent

and I are at the soccer game, but you were there. Too bad. It

is really exciting.

   I'll talk to you soon. Call me.

                       Kathy

STEP 4 COMMUNICATION PRACTICE

EXERCISE 6: Pronunciation

A | *Listen to the sentences. Mark each sentence* **A (Affirmative)** *or* **N (Negative)**. *Circle* **was** *or* **wasn't, were,** *or* **weren't.**

   _N_ **1.** I **was** / (**wasn't**) at school yesterday.

   ____ **2.** It **was** / **wasn't** hot yesterday.

   ____ **3.** They **were** / **weren't** at the rock concert last night.

   ____ **4.** My friend **was** / **wasn't** with me at the movies.

   ____ **5.** She **was** / **wasn't** asleep at midnight.

   ____ **6.** We **were** / **weren't** at the soccer game.

B | *PAIRS: Say each sentence in the affirmative or the negative. Your partner says which one you said.*

EXERCISE 7: Listening

🎧 *Listen to the message on the answering machine. Check (✓) T (True), F (False), or* **NI (No Information).**

		T	F	NI
1.	Mark is at home now.	☐	☑	☐
2.	Josh was at the movies last night.	☐	☐	☐
3.	Amanda was at home last night.	☐	☐	☐
4.	Josh was alone at the movies.	☐	☐	☐
5.	The movie was *Transformers*.	☐	☐	☐
6.	The movie was exciting.	☐	☐	☐
7.	The theater was too hot.	☐	☐	☐

EXERCISE 8: Ask and Answer

PAIRS: Practice asking and answering the questions. Ask a partner. Then your partner asks you.

A: Were you at _____ (school / work / home) (yesterday morning / yesterday afternoon / last night)?

B: No, I wasn't. I was at _____ (the movies / a concert / a game).

A: What _____ (movie / concert / game)?

B: _____.

A: How was it?

B: It was _____ (great / pretty good / pretty bad / awful).

EXERCISE 9: Describe an Event

Tell a partner about a movie, a play, a concert, or a game. How was it? Use the words from the box.

boring	exciting	funny	interesting	scary

> EXAMPLE: **A:** I was at the movies last night. I saw *No Country for Old Men*.
> **B:** Was it good?
> **A:** Yes! It was exciting—and pretty scary.

EXERCISE 10: Writing

A | *Write six sentences about a movie, play, concert, or game. Say what it was, how it was, and who was in it. Use the past of* **be**. *Use vocabulary from the unit.*

> EXAMPLE: I was at a movie last night. The movie was *Julie and Julia*. It was very funny . . .

B | *Check your work. Use the Editing Checklist.*

Editing Checklist

Did you use . . . ?
- ☐ the past of **be** correctly
- ☐ vocabulary from the unit
- ☐ correct spelling

UNIT 7 Review

Check your answers on page UR-1.

Do you need to review anything?

EXERCISE A

Complete the conversation with **was, wasn't, were,** or **weren't.**

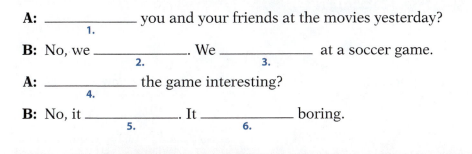

A: _____ you and your friends at the movies yesterday?
     1.

B: No, we _____. We _____ at a soccer game.
          2.   3.

A: _____ the game interesting?
     4.

B: No, it _____. It _____ boring.
           5.   6.

EXERCISE B

Answer the questions with short answers. Then provide more information. Use **was** or **were** and the words in parentheses.

1. Was Tim at home last night?

   No, _____. _____
                                              (He / at the library)

2. Were your brothers at school today?

   No, _____. _____
                                              (They / sick)

EXERCISE C

Correct the errors in the email message. There are five mistakes.

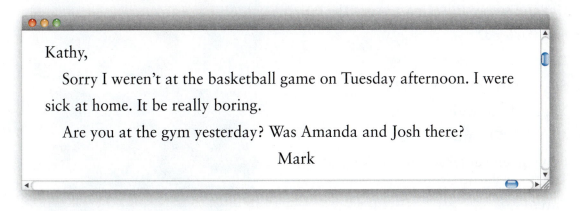

Kathy,

   Sorry I weren't at the basketball game on Tuesday afternoon. I were sick at home. It be really boring.

   Are you at the gym yesterday? Was Amanda and Josh there?

                    Mark

8 Past of *Be*: *Wh-* Questions
TRAVEL AND LEISURE ACTIVITIES

STEP 1 GRAMMAR IN CONTEXT

Before You Read

GROUPS: Talk about your last vacation. Where were you? How was the vacation? How was the weather?

Read

🎧 *Read the conversation.*

JASON: Hi, Mark.

MARK: Hey, Jason.

JASON: Welcome back. **How was** your vacation?

MARK: Great.

JASON: You look good. **Where were** you?

MARK: In Spain.

JASON: Nice. **How long were** you there?

MARK: Ten days. Ten wonderful days.

JASON: That's a long vacation. My parents were there last month. It was hot. **How was** the weather?

MARK: Hot and sunny. But it was cool at the beach.

JASON: And the food?

MARK: Delicious.

JASON: So . . . were you on a tour?

MARK: No, but I was with a guide.

JASON: A guide? **Who was** your guide?

MARK: Remember Kathy? At Amanda's wedding? The travel agent?

JASON: Sure.

MARK: Well, she's in Barcelona this month. She was my guide.

JASON: You lucky man!

After You Read

A | **Practice** *PAIRS: Practice the opening conversation.*

B | **Vocabulary** *Listen and repeat the words. Write new words in a notebook.*

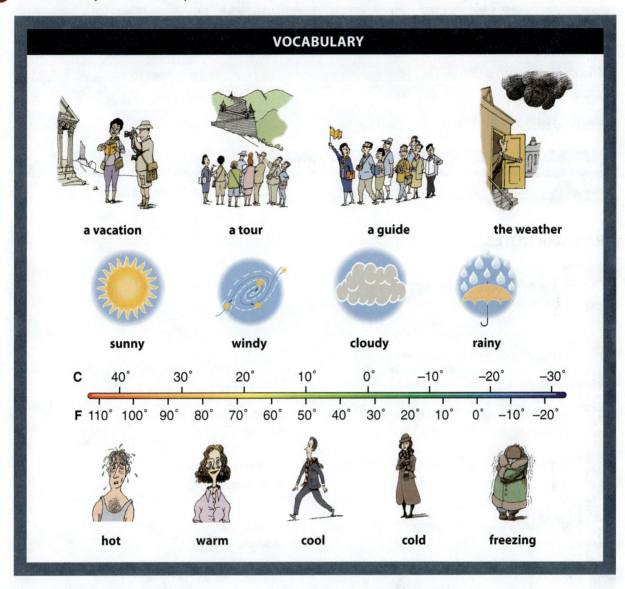

VOCABULARY

a vacation   a tour   a guide   the weather

sunny   windy   cloudy   rainy

C 40° 30° 20° 10° 0° −10° −20° −30°

F 110° 100° 90° 80° 70° 60° 50° 40° 30° 20° 10° 0° −10° −20°

hot   warm   cool   cold   freezing

C | **Vocabulary** *PAIRS: Talk about the weather in your city every day last week. How was the weather each day last week?*

EXAMPLE: **A:** I think it was hot on Monday.   **B:** And it was cloudy on Tuesday.

D | **Comprehension** *Look again at the opening conversation. There are six mistakes in the passage. The first mistake is already corrected. Find and correct five more mistakes.*

> Mark was in Spain for ~~seven~~ *ten* days. The weather was sunny and cool, but it was hot at the beach. Jason's cousins were in Spain last month. The weather was rainy then. The food in Spain was delicious. Mark's trip was great. Amanda's friend Kathy was his guide. She was in Madrid for a month.

PAST OF *BE*: *WH-* QUESTIONS

Wh- Questions	Short Answers	Long Answers
Where were you?	(In) Spain.	I was in Spain.
Who were you with?	Friends.	I was there with friends.
How was the weather?	Hot.	It was hot.
How long were you there?	Ten days.	I was there for ten days.

Questions about the Subject	Short Answers	Long Answers
Who was in Spain?	Mark (was).	Mark was in Spain.

GRAMMAR NOTES

1	Some *wh-* questions start with **where**, **when**, **who**, **what**, **how**, or **how long**. These words ask for information. In informal conversation, **answers** are usually **short**.	**A: How** was your weekend? **B:** Great!
2	Use **where** to ask about a location. Use **when** to ask about a time.	**A: Where** were you? **B:** In Spain. **A: When** were you there? **B:** In June.
3	Use **who** to ask about a person.	**A: Who** was in Spain? **B:** Mark. **A: Who** were you with? **B:** A friend.
4	Use **how** to ask for a description.	**A: How** was your vacation? **B:** Wonderful!
5	Use **how long** to ask for a length of time.	**A: How long** was the game? **B:** Two hours.
6	Use *it* to talk about the weather.	• **It** was hot. • **It** was sunny.

EXERCISE 1: Discover the Grammar

Circle the question word. Underline the past forms of **be**. *Then match the questions and answers.*

_b_ **1.** (Where) were you last night?   **a.** It was warm.

____ **2.** Who was with you?   **b.** I was at a soccer game.

____ **3.** How was the game?   **c.** Two hours.

____ **4.** How long was the game?   **d.** He was on vacation in Miami.

____ **5.** How was the weather?   **e.** My sister.

____ **6.** Where was your brother?   **f.** Exciting.

EXERCISE 2: Word Order   *(Grammar Notes 1–5)*

Put the words in the correct order. Make conversations.

1. A: How / your weekend / was /   **A:** _How was your weekend_____?

   B: was / It / great /   **B:** _____.

2. A: you / were / Where /   **A:** _____?

   B: a jazz concert / At /   **B:** _____.

3. A: was / When / the concert /   **A:** _____?

   B: last night / was / It /   **B:** _____.

4. A: the musician / Who / was /   **A:** _____?

   B: was / Diana Krall / It /   **B:** _____.

5. A: the concert / long / was / How /   **A:** _____?

   B: two hours / It / was /   **B:** _____.

EXERCISE 3: Past *Wh-* Questions

(Grammar Notes 1–5)

Write questions about the underlined words.

1. **A:** *How was the weather* ?

   B: It was <u>sunny</u>.

2. **A:** _____ at the movies?

   B: <u>Mark</u> was.

3. **A:** _____ Pierre on Monday?

   B: He was <u>in Paris</u>.

4. **A:** _____?

   B: The party was <u>yesterday</u>.

5. **A:** _____?

   B: Mark and Jason were with <u>Kathy</u>.

6. **A:** _____ the movie?

   B: The movie was <u>three hours long</u>.

7. **A:** _____?

   B: His parents were <u>in Spain</u>.

8. **A:** _____?

   B: Our guide was <u>great</u>.

EXERCISE 4: Past *Wh-* Questions

(Grammar Notes 1–5)

*Complete the conversation with past **wh-** questions.*

A: You weren't in class last week. Where _____?
                                                           1.

B: I was in London.

A: In London? Why?

B: It was my brother's wedding. His wife is British.

A: How _____?
              2.

B: The wedding was wonderful.

A: How long _____?
                      3.

B: I was in London for just four days.

A: How _____?

⁴·

B: It wasn't so nice. It was cold and rainy, but the people were great, and we had a terrific time.

EXERCISE 5: Editing

There are eight mistakes in the conversations. The first mistake is already corrected.
Find and correct seven more mistakes.

1. **A:** How ~~were~~ *was* your weekend?

   B: Saturday evening was great.

   A: Where was you?

   B: At a soccer game.

   A: How the game was?

   B: Exciting and long.

   A: How long were it?

   B: Three hours.

2. **A:** How were your vacation?

   B: OK.

   A: Where you were?

   B: Was at the beach.

   A: How the weather?

   B: Cool and rainy.

   A: That's too bad.

STEP 4 COMMUNICATION PRACTICE

EXERCISE 6: Listening

A | *Listen to the conversation. Circle the correct letter.*

1. How was Jason's weekend?
   a. Very good.
   b. Good.
   c. Not so good.

2. How was Mark's weekend?
   a. Very good.
   b. Good.
   c. Not so good.

B | *Listen again. Circle the correct letter to complete the sentences.*

1. Jason was at _____.
   a. the beach
   b. the movies
   c. home

2. The weather was _____.
   a. sunny and cool
   b. sunny and hot
   c. sunny and cold

3. Mark was at _____.
   a. the beach
   b. the movies
   c. home

4. Mark was busy with _____.
   a. work
   b. homework
   c. friends from high school

EXERCISE 7: Pronunciation

A | *Listen to the* **wh-** *words in the questions. Circle the question words that begin with the /w/ sound.*

1. (Where) were you?

2. Who were you with?

3. When were you there?

4. What was your flight number?

5. What was the weather like on Saturday?

6. Who was in Seoul?

B | *Listen again and practice.*

EXERCISE 8: Clarification

Read a sentence to your partner. Cough at the blank. Your partner says, "What was that?" and asks a question. Answer the question.

EXAMPLE: **Student A:** It was *(COUGH)* and rainy yesterday.
Student B: What was that? How was the weather?
Student A: It was cold and rainy.

1. It was _____ and rainy yesterday.

2. My cousin was in _____ for a week.

3. _____ was at a concert last night.

4. We were on vacation for _____ days.

5. My uncle was in Venice last _____.

6. It was _____ and sunny in Miami every day last week.

7. My friends were in _____ last summer.

8. I was in _____ on Monday.

9. _____ were in Tokyo on Tuesday.

10. It was _____ and cold on Wednesday.

EXERCISE 9: Who Was Really There?

A | *GROUPS OF THREE: Choose a place where only one student was.*

All three students say, "I was in _____."

    EXAMPLE: **Student A:** I was in Mexico City.
                       Student B: I was in Mexico City.
                       Student C: I was in Mexico City.

B | *The class asks the three students questions.*

    EXAMPLES: Where is Mexico City? What is a famous landmark? How big is the city? What kind of public transportation is there?

C | *Students A, B, and C answer the questions. The class guesses who was really there.*

EXERCISE 10: Writing

A | *Write about your last vacation. Tell about the weather. Use vocabulary from the unit. Use the past of* **be**.

B | *Check your work. Use the Editing Checklist.*

Editing Checklist
Did you use . . . ? ☐ vocabulary from the unit ☐ the past of **be** correctly ☐ correct spelling

C | *PAIRS: Read your sentences to your partner. Ask questions.*

Check your answers on page UR-1.

Do you need to review anything?

EXERCISE A

Put the words in the correct order. Make a conversation.

A: were / Where / last night / you _____?

B: at the movies / was / I / _____.

A: the movie / was / How / _____?

B: funny / was / It / _____.

A: you / with / were / Who / _____?

B: with Jane and Andrew / I / was / _____.

EXERCISE B

Complete the conversations with **Who, Where, When, How,** *or* **How long.**

1. **A:** _____ were you last night?

   B: At the supermarket.

2. **A:** _____ was the weather?

   B: It was freezing.

3. **A:** _____ was with you?

   B: My roommate.

4. **A:** _____ was the concert?

   B: One hour.

5. **A:** _____ were you at the beach?

   B: Yesterday.

EXERCISE C

Correct the conversation. There are four mistakes.

A: Hi. How were your vacation?

B: It great.

A: Where was you?

B: In London.

A: In London? How the weather was?

B: It was rainy.

Imperatives; Simple Present: Statements

UNIT	GRAMMAR FOCUS	THEME
9	Imperatives	Giving Directions
10	Simple Present: Statements	Likes and Dislikes

Imperatives

GIVING DIRECTIONS

STEP 1 ### GRAMMAR IN CONTEXT

Before You Read

PAIRS: Name a good restaurant. Your partner asks, "Where is it? How do you get to it?"

Read

🎧 *Read the conversation.*

MARK: Is the restaurant close? I'm hungry.

STEVE: Yes, it is.

MARK: Is it good?

STEVE: **Don't worry.** It's very good. It's Indian.

MARK: Great. I love Indian food.

STEVE: Now **drive** to the corner and **turn** left at Jackson Street.

MARK: At the gas station?

STEVE: Yes. Then **go** two blocks on Jackson.

MARK: Got it.[1]

STEVE: OK. **Turn** right at the next corner.

MARK: At Third Avenue?

STEVE: Yes. The restaurant is on the corner on your right.

MARK: Is that it?

STEVE: Yes, it is. **Don't park** here. It's a bus stop. **Park** behind the truck.

MARK: OK. **Please hand** me my jacket. . . . Uh, **wait** a second . . . Steve? The restaurant is empty.

STEVE: Really? It's usually packed.[2]

MARK: Is that a sign on the door?

STEVE: Uh-huh . . . Closed for vacation.

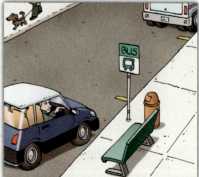

---

[1] **Got it:** I understand.
[2] **packed:** filled with people

After You Read

A | **Practice** *PAIRS: Practice the opening conversation.*

B | **Vocabulary** *Listen and repeat the words. Write new words in a notebook.*

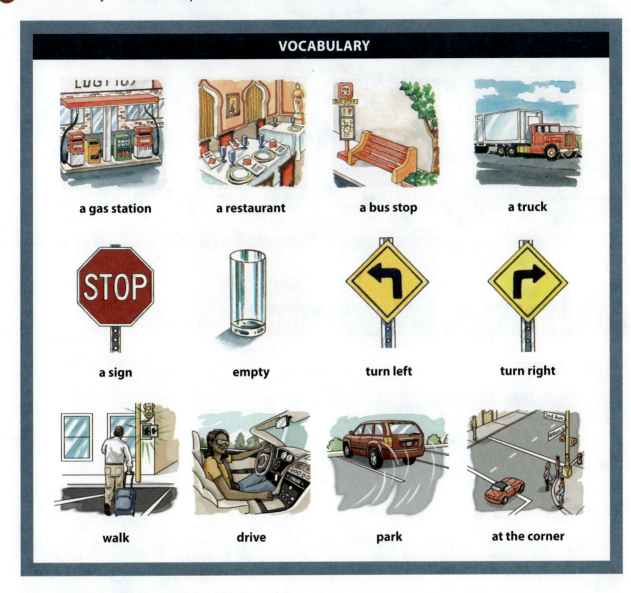

VOCABULARY

a gas station

a restaurant

a bus stop

a truck

a sign

empty

turn left

turn right

walk

drive

park

at the corner

C | **Vocabulary** *PAIRS: Are these signs near your school? Where are they?*

a. Walk / Don't walk
b. Drive slowly
c. Stop
d. Don't walk on the grass

D | Comprehension *PAIRS: Look again at the opening conversation. Then look at the map. Draw Mark's route. Draw an **X** at the restaurant.*

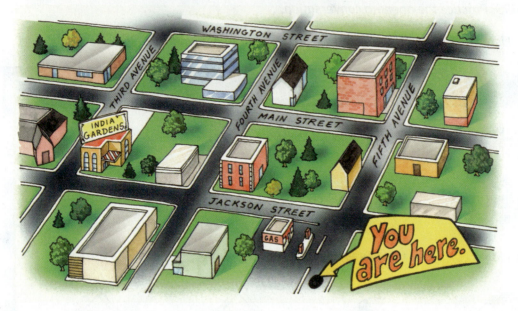

IMPERATIVES

Affirmative	Negative
Turn left.	**Don't turn** right.
Park here.	**Don't park** there.

GRAMMAR NOTES

1	Use the imperative for **directions, instructions,** and **requests**.	• **Turn** left. (direction) • **Answer** the questions. (instruction) • **Please hand** me my jacket. (request)
2	Use the **base form** of the verb for the imperative.	• **Open** the door.
3	Use *do not* + the **base form** for the negative form of the imperative. *Don't* is the short form (contraction) of *do not*.	• **Do not park** here. • **Don't park** here.
4	*Please* makes a request more **polite**. *Please* comes at the beginning or at the end of the sentence.	• **Please** help me. OR • Help me, **please**.

EXERCISE 1: Discover the Grammar

Read the sentences. Underline the negative imperatives. Then match the sentences.

___c___ **1.** <u>Don't walk</u>.

_____ **2.** Don't park there.

_____ **3.** My hands are full.

_____ **4.** Don't turn left at the corner.

_____ **5.** Don't worry.

_____ **6.** Please hand me the dictionary.

a. Please open the door.

b. Turn right.

~~c.~~ Take a bus.

d. It's a bus stop.

e. It's next to you.

f. You're not late.

EXERCISE 2: Directions

(Grammar Notes 1–3)

Look at the pictures. Write the correct sentences from the box.

| Don't park here. | Make a U-turn. | Turn left. | Turn right. |

1. _____

2. _____

3. _____

4. _____

EXERCISE 3: Commands and Requests

(Grammar Notes 1–4)

Look at the pictures. What are the people saying? Write the correct sentences from the box.

Close the window, please.	Listen to this CD.	Please turn to page six.
Don't go in the deep water.	Please don't smoke.	Try this cake.
Don't read this book.	~~Please sit down.~~	

1. *Please sit down.*

2. _____

3. _____

4. _____

5. _____

6. _____

7. _____

8. _____

EXERCISE 4: Responding to Imperatives

(Grammar Notes 1–4)

A | *Look at sentence A. Follow the instructions.*

- Circle the word *open*.
- Underline the word *not*.
- Change the word *window* to *door*.
- Change *do not* to the short form.
- Write the new sentence on the line.

A. Do not (open) the window.

_____

B | *Look at sentence B. Follow the instructions.*

- Add *please* to the sentence.
- Change *do not* to the short form.
- Change *driveway* to *garage*.
- Write the new sentence on the line.

B. Do not park in the driveway.

_____

EXERCISE 5: Editing

There are seven mistakes in the sentences. The first mistake is already corrected. Find and correct six more mistakes.

1. Please ~~not to~~ *don't* open your book.

2. You no sit here. It's not your seat.

3. Study please page 3.

4. Completes the sentences.

5. Don't please drive fast.

6. No close the window. Keep it open.

7. Don't to turn left. Turn right at the corner.

STEP 4 COMMUNICATION PRACTICE

EXERCISE 6: Listening

A | *Listen to the conversation between a new and an old student. Read the question. Then listen again. Complete the sentence.*

The woman asks for directions to two places. What places are they?

The _____ and the _____.

B | *Listen again. Complete the sentences with directions to both places.*

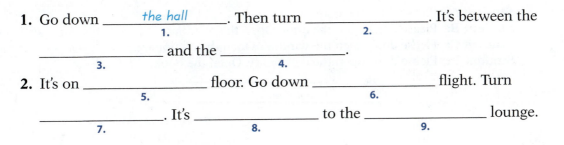

1. Go down _____*the hall*_____. Then turn _____. It's between the
                1.   2.

   _____ and the _____.
        3.   4.

2. It's on _____ floor. Go down _____ flight. Turn
              5.   6.

   _____. It's _____ to the _____ lounge.
      7.   8.   9.

EXERCISE 7: Pronunciation

A | *Listen and practice.*

1. **a. sit** — Don't **sit** there.   **b. seat** — Take this **seat**.

2. **a. hit** — Don't **hit** me.   **b. heat** — Turn on the **heat**.

3. **a. Kip** — Please feed **Kip**.   **b. keep** — **Keep** your cell phone on.

4. **a. his** — **His** name is Steve.   **b. he's** — **He's** a teacher.

5. **a. it** — **It** isn't good.   **b. eat** — Don't **eat** the orange.

B | *Listen to the sentences. Check (✓) the sounds you hear.*

	/ɪ/ (b*i*t, h*i*t)	/i/ (b*ea*t, h*ea*t)
1.		✓
2.		
3.		
4.		
5.		
6.		
7.		
8.		
9.		

EXERCISE 8: Make Requests

GROUPS OF FOUR: Student A, make a request. Use a verb from the box. Student B, say the negative and make a new request. Students C and D do the same. Then Student D starts a new round with a new verb.

close	give me	hand me	open	turn to	write

EXAMPLE: **Student A:** Please open the door.
                Student B: Please don't open the door. Open the window.
                Student C: Please don't open the window. Open the dictionary.
                Student D: Please don't open the dictionary. Open the book.

EXERCISE 9: Directions

A | *PAIRS: Look at the map. Read the directions to a park aloud. Your partner listens and checks (✔) the correct park.*

Directions: *You are at Union Street and Third Avenue. Walk two blocks on Third Avenue to Pine Street. Turn right. Then go one block. Where are you?*

____ **1.** Westlake Park

____ **2.** Victor Steinbrueck Park

____ **3.** Regrade Park

B | *Switch roles. Start at the same place. Give directions to the other parks. Your partner names the park.*

EXERCISE 10: Writing

A | *Write directions to a place near your school. Use vocabulary from the unit. Use the imperative.*

B | *Check your work. Use the Editing Checklist.*

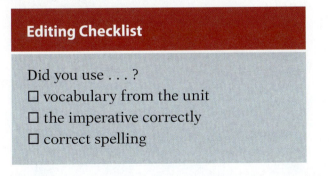

Editing Checklist

Did you use . . . ?
☐ vocabulary from the unit
☐ the imperative correctly
☐ correct spelling

C | *Read your directions to the class. The class names the place.*

EXAMPLE: **Student A:** Turn right at the corner. Go two blocks. It's in the middle of the block.
Student B: Is it the public library?
Student A: Yes, it is.

UNIT 9 Review

Check your answers on page UR-1.

Do you need to review anything?

EXERCISE A

Complete the sentences. Write the correct forms of the words from the box.

not, eat	**not, worry**	**turn**
not, open	**read**	

1. Please _____ the window. It's cold.

2. _____ this book. It's really interesting

3. _____ those muffins. They're terrible.

4. _____. We aren't late.

5. _____ left at the next corner.

EXERCISE B

Look at the sentence. Follow the instructions.

1. Circle the word *not*.
2. Underline the word *start*.
3. Change *do not* to the short form.
4. Change the number *9* to *10*.
5. Write the new sentence on the line.

Do not start Unit 9.

_____

EXERCISE C

Correct the sentences. There are five mistakes.

1. Please to stop at the corner.

2. You not make a U-turn.

3. Turns right, please.

4. Don't please park here.

5. Don't to turn left.

UNIT 10

Simple Present: Statements
LIKES AND DISLIKES

STEP 1 GRAMMAR IN CONTEXT

Before You Read

PAIRS: Which of these things or activities do you like? Which don't you like? Say "I like"
or "I don't like" for each one.

cars	computers	magazines	parties	sports	travel
classical music	exams	novels	rap music	texting	TV

EXAMPLE: I like TV. OR I don't like TV.

Read

🎧 *Read the conversation.*

JUDY: I **need** more coffee. Would you like some?

MARK: Yes, please.

JUDY: Here you go.

MARK: Thanks.

JUDY: Oh! New photos?

MARK: Yes . . . Look at this one. This **is** my brother, Nick.
He **lives** in Kenya. He **teaches** English there.

JUDY: In Kenya? Wow! . . . He **looks** like you.

MARK: I **know**. We both **have** brown hair and green eyes.

JUDY: And you**'re** both tall.

MARK: But we**'re** different in a lot of ways.

JUDY: How?

MARK: Well, I **like** people and parties. Nick **likes**
computers. Nick **doesn't like** parties.

JUDY: Anything else?

MARK: Uh-huh. I **speak** Chinese. Nick **speaks** Swahili.
I **read** newspapers and magazines. Nick **reads**
novels. I **call** my friends. I **watch** DVDs almost
every night, but Nick **surfs** the Internet. He
emails me a lot. He **writes** a blog too.

JUDY: Yeah? He **sounds** interesting.

A | Practice *PAIRS: Practice the opening conversation.*

B | Vocabulary *Listen and repeat the words. Write new words in a notebook.*

VOCABULARY

look like	**surf the Internet**	**a magazine**
a novel	**a newspaper**	**a blog**

LANGUAGES

Arabic	Chinese	English	French
عربي	中文		Français
Portuguese	**Russian**	**Spanish**	**Swahili**
Portugues	Русский	Español	Kiswahili

C | Vocabulary *PAIRS: Where do people speak the languages in the box?*

EXAMPLE: They speak Arabic in Iraq.

D | Comprehension *Look again at the opening conversation. Write **T (True)** or **F (False)**.*

____F____ **1.** Mark's brother Nick lives in the United States.

_____ **2.** Nick is a writer.

_____ **3.** Mark looks like Nick.

_____ **4.** Nick likes computers.

_____ **5.** Nick speaks Chinese.

_____ **6.** Nick writes a blog.

THE SIMPLE PRESENT: STATEMENTS

Affirmative Statements		
Subject	**Verb**	
I You* We They	**come**	from Brazil.
He She It	**comes**	

Negative Statements			
Subject	***Do not / Does not***	**Base Form of Verb**	
I You* We They	**do not don't**	**come**	from China.
He She It	**does not doesn't**	**come**	from China.

You is both singular and plural.

GRAMMAR NOTES

1	Use the **simple present** to talk about **facts** or things that **happen again and again**.	• I **live** in Kenya. (*a fact*) • He **watches** TV every night. (*a thing that happens again and again*)
2	In **affirmative statements**, use the **base form** of the verb with *I*, *you*, *we*, and *they*. Add *-s* or *-es* only with the **third-person singular** (*he*, *she*, *it*). Add *-s* to most verbs. Add *-es* to verbs that end in *ch*, *o*, *ss*, *sh*, *x*, or *z*.	• We **live** in Redmond. • They **have** a house in Seattle. • It **rains** a lot here. • She **rushes** home after work. • He **reads** travel books. • She **watches** TV at night. • She **does** her homework after class.
3	Use *do not* or *does not* + the **base form** of the verb to make a **negative statement**. We often use the contractions *don't* and *doesn't* in speaking and informal writing.	• They **do not live** in the city. • He **does not speak** Chinese. • They **don't live** in the city. • He **doesn't speak** Chinese.
4	*Be* and *have* are **irregular verbs**. **NOTE:** Look at Unit 13 for more practice with *be* and *have*.	• I **am** a teacher. Steve **is** a teacher too. • I **have** a lot of students. Steve **has** a lot of students too.

EXERCISE 1: Discover the Grammar

A | *Check (✔) the sentences in the simple present.*

_____ **1.** Please speak English. Please don't speak Spanish.

__✔__ **2.** My brother Nick looks like me.

_____ **3.** Jessica speaks Spanish. She doesn't speak Italian.

_____ **4.** I have brown eyes. I don't have blue eyes.

_____ **5.** Drive to the corner and turn left.

_____ **6.** Jeremy has a brother and a sister.

_____ **7.** Nick writes a blog.

_____ **8.** Don't be late for dinner.

B | *Check (✔) the sentences in the third-person singular.*

_____ **1.** Annie and I don't like fish.

__✔__ **2.** Miryam speaks Arabic.

_____ **3.** It doesn't snow in Brazil.

_____ **4.** She doesn't speak Italian.

_____ **5.** Nick likes computers.

_____ **6.** They come from Hong Kong.

_____ **7.** It rains a lot here in the winter.

_____ **8.** I don't like pizza.

EXERCISE 2: Third Person   *(Grammar Notes 1–2)*

Write two sentences about the people.

1.   Name: Heng

   Place: Beijing, China *Heng lives in Beijing, China.* _____

   Language: Chinese *Heng speaks Chinese.* _____

2.   Name: Ali

   Place: Amman, Jordan _____

   Language: Arabic _____

3.   **Names:** Antonio and Rosa

     Place: Salvador, Brazil _____

  Language: Portuguese _____

4.   **Name:** Elena

     Place: Santiago, Chile _____

  Language: Spanish _____

5.   **Names:** Maureen and James

     Place: Dublin, Ireland _____

  Language: English _____

EXERCISE 3: *Want*   *(Grammar Notes 2–3)*

Complete the conversation. Use the simple present form of **want.** *Use the affirmative or negative.*

WAITER: Can I help you?

TIM: Yes, thanks. The children _____*want*_____ ice cream. My son
                                1.

    _____ chocolate.
       2.

BEN: No, Dad. I _____ chocolate. I _____ vanilla.
             3. (not)   **4.**

ANNIE: I _____ chocolate.
        5.

TIM: OK. My son _____ vanilla. My daughter _____
                6.   **7.**

   chocolate.

WAITER: And you, sir?

TIM: I _____ ice cream. I just _____ a soda.
      8. (not)   **9.**

WAITER: Is that all?

TIM: Yes, thanks.

EXERCISE 4: Affirmative and Negative

(Grammar Notes 1, 3–4)

Look at the pictures. Complete the sentences. Use the correct forms of the verbs in parentheses. Use the affirmative or negative.

1. Jeremy _____ *has* _____ an old car.
   (have)
   He _____ *doesn't have* _____ a new car.

2. Annie _____ pizza.
   (like)
   She _____ salad.

3. The man _____ water.
   (need)
   He _____ ice cream.

4. Judy _____ tea.
   (want)
   She _____ coffee.

EXERCISE 5: Editing

There are eight mistakes in the letter. The first mistake is already corrected. Find and correct seven more mistakes.

> Dear Mary,
>
>   Spain is great. The Spanish people are very friendly, but they ~~speaks~~ *speak* so fast. Jim speak Spanish very well. He don't understand everything, but he understand a lot. I speak a little Spanish. I don't understand much yet.
>
>   It's rainy here! People say it don't usually rain much in the summer here.
>
>   We're at my cousin's house. He and his wife lives in a beautiful apartment in Madrid. Juan work in an office downtown. His wife Alicia no work. She stays at home with the children.
>
>   See you soon.
>
>   Rose

STEP 4 COMMUNICATION PRACTICE

EXERCISE 6: Listening

A | *Listen to the conversation between Tim Olson and a man he meets on a train. Then listen again. Circle the correct letter to complete the sentences.*

1. They're going to _____.
   a. Chicago   **(b.)** Seattle   **c.** Bucharest

2. The man doesn't live in _____.
   a. Romania   **b.** Bucharest   **c.** Chicago

3. The man comes from _____.
   a. Romania   **b.** Russia   **c.** Rwanda

4. A lot of people in the man's country know some _____.
   a. English   **b.** French   **c.** Russian

5. The man speaks _____ languages.
   a. one   **b.** two   **c.** three

6. Tim doesn't speak any _____.
   a. English   **b.** French   **c.** Spanish

B | *Listen again. What does Tim think about the man's English? Complete the sentence.*

He thinks his English _____.

EXERCISE 7: Pronunciation

A | *Read and listen to the Pronunciation Note.*

Pronunciation Note
In third-person singular present verbs the final sound is:
/s/ after voiceless sounds, such as /p/, /t/, /k/.
EXAMPLES: books, cats
/z/ after voiced sounds, such as /b/, /d/, /g/.
EXAMPLES: beds, dogs
/ɪz/ after such sounds as /ch/ and /sh/.
EXAMPLES: churches, wishes

B | *Listen to the next part of the conversation. Listen carefully to the verbs in the third-person singular. What is the last sound? Check (✔) the sounds you hear.*

Verb	/s/	/z/	/ɪz/
has		✓	
teaches			
writes			
sounds			
watches			
understands			
works			

C | *Listen and repeat the verbs.*

EXERCISE 8: True or False?

A | *PAIRS: Take turns. Use the words to make affirmative sentences in the simple present. Three of the statements are true, and four are false. Correct the false statements.*

> **EXAMPLE:** Most people / Beijing / speak Spanish
> **A:** Most people in Beijing speak Spanish.
> **B:** False. Most people in Beijing speak Chinese.

1. Antonio Banderas / come from / Spain
2. Most people / China / eat with chopsticks
3. People / Japan / drive / on the right
4. People / Great Britain / drive / on the right
5. People / live / at the North Pole
6. Penguins / live / in deserts
7. It / snow / Chile / in July

B | *Check your answers on page P-1.*

EXERCISE 9: Writing

A | *Write true statements about yourself.*

I live in _____. I don't like _____.

I work in _____. I need _____.

I speak _____. I don't need _____.

I don't speak _____. I want _____.

I like _____. I don't want _____.

B | *Now work with a partner. Tell your partner five things about yourself.*

> **EXAMPLE:** I work in a department store. I speak two languages. I like chocolate ice cream. I don't like pizza. I need a job.

C | *Now write five sentences about your partner.*

> **EXAMPLE:** She works in a department store . . .

D | *Check your work. Use the Editing Checklist.*

Editing Checklist

Did you use . . . ?
☐ the simple present correctly
☐ correct spelling

Check your answers on page UR-1.

Do you need to review anything?

EXERCISE A

Complete the sentences. Use the correct forms of the verbs in parentheses. Use contractions whenever possible.

1. My roommate _____ rap music. He
   (like)
   _____ classical music.
   (not, like)

2. My children _____ apples. My son
   (not, want)
   _____ ice cream. My daughters
   (want)
   _____ chocolate.
   (want)

EXERCISE B

Circle the correct words to complete the sentences.

1. My sister and I **live / lives** in different cities.

2. She **like / likes** to surf the Internet, and I **like / likes** to read.

3. She **has / have** blue eyes, and I **has / have** brown eyes.

EXERCISE C

Correct the sentences. There are five mistakes.

1. Look at this photo.

2. This is my cousin Juan. He don't look like me!

3. Juan and his wife, Alicia, lives in Spain.

4. Alicia is stay at home with the children, and Juan work in an office.

5. They both speaks Spanish very well.

PART V

SIMPLE PRESENT: QUESTIONS, *Be* AND *Have*; ADVERBS OF FREQUENCY

Simple Present: *Yes / No* Questions
SHOPPING FOR ELECTRONICS

Before You Read

PAIRS: Name one electronic device (TV, DVD player, cell phone, computer) that you have and one you don't have but want to get.

Read

🎧 *Read the conversation.*

AMANDA: Uh . . . Steve, that TV is pretty old. **Do** you **need** a new one? **Do** you **want** a flat screen TV?

STEVE: No, I don't think so. This old TV works very well.

AMANDA: How about a smart phone? **Do** you **want** a smart phone? Josh and I use our smart phones all the time.

STEVE: Not really. Why?

AMANDA: There's a huge sale at Goodbuys. It starts today.

STEVE: Goodbuys? **Do** you **mean** the store on Main Street?

AMANDA: Uh-huh. Everything is 30 percent off. They have some great deals.*

STEVE: I don't need anything. People have too many things.

AMANDA: Well, what about Jessica? **Does** she **need** anything? **Does** she **have** a GPS? They're really helpful. **Do** Tim, Jeremy, or Ben **want** anything?

STEVE: I don't know. Amanda, why are you telling me about Goodbuys? **Do** you **work** there?

AMANDA: Actually, I do. I'm a new manager.

STEVE: Really? That's great. Wait a second. **Do** they **fix** things?

AMANDA: Yes, they do. The service department is great.

STEVE: Well, that sounds good. My radio doesn't work.

AMANDA: Uh . . . Steve. Is that the radio?

STEVE: Yes.

AMANDA: Steve! That radio is older than all of our technicians. I'm not sure they can fix it.

---

* **great deals:** things you can buy at a very low price

SHOP AT
GOODBUYS!
SALE Starts today
ALL TVs, DVDs, phones, stereos 30% OFF
HURRY WHILE THINGS LAST!

After You Read

A | Practice *PAIRS: Practice the opening conversation.*

🎧 **B | Vocabulary** *Listen and repeat the words. Write new words in a notebook.*

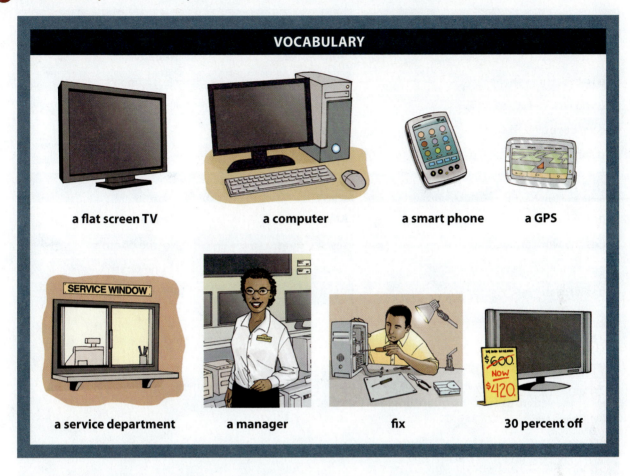

VOCABULARY

a flat screen TV   a computer   a smart phone   a GPS

a service department   a manager   fix   30 percent off

C | Vocabulary *PAIRS: Tell about an electronics store near your school. What do they sell? Do they have great deals? Do they fix things?*

> **EXAMPLE:** Electronics Plus is near our school. It's on 86th Street. They sell TVs, computers, and other electronics. They have great deals. They don't have a service department.

D | Comprehension *Look again at the opening conversation. Write* **Yes, No,** *or* **I don't know.**

1. Does Steve work at Goodbuys? _____*No*_____

2. Does Steve want a new TV? _____

3. Do Amanda and Josh like their flat screen TV? _____

4. Does the sale start tomorrow? _____

5. Do they have a service department at Goodbuys? _____

6. Does Steve want to go to Goodbuys? _____

7. Does Steve have a new radio? _____

SIMPLE PRESENT: *YES / NO* QUESTIONS

Yes / No Questions	Short Answers	
Do	**Affirmative**	**Negative**
Do I **need** a new phone?	Yes, you **do**.	No, you **don't**.
Do you **want** a flat screen TV?	Yes, I **do**.	No, I **don't**.
Do we **have** a good deal?	Yes, we **do**.	No, we **don't**.
Do they **have** a service department?	Yes, they **do**.	No, they **don't**.

Yes / No Questions	Short Answers	
Does	**Affirmative**	**Negative**
Does she **work** at Goodbuys?	Yes, she **does**.	No, she **doesn't**.
Does he **have** time on Wednesday?	Yes, he **does**.	No, he **doesn't**.
Does it **mean** "yes"?	Yes, it **does**.	No, it **doesn't**.

GRAMMAR NOTES

1	Use *do* or *does* + a **subject** + the **base form** of the verb to ask *yes / no questions* in the simple present. Use *do* with *I*, *you*, *we*, and *they*. Use *does* with *he*, *she*, and *it*.	• **Do** you **work** there? • **Does** he **have** a smart phone?
2	We usually use **short answers** in conversation. Sometimes we use **long answers**.	**A:** Do they have a service department? **B: Yes.** OR **Yes, they do.** **B: Yes. They have a service department.**

EXERCISE 1: Discover the Grammar

Read the sentences. Underline the six **yes / no** *questions. Then match the questions and the answers.*

_____ **1.** Do you want a TV?

_____ **2.** Do these TVs cost $1,000?

_____ **3.** Does that TV have a warranty?

_____ **4.** Do you deliver?

a. Yes, we do, but there's a $50 charge. Do you have a big car? We can help you get it in.

b. Yes, we do. Our old TV doesn't work.

c. Yes, it does. It comes with a 90-day warranty.

d. No, they cost $850. They're on sale. Do you like them? They're very popular.

EXERCISE 2: *Do* or *Does*

(Grammar Note 1)

Complete the conversations. Use **Do** *or* **Does** *and the correct words from the box.*

cost	~~know~~	like	live	mean	need	use

1. A: _____ *Do* _____ you _____ *know* _____ a good electronics store?

   B: Yes, I do. I get all my electronics at Goodbuys.

2. A: _____ that smart phone _____ a lot?

   B: No, it's not expensive.

3. A: _____ I _____ a case for my phone?

   B: No, but it's a good idea to get one.

4. A: _____ she _____ near Goodbuys?

   B: Yes, she does. Her home is close to the electronics store.

5. A: _____ Amanda _____ her job?

   B: Yes. She likes it a lot.

6. A: _____ Josh and Amanda _____ their smart phones to read email?

   B: Yes, they do. They use their phones for a lot of things.

7. A: _____ "fix" _____ "repair"?

   B: Yes, it does.

EXERCISE 3: Yes / No Questions

(Grammar Note 1)

Write **yes / no** questions. Use **Do** or **Does** and the simple present of the words in parentheses.

1. (you / like computer games) ___Do you like computer games___?

2. (you / know a good electronics store) _____?

3. (your family / have a lot of electronics) _____?

4. (your friends / spend a lot of time online) _____?

5. (your friends / spend a lot of money on electronics) _____?

6. (your cell phone / have a case) _____?

EXERCISE 4: Yes / No Questions

(Grammar Notes 1–2)

Write **yes / no** questions. Use the words in parentheses. Read Jeremy's note to Amanda and Josh. Then answer the questions with short answers.

> Dear Amanda and Josh,
>   Thanks so much for the smart phone. I use it all the time. I check my email. I text my friends. I listen to music. I take photos. I use the calculator, and, of course, I make calls.
>   It was a terrific birthday gift. It was great seeing you both. I'm glad you live nearby.
> Love,
> Jeremy

1. (Jeremy / like his smart phone)

   A: ___Does Jeremy like his smart phone___?

   B: ___Yes, he does___.

2. (Jeremy / use the phone for different things)

   A: _____?

   B: _____.

3. (Jeremy / check / email from the phone)

   A: _____?

   B: _____.

4. (Jeremy / listen to music from the phone)

A: _____?

B: _____.

5. (Jeremy / watch TV shows from his phone)

A: _____?

B: _____.

6. (Jeremy and his friends / send text messages)

A: _____?

B: _____.

7. (Amanda and Josh / live near Jeremy)

A: _____?

B: _____.

EXERCISE 5: Editing

There are five mistakes in the conversation. The first mistake is already corrected. Find and correct four more mistakes.

A: Do you ~~knows~~ *know* a good electronics store?

B: Yes, I do. It's on Main Street.

A: Does it stays open late?

B: Yes, it do.

A: What's the name of the store?

B: Goodbuys.

A: Do you spells it G-O-O-D-B-U-Y?

B: Uh-huh, but it has an *s* at the end.

A: Cost electronics at Goodbuys a lot?

B: No, they don't. Everything there is a good buy.

A: That's terrific.

EXERCISE 6: Listening

A | *Listen to the conversation between Mark and Judy. Complete the sentence. Circle the correct letter.*

Mark wants a gift for _____.

a. his mother's birthday

b. his grandmother's anniversary

c. his grandmother's birthday

B | *Listen again. Circle the correct letter.*

1. Do Judy and Mark go to the game?

    a. Yes, they do.

    b. No, they don't.

2. Does Mark's grandmother like music?

    a. Yes, she does.

    b. Mark doesn't know.

3. Does Mark's grandmother like chocolate?

    a. Yes, she does.

    b. Mark isn't sure.

4. Judy says, "I know the perfect gift." What is it?

    a. a gift of time

    b. a gift of money

EXERCISE 7: Pronunciation

A | *We usually stress important words (for example, nouns and verbs) in a sentence. Listen and repeat the sentences.*

1. Do you **want** a **smart phone**?

2. Does he **need** a **battery**?

3. Does it **come** with a **case**?

4. Does she **like** her **computer**?

5. Do they **like music**?

B | *Listen and underline the important words.*

1. Does he <u>fix</u> <u>computers</u>?

2. Does he want a phone?

3. Do you sell cameras?

4. Do you have a computer?

5. Do they use their GPS?

C | *Listen again and repeat.*

EXERCISE 8: Do You . . . ?

A | *Write* **yes** / **no** *questions. Ask four classmates. Follow the example.*

EXAMPLE: **Tuan:** Do you check your email every day?
Annette: Yes, I do.
Pablo: No, I don't.

1. ~~check email every day~~	3. like electronics	5. send e-cards
2. have a GPS	4. play computer games	6. shop online

Yes / No Questions	Student A	Student B	Student C	Student D
1. Do you check your email every day?				
2.				
3.				
4.				
5.				
6.				

B | *Tell the class about your classmates.*

EXAMPLE: **Tuan:** Annette checks her email every day. Pablo doesn't check his email every day.

EXERCISE 9: Writing

A | *Write five* **yes** / **no** *questions in the simple present about electronic devices. Use vocabulary from the unit.*

B | *Check your work. Use the Editing Checklist.*

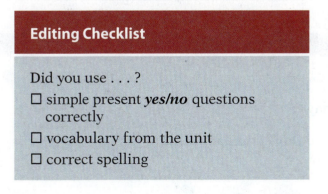

Editing Checklist

Did you use . . . ?
☐ simple present *yes/no* questions correctly
☐ vocabulary from the unit
☐ correct spelling

C | *GROUPS: Ask your partners your questions. Report their answers to the class.*

EXAMPLES: Do you have a cell phone? Do you call five or more people a day? Everyone in our group has a cell phone, and everyone calls more than five people every day.

Check your answers on page UR-1.

Do you need to review anything?

EXERCISE A

Match the questions and answers.

_____ **1.** Do you have a flat screen TV?   **a.** Yes, they do.

_____ **2.** Do they fix radios?   **b.** No, I don't.

_____ **3.** Does Josh have a smart phone?   **c.** Yes, he does.

_____ **4.** Does this car have a GPS?   **d.** No, it doesn't.

EXERCISE B

*Write **yes** / **no** questions. Use **do** or **does** and the words in parentheses. Then answer the questions.*

1. (Steve's radio / work)

    A: _____?

    B: No, _____.

2. (the store / have radios)

    A: _____?

    B: Yes, _____.

3. (Tim and Jeremy / work at Goodbuys)

    A: _____?

    B: No, _____.

EXERCISE C

Correct the conversation. There are five mistakes.

A: Does you want to go to the park today?

B: Sorry. I need to get a gift for my sister. Do you has any ideas?

A: Sure. Does she likes music? CDs are a good gift.

B: No, she don't.

A: Well, does she like books?

B: Yes, she is. Thanks. That's a great idea!

Simple Present: *Wh-* Questions
CROSS-CULTURAL DIFFERENCES

STEP 1 GRAMMAR IN CONTEXT

Before You Read

PAIRS: Talk about everyday activities. Ask, "What time do you get up in the morning? What time do you go to bed at night?"

Read

Read the conversation.

JEREMY: So **how do** you **like** the United States?

YOSHIO: I like it a lot. But it's really different from Japan.

JEREMY: **What do** you **mean?**

YOSHIO: I think in Japan we stay up later.

JEREMY: **What time do** Japanese people **go** to bed?

YOSHIO: Students stay up till midnight or later. And my father stays up till 1:00 or 2:00 A.M.

JEREMY: Really? **Why does** he **stay up** so late? **What does** he **do?**

YOSHIO: He's a businessman. He meets clients* in the evening.

JEREMY: **What time do** people **get up** in Japan?

YOSHIO: Oh, maybe 7:00 or 7:30.

JEREMY: That's pretty much like here. . . . **What else is** different?

YOSHIO: Well, in the United States, most people wear their shoes in the house. In Japan we take our shoes off.

JEREMY: Wow! That's different. . . . So **what do** you **like** best about the United States?

YOSHIO: People here are open and friendly. I have a lot of friends here.

JEREMY: That's good. Hey, we have calculus!

YOSHIO: Uh-oh! **What time does** it **start?**

JEREMY: Two o'clock. It's almost 2:00 now.

YOSHIO: OK, let's go.

---

* **clients:** people who pay for help and advice

After You Read

A | Practice *PAIRS: Practice the opening conversation.*

B | Vocabulary *Listen and repeat the words. Write new words in a notebook.*

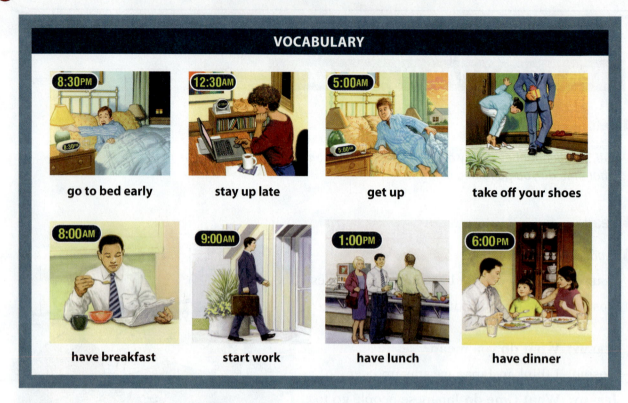

go to bed early	stay up late	get up	take off your shoes
have breakfast	start work	have lunch	have dinner

C | Vocabulary *PAIRS: Ask your partner questions about his or her everyday activities.*

EXAMPLE: **A:** Do you stay up late / go to bed early / get up early?
B: Yes, I do. / No, I don't.
B: How late do you stay up?
A: Eleven or 11:30.
A: What time do you have lunch?
B: About 1:00. What about you?

D | Comprehension *Look again at the opening conversation. Write **T** (True) or **F** (False).*

___T___ **1.** Yoshio likes the United States.

_____ **2.** Japanese students go to bed early.

_____ **3.** Yoshio's father works in the evening.

_____ **4.** People in Japan wear their shoes in the house.

_____ **5.** Yoshio doesn't have many friends in the United States.

_____ **6.** Jeremy and Yoshio have a math class at 2:00.

SIMPLE PRESENT: *WH-* QUESTIONS

Wh- Questions	Answers
How do I **get** there?	Take the number 3 bus.
Why do you **go** to bed so early?	I start work at 6 A.M.
When do we **leave**?	After work.
Where do they **live**?	In Seattle.
What does he **do**?	He's a bus driver.
How late **does** she **stay up**?	At least until midnight.
What time does it **start**?	At seven o'clock.

Wh- Questions about the Subject	Answers
Who wakes you **up**? Your mom? **What happens** on Saturday?	No. My alarm clock does. We sleep in.

GRAMMAR NOTES

1

Wh- **questions** ask for **information**. They often start with *how*, *when*, *why*, *where*, *what*, *who*, or *what time*.

Use a *wh-* **word** + *do* or *does* + the subject + the **base form** of the verb.

BE CAREFUL! Use *do* with *I*, *you*, *we*, and *they*. Use *does* with *he*, *she*, and *it*.

- **What time do** you **start** work?
- **What time does** he **get up**?
- **Where does** Annie **go** to school?
- **How does** she **get** to school?

2

To ask a **question about the subject**, use *who* or *what* + the third-person singular form of the verb. Do not use *do* or *does*.

- **Who wakes** you **up**? Your mom?
  Not: Who ~~does wake~~ you up?
- **What happens** on Sunday?

3

To ask about the meaning of a word, say *"What does . . . mean?"*

To answer, say, *" . . . means . . . "*

To ask about the spelling of a word, say *"How do you spell . . . ?"*

A: **What does** *little* **mean**?
  Not: ~~What means *little*?~~
  Not: ~~What does mean *little*?~~
B: *Little* **means** "small."

A: **How do you spell** *shoes*?
B: S-H-O-E-S.

4

REMEMBER: In pronunciation, we use falling intonation for *wh-* questions.

- Where do you live?

EXERCISE 1: Discover the Grammar

Read the conversation. Underline the wh- *questions in the simple present.*

MARK: So . . . <u>what do you think of your new job</u>?

 JOSH: Great. I love it. But it's really different.

MARK: What do you mean?

 JOSH: Well, I have to go to bed early and get up early.

MARK: What time do you go to bed?

 JOSH: About 10:30.

MARK: Who wakes you up? Amanda?

 JOSH: Amanda? No way! My alarm clock does.

MARK: Hmm. Do you like your boss?

 JOSH: Yes, she's nice. And I like the other guys in the office. We eat lunch together and have great conversations.

MARK: What do you talk about?

 JOSH: Everything. Sports. Travel. Movies.

MARK: That's great.

EXERCISE 2: *Wh-* Questions

(Grammar Note 1)

Josh's niece is interviewing him for her school newspaper. Write her **wh-** *questions. Use the simple present and the words in parentheses.*

1. (Where / you / work) *Where do you work* _____?

2. (What time / you / start work) _____?

3. (What / you / do in your job) _____?

4. (Who / you / work with) _____?

5. (How late / you / stay up on weeknights) _____?

6. (What sport / you / really like) _____?

7. (Why / you / like it) _____?

8. (When / you / play it) _____?

EXERCISE 3:   *Wh-* Questions

(Grammar Notes 1–3)

Write **wh-** *questions about the underlined words. Use* **how, who, what, where, why,** *or* **what time.**

1. A: _Where do they live_____?

   B: They live on <u>40th Street in Redmond</u>.

2. A: Jeremy, _____?

   B: I go to bed <u>at 11:00 or 11:15</u>.

3. A: Annie, _____?

   B: I feel <u>good</u>.

4. A: Ben, _____?

   B: I play soccer <u>because it's very exciting</u>.

5. A: Mom, _____?

   B: *Fascinating* means "<u>very interesting</u>."

6. A: _____?

   B: <u>S-L-E-E-P-Y</u>.

7. A: Yoshio, _____?

   B: <u>My mother</u> wakes my father up in the morning.

EXERCISE 4:   Editing

There are five mistakes in the conversation. The first mistake is already corrected. Find and correct four more mistakes.

A: Hey! I have a new job.

B: Really? Where you work?   *do*

A: At a bookstore.

B: What you do?

A: I'm a salesperson.

B: What time you do start?

A: Eight-thirty in the morning.

B: How you like the work?

A: It's challenging.

B: *Challenging?* I don't know that word. What means *challenging?*

A: It means "hard but interesting."

EXERCISE 5: Listening

A Listen to the conversation about Jason's first day on the job. Check (✓) the true sentence.

_____ **1.** Jason and Margaret both drive to work.

_____ **2.** Jason and Margaret are both accountants.

_____ **3.** Jason and Margaret both live in the same town.

B Listen to the conversation again and answer the questions in complete sentences.

1. Who is new in the company? _Jason is new in the company_____.

2. What does Jason do? _____.

3. What does Margaret do? _____.

4. Does Jason like the company? _____.

5. What does Jason dislike? _____.

6. Where do Jason and Margaret live? _____.

7. How does Margaret get to work? _____.

8. What time does Margaret catch the bus? _____.

EXERCISE 6: Pronunciation

🎧 *Listen to the sentences. Circle the word in each sentence with the most stress.*

EXAMPLES: Where do you (live)?   Where do (you) live?

1. What do you (do)?

2. What do you do?

3. Where do you catch the bus?

4. Where do you catch the bus?

5. Why don't you take the bus tomorrow?

6. Why don't you take the bus tomorrow?

7. How long does the bus take?

8. How long does the bus take?

EXERCISE 7: Ask and Answer

PAIRS: Ask your partner questions using **how, what, what time, when,** *and* **where** *and the words from the box.*

do (occupation)	get to school	live	start work / class	study

EXAMPLE: **A:** Where do you WORK?
            B: I work at a supermarket. Where do YOU work?
            A: I work at . . .
               OR I don't work. I go to school full-time.

EXERCISE 8: Information Gap

PAIRS: Student A, ask Student B about the meaning of a word from your list. Write the answer. Then answer Student B's question. Choose an answer from your list. Take turns.

Student B, look at the Information Gap on page 115 and follow the instructions there.

EXAMPLE: **A:** What does *tiny* mean?
            B: *Tiny* means "very small." What does *large* mean?

Student A's Words

1. tiny: *very small*

2. boring: _____

3. noon: _____

4. midnight: _____

5. super: _____

6. unhappy: _____

7. terrible: _____

8. nice: _____

big

not married

between first and third

the children of your aunt or uncle

good-looking

totally different

intelligent

your parents, brothers, sisters, grandparents, and so on

▶ *To check your answers, go to the Answer Key on page P-1.*

EXERCISE 9: Writing

A | *A student from another country is visiting your class. Write five interview questions using* **wh-** *words.*

>   EXAMPLE: **A:** Where do you come from?
>   **B:** I come from Tanzania.

1. _____?

2. _____?

3. _____?

4. _____?

5. _____?

B | *Check your work. Use the Editing Checklist.*

Editing Checklist

Did you use . . . ?
☐ **wh-** questions correctly
☐ correct spelling

INFORMATION GAP FOR STUDENT B

Student B, answer Student A's questions. Choose an answer from your list. Then ask
Student A about the meaning of a word from your list. Write the answer. Take turns.

EXAMPLE: **B:** *Tiny* means "very small." What does *large* mean?
            A: *Large* means "big."

Student B's Words

1. large: _big_____

2. relatives: _____

3. opposite: _____

4. smart: _____

5. cousins: _____

6. cute: _____

7. single: _____

8. second: _____

Student B's Answers

12:00 A.M.

not interesting

12:00 P.M.

sad

good

very bad

great

very small

▶ *To check your answers, go to the Answer Key on page P-1.*

Check your answers on page UR-1.

Do you need to review anything?

EXERCISE A

Complete the conversation with **What, What time, Who,** or **Why.**

A: _____ do you wake up? **B:** At 5 A.M.

A: At 5 A.M.? That's early! _____ wakes you up? **B:** My cat.

A: _____ does it wake you up at 5:00? **B:** It wants breakfast!

A: _____ does your cat eat for breakfast? **B:** Chicken and eggs.

EXERCISE B

Put the words in the correct order. Make **wh-** questions in the simple present.

1. (your cousins / Where / live) _____?

2. (start work / your father / When) _____?

3. (do / What / he) _____?

4. (like / he / How / his job) _____?

5. (you and your sister / walk to school / Why) _____?

6. (your cat / What time / wake up) _____?

EXERCISE C

Correct the conversation. There are five mistakes.

A: I have a new job. **B:** Really? Where you do work?

A: At Goodbuys. **B:** What does you do?

A: I'm an electronic technician. **B:** What means *electronic technician*?

A: An electronic technician fixes electronic devices. **B:** How are you like the work?

A: I like it a lot. **B:** What time you start?

A: At 9:00 in the morning.

UNIT 13 Simple Present: *Be* and *Have*
DESCRIBING PEOPLE

STEP 1 GRAMMAR IN CONTEXT

Before You Read

GROUPS: Look at your group and answer the questions. Write numbers. Then report to the class.

How many have

____ short hair?   ____ dark hair?

____ long hair?   ____ light hair?

EXAMPLE: Three of us have short hair. José has long hair.

Read

Read the conversation.

RICK: You**'re** in Music Appreciation 101, **aren't** you?

JUDY: Uh-huh . . .

RICK: Could you please give these tickets to Sonia Jones? She**'s** in your music class.

JUDY: Sure. But I don't know her. What does she look like?

RICK: Well, she **has** dark hair and dark eyes.

JUDY: Half the women **have** dark hair and dark eyes. And there **are** 100 students in my class.

RICK: She**'s** tall and thin.

JUDY: OK, but a lot of women **are** tall and thin.

RICK: She**'s** in her early twenties.

JUDY: Rick! Almost everyone at school **is** 20-something. **Is** there something unusual about her?

RICK: She **has** two heads.

JUDY: Rick!

RICK: Sonia**'s** eight months pregnant.

JUDY: Why didn't you say so?

Simple Present: *Be* and *Have*   **117**

A | Practice *PAIRS: Practice the opening conversation.*

B | Vocabulary *Listen and repeat the words. Write new words in a notebook.*

VOCABULARY

tall   average height   short   thin   average weight   heavy   pregnant

wavy black hair   curly red hair   straight blond hair   dark brown hair   light brown hair

C | Vocabulary *PAIRS: Look at the pictures. Describe one of the people. Don't say the name. Use the vocabulary words. Your partner names the person.*

Ewa   Nuttapong   Hanan   Hatimi

D | Comprehension *Look again at the opening conversation. Underline the correct answers.*

1. Is Sonia in Music Appreciation 1?
   <u>Yes, she is.</u> / No, she isn't.

2. Does Sonia have dark hair and light eyes?
   Yes, she does. / No, she doesn't.

3. Is Judy's class small?
   Yes, it is. / No, it isn't.

4. Are Judy and Rick in the same Music Appreciation class?
   Yes, they are. / No, they aren't.

5. Are most of the students between the ages of 20 and 29?
   Yes, they are. / No, they aren't.

6. Is Sonia pregnant?
   Yes, she is. / No, she isn't.

7. Does Sonia have two heads?
   Yes, she does. / No, she doesn't.

STEP 2 GRAMMAR PRESENTATION

SIMPLE PRESENT: *BE* AND *HAVE*

Be	Have
Affirmative Statements	**Affirmative Statements**
I **am** short.	I **have** brown eyes.
He **is** tall.	She **has** blue eyes.
We **are** late.	We **have** a problem.
Negative Statements	**Negative Statements**
I'**m not** tall.	I **don't have** green eyes.
He'**s not** short. OR He **isn't** short.	She **doesn't have** green eyes.
We'**re not** early. OR We **aren't** early.	We **don't have** time.
Yes / No **Questions**	*Yes / No* **Questions**
Am I late?	**Do** I **have** any gray hair?
Is he 25 years old?	**Does** he **have** black hair?
Are we early?	**Do** we **have** time?
Wh- **Questions**	*Wh-* **Questions**
Where am I?	**When does** he **have** his class?
Who is in your class? OR **Who's** in your class?	**Who has** the tickets?
What are the tickets for?	**What does** she **have** in her bag?

GRAMMAR NOTES

1	*Be* and *have* are common irregular verbs. *Be* has three forms in the simple present: *am*, *is*, and *are*.	• I **am** short. • He **is** tall. • They **are** tall.
	Have has two forms in the simple present: *have* and *has*. Use *have* with *I*, *you*, *we*, and *they*.	• **I have** black hair. • **You have** blue eyes. • **We have** blue eyes. • **They have** brown eyes.
	Use *has* with *he*, *she*, and *it*.	• **He has** brown hair. • **She has** blond hair. • **It has** green eyes.
2	In **negative statements** with *be*, use *am not*, *is not*, and *are not* or their contractions.	• I'm **not** home. • She**'s not** tall. • We **are not** musicians.
	In negative statements with *have*, use *do not have* or *does not have* or their contractions.	• I **don't have** blue eyes. • He **doesn't have** green eyes.
	Contractions are more common in speaking and informal writing.	
3	In a *yes / no* **question** with *be*, put *am*, *is*, or *are* before the subject.	• **Are you** a student?
	In a *yes / no* **question** with *have*, use *do* or *does* + the subject + *have*.	• **Do you have** blue eyes? • **Does he have** brown eyes?
4	For *wh-* **questions** with *be*, use the question word + *yes / no* question word order.	• **Where am** I? • **What is** her name? • **How are** his parents?
	Most *wh-* **questions** with *have* use the *wh-* question word + *do* or *does* + a subject + the **base form** of the verb.	• **What does** he **have** for lunch? • **When do** they **have** dinner?
	Questions about the subject: Use statement word order. These questions do not use *do* or *does*.	• **Who has** green eyes? Not: Who ~~does have~~ green eyes?
5	Use *be* to talk about **age**.	A: How old **are** you? B: **I am** 21 years old. Not: I ~~have~~ 21 years.

EXERCISE 1: Discover the Grammar

*Underline **be** verbs once. Underline **have** verbs twice. Then match the questions and answers.*

_c_ **1.** How old is he?

____ **2.** Does he have short hair?

____ **3.** Who has the tickets?

____ **4.** Is she in your class?

____ **5.** Do you have a music class?

____ **6.** Are those girls pregnant?

a. He has them.

b. Yes, they are both in their eighth month.

c. He's 20.

d. No, I don't have music this year.

e. Yes, she's in my music class.

f. No, it's long.

EXERCISE 2: *Be* and *Have*   (Grammar Notes 1, 5)

*Complete the passage. Use the correct forms of **be** or **have**. Find the answer on page P-1.*

Who _____ I?
   1.   *am*

It is 1764. I _____ eight years old. I _____ from Austria. I _____
            2.   3.   4.

in England now with my family. My father _____ a violinist. I _____
                                        5.   6.

an older sister. She _____ a violinist too. I play the violin and the harpsichord.
                  7.

I also write music. People say, "You _____ a beautiful voice." They say, "You
                                    8.

_____ amazing." The kings and queens of Europe love my music. My middle name
    9.

_____ Amadeus.
  10.

EXERCISE 3: *Be* and *Have*   (Grammar Notes 3–4)

*Write questions. Use the correct forms of **be** or **have** and the words in parentheses.*

A: (Who / Midori) _____ *Who is Midori* _____?
                                      1.

B: She's a great violinist. She performs all over the world.

A: (Where / she / from) _____?
                                      2.

B: She's from Osaka, Japan.

A: (she / in Japan / now) _____?
                                      3.

(continued on next page)

B: No. She lives in Los Angeles.

A: (she / any sisters or brothers) _____ ?
4.

B: She has a brother, Ryu Goto.

A: (he / a violinist) _____ ?
5.

B: Yes, he is. He's very talented too.

A: (Midori / other interests) _____ ?
6.

B: Yes, she does. She writes, teaches, and brings music to children all over the world.

EXERCISE 4: Editing

There are six mistakes in the conversation. The first mistake is already corrected. Find and correct five more mistakes.

JUDY: Who was on the phone?

MARK: My cousin, Francisco.

JUDY: How old ~~has~~ *is* he?

MARK: Twenty-five.

JUDY: Where he from?

MARK: São Paulo.

JUDY: Is he a writer like you?

MARK: No. He a musician. He plays the guitar.

JUDY: He cute?

MARK: Yes, he is. He looks like me.

JUDY: Does he has a girlfriend?

MARK: Yes, he do.

JUDY: That's too bad.

EXERCISE 5: Listening

 A | *Judy is telling Mark about a new friend. Listen and answer the questions about Judy's friend Olivia.*

    1. What does Olivia do? _____

    2. Where is she from? _____

 B | *Listen again. Complete the paragraph about Olivia. Then circle her in the picture.*

She's _____average_____ height and

_____ weight. She has _____

_____ hair. It's very _____.

She's a _____ saxophone

_____.

EXERCISE 6: Pronunciation

 A | *Read and listen to the Pronunciation Note.*

> **Pronunciation Note**
>
> **The /h/ sound: /h/ is a breathing sound.**
>
> The **/h/** sound is sometimes dropped in the words *he, his, her, have,* and *has* when they are unstressed inside a sentence. The **/h/** sound is not dropped when those words start a sentence or are in short answers.

 B | *Listen to the /h/ sound in the underlined words. Then listen again and repeat.*

His hair is black.
Last week his hair was gray.
He's a happy man.

I think he's sad.
Her husband is 40 years old.
I don't know her husband.

 C | *Listen and repeat. Practice with a partner.*

    A: Is he tall?

    B: Yes, he is.

    A: When does her concert start?

    B: Her concert starts at 9:00.

    A: What's his last name?

    B: His last name is Kim.

    A: Give him the tickets.

    B: Where is he?

EXERCISE 7: Describe People

Work with a partner. Describe one of the people in Exercise 5 to your partner. Your partner points to the person. Take turns.

EXERCISE 8: Writing

A | *Write a description of a famous person. Use the vocabulary from the unit. Use* **be** *and* **have.**

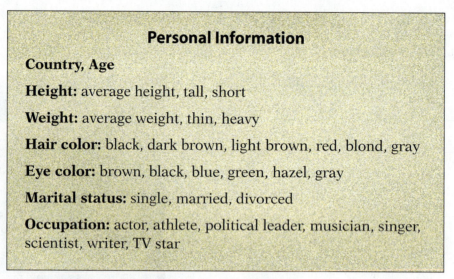

Personal Information

Country, Age

Height: average height, tall, short

Weight: average weight, thin, heavy

Hair color: black, dark brown, light brown, red, blond, gray

Eye color: brown, black, blue, green, hazel, gray

Marital status: single, married, divorced

Occupation: actor, athlete, political leader, musician, singer, scientist, writer, TV star

EXAMPLE: **(Meryl Streep)** She's from New Jersey in the United States. She's in her 60s. She's tall and average weight. She has blond hair and blue eyes. She's married. She's the star of many movies, including *Doubt, Sophie's Choice, Silkwood, Mamma Mia,* and *Out of Africa.* Some say she's the greatest American actress living today.

B | *Check your work. Use the Editing Checklist.*

Editing Checklist

Did you use . . . ?
- ☐ vocabulary from the unit
- ☐ *be* and *have* correctly
- ☐ correct spelling

C | *GROUPS: Each student describes the person he or she wrote about. Do not tell the name. The others in the group guess the person.*

EXERCISE A

Match the questions and answers.

_____ **1.** Who has the tickets?

_____ **2.** Is she a student?

_____ **3.** Do you have a cell phone?

_____ **4.** Are those girls sisters?

_____ **5.** Does he have two brothers?

a. Yes, she is.

b. Yes, I do.

c. Yes, they are.

d. No, he doesn't.

e. Jane does.

EXERCISE B

Complete the conversation. Use the correct forms of **be** *or* **have**.

A: What does Ken look like?

B: He _____ tall and average weight.

A: What color hair _____ he _____?

B: He _____ red hair.

A: _____ he _____ any sisters?

B: Yes, but they _____ not tall!

EXERCISE C

Correct the conversation. There are five mistakes.

A: Could you please meet my friend Maria at the bus stop?

B: OK. What does she look like?

A: She thin, and she have brown hair and brown eyes.

B: Has she tall or short?

A: She has average height.

B: Is she have short hair?

A: No, it's long.

Simple Present with Adverbs of Frequency
HABITS

Before You Read

PAIRS: Talk about your habits. Ask, "What do you always do in the morning? What do you never do in the morning?"

> **EXAMPLE:** I always get up early. I never eat breakfast.

Read

Read the conversation.

JOSH: How's it going, Steve? You look kind of tired.

STEVE: Well, things are OK, but I *am* a little tired.

JOSH: Any idea why?

STEVE: Maybe I'm not getting enough sleep.

JOSH: How much do you get?

STEVE: Oh, about six hours a night.

JOSH: What time do you go to bed?

STEVE: I **usually** stay up till 12:30 or 1:00. And I get up at 6:30 or 7:00.

JOSH: Do you **ever** sleep late?

STEVE: **Sometimes**—on the weekend.

JOSH: And I hear you **always** have fast food for lunch.

STEVE: And I **sometimes** skip breakfast.

JOSH: So you don't eat three meals a day?

STEVE: **Rarely.** I'm **usually** in a hurry in the morning. So I skip breakfast.

JOSH: Not good, my friend. What about lunch and dinner?

STEVE: I **always** have a good dinner. But lunch . . . well, I'm **always** in a hurry then. So I **usually** go to a fast-food place near the university. I know fast food isn't always healthy.

JOSH: Hmm. Not enough sleep. No breakfast. Fast food for lunch. You're living dangerously.

STEVE: Maybe. But I have one good habit. I exercise.

JOSH: Great. **How often**?

STEVE: Two or three times a year.

After You Read

A | **Practice** *PAIRS: Practice the opening conversation.*

B | **Vocabulary** *Listen and repeat the words. Write new words in a notebook.*

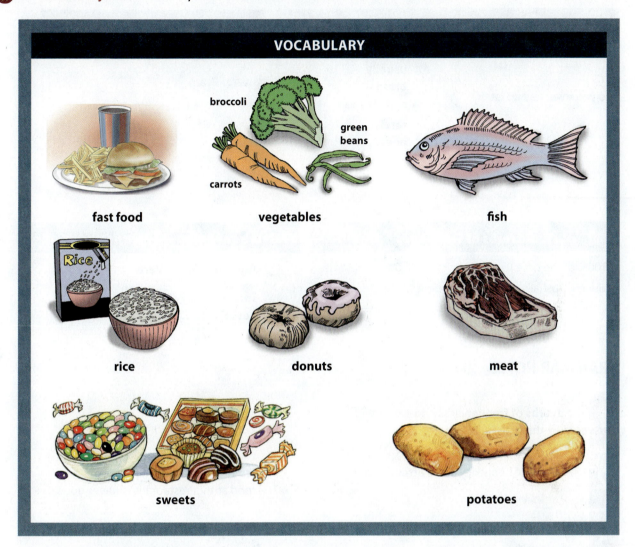

VOCABULARY

fast food

broccoli

green beans

carrots

vegetables

fish

rice

donuts

meat

sweets

potatoes

C | **Vocabulary** *PAIRS: Look at the vocabulary words. Say what you **never, sometimes**, or **often** eat.*

EXAMPLE: **A:** I never eat carrots.
　　　　　B: Really? I often eat carrots. I never eat meat.
　　　　　A: I sometimes eat meat.

D | **Comprehension** *Look again at the opening conversation. Circle the correct answers.*

1. Steve **is / isn't** getting enough sleep.

2. Steve usually goes to bed **before / after** midnight.

3. Steve **always / sometimes** skips breakfast.

4. Steve **usually / sometimes** eats fast food for lunch.

5. Steve **usually / rarely** eats three meals a day.

6. Steve exercises **a lot / a little**.

ADVERBS OF FREQUENCY

Yes / No Questions	Short Answers		
Do you **ever** stay up late?	Yes, I	always usually often sometimes	do.
	No, I	rarely never	

Adverbs of Frequency with *Be*

	Be	Adverb	
I	am		
He She It	is	always usually often rarely	late.
We You They	are		

Adverbs of Frequency

100% of the time ⟷ 0% of the time

always   usually   often   sometimes   rarely   never

Adverbs of Frequency with Other Verbs

	Adverb	Verb	
I	sometimes	skip	lunch.
He	never	eats	breakfast.

GRAMMAR NOTES

1	**Adverbs of frequency** say **how often** something happens.	• I **often skip** breakfast. • She **sometimes skips** lunch.
2	Adverbs of frequency come **after** the verb *be*.	• I'm **usually** tired in the morning. • The food at that restaurant **is never** good.
3	Adverbs of frequency usually come **before other verbs**. **NOTE:** *Usually* and *sometimes* can also come at the beginning or end of a sentence.	• He **usually goes** to a fast-food place. • It **always rains** on the weekends. • **Usually** I get up at 8:00. OR I get up at 8:00, **usually**. • **Sometimes** I skip breakfast. OR I skip breakfast, **sometimes**.
4	Use *ever* in *yes / no* questions. *Ever* means "at any time." **BE CAREFUL!** Do not use *ever* in affirmative statements.	**A:** Do you **ever sleep** late? **B: Often.** OR I **often do.** • I sleep late. NOT: I ~~ever~~ sleep late.
5	Use *how often* to ask about frequency.	**A: How often** do you exercise? **B:** I usually exercise **three times a week**.

EXERCISE 1: Discover the Grammar

Read the paragraph about Josh Wang. Circle the 14 adverbs of frequency.

Josh Wang has an active life. He (usually) gets up at 6 A.M. He always runs 2 or 3 miles with his dog. Sometimes he feels tired, but he still runs. When he gets home from running, he has breakfast. He often has eggs, juice, toast, and coffee, but sometimes he has cereal and fruit. Then Josh goes to work, and he's never late. He works from 9:00 until 5:00. He rarely stays late. In the evening, Josh always has a healthy dinner. He often has fish with rice and vegetables. He never has fast food. He rarely eats sweets. After dinner Josh sometimes reads. Josh is also an artist, so sometimes he paints. He's always in bed by 10:30.

EXERCISE 2: Adverbs of Frequency
(Grammar Notes 1–5)

Put the words in the correct order. Make conversations.

1. **A:** Do you ever stay up late _____?
   (late / ever / Do / up / stay / you)

   B: _____.
   (do / Yes, / often / I)

2. **A:** _____?
   (tired / morning / you / Are / the / in / ever)

   B: _____.
   (then / always / I'm / tired)

3. **A:** _____?
   (often / exercise / How / you / do)

   B: _____.
   (week / a / five / usually / I / exercise / times)

4. **A:** _____?
   (usually / evening / you / do / What / the / in / do)

   B: _____.
   (piano / the / practice / I / often)

EXERCISE 3: Adverbs of Frequency

(Grammar Notes 2–3)

Look at the pictures. Write sentences about Jessica Olson on the next page. Use **always**, **usually**, **sometimes**, or **never** and the words in parentheses.

	Sun	Mon	Tues	Wed	Thurs	Fri	Sat
1	✓	✓	✓	✓	✓	✓	✓
2							
3		✓	✓		✓	✓	
4		✓		✓		✓	

EXAMPLE: Jessica always gets up early.

1. (take a shower) _____

_____

2. (drive to work) _____

_____

3. (arrive at work on time)_____

_____

4. (cook dinner) _____

_____

EXERCISE 4: Editing

There are six mistakes in the conversation. The first mistake is already corrected. Find and correct five more mistakes.

JESSICA: Domingo, you're a great soccer player. How do you exercise?
often
          ^

DOMINGO: I exercise six or seven days a week.

JESSICA: Do ever you get tired of exercising?

DOMINGO: Sure I do. But always I do it.

JESSICA: OK. How often do you travel?

DOMINGO: I travel a lot—at least three times a month.

JESSICA: Does ever your wife get unhappy because you travel so much?

DOMINGO: No, never she gets unhappy. She travels usually with me.

JESSICA: That's great, Domingo. Now, good luck in your next game.

EXERCISE 5: Listening

🎧 **A** | *Listen to the telephone conversation between Ken and his grandmother. Then check (✓) the two true statements.*

_____ **1.** Ken's birthday is today.

_____ **2.** Ken is always tired.

_____ **3.** Ken has a job.

_____ **4.** Ken gets eight hours of sleep a night.

🎧 **B** | *Listen again. Complete the statements.*

1. Grandma calls Ken because tomorrow is _his birthday_____.

2. Grandma is usually _____.

3. Ken is always _____.

4. Ken usually starts work at _____.

5. He never has time _____.

6. Ken sometimes stays up late _____.

7. Ken usually gets _____ of sleep.

8. Grandma says Ken needs _____ of sleep every night.

EXERCISE 6: Pronunciation

🎧 **A** | *Read and listen to the Pronunciation Note.*

> **Pronunciation Note**
>
> To make the /r/ sound, put the sides of your tongue on your upper back teeth. The tip of your tongue doesn't touch anything.

🎧 **B** | *Listen to the words. Check (✓) the words that have an /r/ sound.*

| _____ 1. | _____ 3. | _____ 5. | _____ 7. | _____ 9. |
| ✓ 2. | _____ 4. | _____ 6. | _____ 8. | _____10. |

C | *PAIRS: Practice words with the /r/ sound.*

| 1. ever | 3. hours | 5. wear | 7. ride | 9. right |
| 2. tired | 4. sure | 6. morning | 8. work | 10. rare |

EXERCISE 7: About You

A | *Write true statements about yourself. Use the words in parentheses and an adverb of frequency.*

EXAMPLE: I'm always on time to class.

1. (be on time to work) _____

2. (be tired in the morning) _____

3. (eat breakfast) _____

4. (eat fast food) _____

5. (ride a horse) _____

6. (go to the movies) _____

7. (wear boots) _____

8. (get enough sleep) _____

B | *PAIRS: Tell your partner about your habits.*

EXERCISE 8: Writing

A | *PAIRS: Change the statements you wrote in Exercise 7 to* **yes** / **no** *questions with* **you***. Use adverbs of frequency. Ask your partner each question. Then tell the class three things about your partner.*

EXAMPLE: **A:** Are you always on time to class?
           B: No, I'm rarely on time to class.
           A: Alicia is rarely on time to class.

B | *Check your work. Use the Editing Checklist.*

> **Editing Checklist**
>
> Did you use . . . ?
> ☐ *yes / no* questions with "you" correctly
> ☐ adverbs of frequency correctly
> ☐ correct spelling

UNIT 14 Review

Check your answers on page UR-2.

Do you need to review anything?

EXERCISE A

Match the sentences with similar meanings.

_____ **1.** They always exercise.

_____ **2.** They rarely exercise.

_____ **3.** They sometimes exercise.

_____ **4.** They usually exercise.

a. They exercise on weekends.

b. They exercise five days a week.

c. They exercise every day.

d. They exercise once a month.

EXERCISE B

Put the words in the correct order. Make conversations.

1. A: _____?
(often / skip / How / you / do / lunch)

    B: _____.
(lunch / sometimes / I / skip)

2. A: _____?
(usually / weekends / you / do / What / the / on / do)

    B: _____.
(movies / the / go / I / often / to)

3. A: _____?
(breakfast / ever / Do / donuts / eat / you / for)

    B: _____.
(do / No, / never / I)

EXERCISE C

Correct the conversation. There are five mistakes.

A: Do you always to eat healthy food?

B: Oh, yes. I am usually eat a lot of fruit and vegetables.

A: Do you have ever fast food?

B: Rarely—and only on the weekend.

A: And I hear you have always breakfast.

B: Yes, I skip breakfast never. Breakfast is very important!

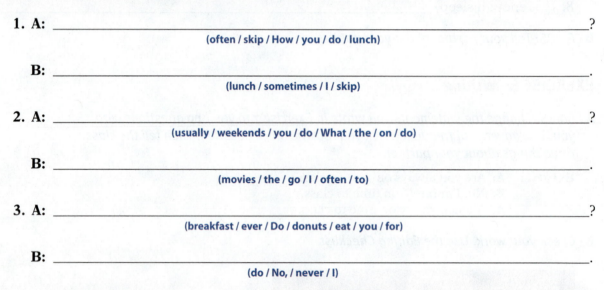

PRESENT PROGRESSIVE

Present Progressive: Statements
A FRIEND FROM LONG AGO

Before You Read

A | *Look at your classmates. Complete the sentences.*

1. _____ is sitting next to a window.

2. _____ is wearing glasses.

3. _____ is talking.

4. _____ is smiling.

5. _____ is not smiling.

B | *PAIRS: Compare your sentences.*

> **EXAMPLE:**   **A:** Eun Young is sitting next to a window.
> **B:** Sahra is sitting next to a window too.

Read

Read the email on the next page from Jessica to her friend Lauren.

Dear Lauren,

I was so surprised and happy to get your email. Yes, I'm the Jessica Beck from Seattle High School. And of course I remember you. We were together in math for four years.

I'm living in Redmond with my husband and children. Here are some photos of us.

Tim is my husband. **He's wearing** the gray sweatshirt. **He's sitting** next to my brother, Steve. **They're watching** a ball game. **They're not smiling** because **their team is losing**. I'm sure you remember Steve. Believe it or not, he's a professor now.

My son Jeremy is in the chair. He's fifteen. **He's texting** friends. He's a great kid. Annie and Ben **are playing** cards. Annie is ten, and Ben is seven. They keep us busy.

In this photo **I'm standing** between my parents. **They're not working** now. Mom is happy, but Dad misses work.

Please call as soon as you get to Washington. My cell phone number is 555-460-9878. I'll meet you at the airport.

Love from your long-lost friend,

Jessica

After You Read

A | Practice *PAIRS: Practice the opening reading. Each person reads a paragraph.*

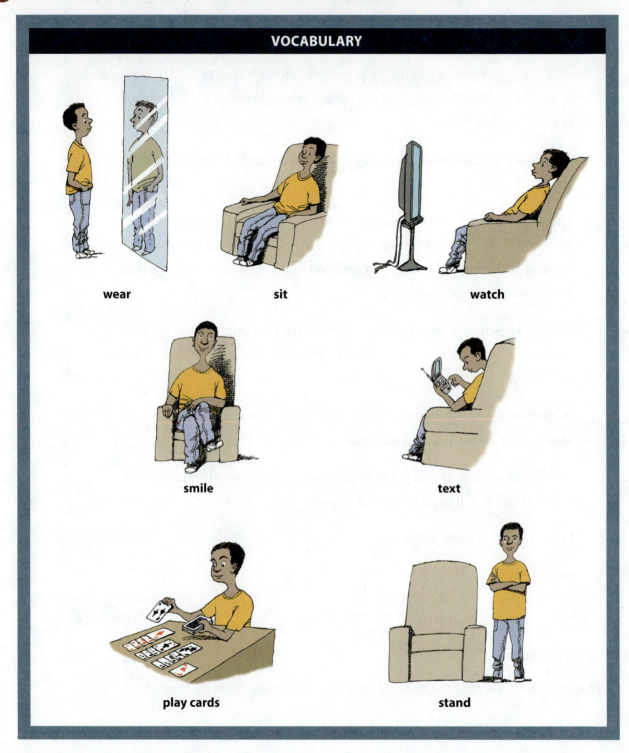

VOCABULARY

wear

sit

watch

smile

text

play cards

stand

C | **Vocabulary** *PAIRS: Look at a classmate. Follow the example. Tell about the classmate. Your partner guesses who it is.*

EXAMPLE: **A:** He's wearing a red sweater. He's sitting near the door. He's not smiling. He's not texting. He's not playing cards. He's not standing.

B: Is it Ernesto?

A: Right!

D | Comprehension *Look again at the opening email. Match the sentence beginnings and endings. The first one is done for you.*

_b_ **1.** Tim is wearing	**a.** between her mom and dad.
____ **2.** Steve and Tim are watching	**b.** a gray sweatshirt.
____ **3.** They're not smiling because	**c.** a sports event on TV.
____ **4.** Jeremy is texting	**d.** their team is losing.
____ **5.** Annie and Ben are playing	**e.** friends.
____ **6.** Jessica is standing	**f.** cards.

STEP 2 GRAMMAR PRESENTATION

PRESENT PROGRESSIVE: STATEMENTS

Affirmative Statements		
am	**is**	**are**
I **am listening**.	He **is standing**. She **is sitting**. It **is raining**.	We **are sitting**. You **are standing**. They **are smiling**.
Contractions		
I'm listening.	**He's** standing. **She's** sitting. **It's** raining.	**We're** sitting. **You're** standing. **They're** smiling.

Negative Statements		
am not	**is not**	**are not**
I **am not talking**.	He **is not standing**. She **is not reading**. It **is not snowing**.	We **are not working**. You **are not listening**. They **are not working**.
Contractions		
I'm not talking.	**He's not** standing. Jeremy **isn't** listening. **She's not** talking. Annie **isn't** talking. **It's not** snowing.	**We're not** talking. Tim and I **aren't** talking. **You're not** talking. You and Annie **aren't** talking. **They're not** talking. Tim and Jeremy **aren't** talking.

GRAMMAR NOTES

1	Use the **present progressive** to talk about an action that is **happening now**. **Now** Past ←————————→ Future *She's talking.*	• The president **is talking**. I**'m listening** to her.
2	Use a form of **be** + the **verb** + **-ing** to form the present progressive. **NOTE:** If the **base verb ends in -e**, drop the **-e** and add **-ing**. If the **base verb is one syllable and it ends in consonant + vowel + consonant, double the last consonant**. Then add **-ing**. **EXCEPTIONS: Do not double** the last consonant if it is **w**, **x**, or **y**.	• I **am listening**. (listen) • She **is talking**. (talk) • He is writ**ing**. (write) • She is run**ning**. (run) • They're sit**ting**. (sit) • We're shop**ping** (shop) • We're gro**wing** tomatoes. • He's fi**xing** his computer. • She's pla**ying** ball.
3	We often use **contractions** in speaking and informal writing.	• He**'s** playing cards. • I**'m** reading. • They**'re** smiling.
4	Use a form of **be** + **not** + the **verb** + **-ing** for **negative statements**. There are **two contractions** for **is not** and **are not**.	• I**'m not wearing** a hat. • Jeremy **isn't talking**. OR He**'s not talking**. • Annie and Ben **aren't reading**. OR They**'re not reading**.

5	**Be**, **have**, **like**, **need**, and **want** are **non-action (stative) verbs**. We usually use these verbs in the **simple present**, not the present progressive.
	
	NOTE: Look at Units 10 and 11 for more practice with these verbs.
		• Ali **is** a lawyer.
		  NOT: Ali ~~is being~~ a lawyer.
		• Septi **likes** apples.
		  NOT: Septi ~~is liking~~ apples.
		• Bob **doesn't have** a car.
		  NOT: Bob ~~isn't having~~ a car.

6	When you want to connect **one subject** with **two verbs, do not repeat** a form of **be**.	• He's **eating** and **watching** TV. NOT: He's eating and ~~is~~ watching TV.

EXERCISE 1: Discover the Grammar

Read the email to Jessica from Lauren. Underline all examples of the present progressive.

Hi Jessica,

I'm at the airport. <u>We're waiting</u> to board the plane. It's snowing in New York, so our flight is late. My new arrival time is 2:30.

I'm looking at your photos and smiling. Tim looks like your first boyfriend, Adam. But Tim isn't wearing torn jeans, and Tim's hair is short.

It's really nice of you to meet me at the airport.

I'll be easy to find. I'm wearing a red jacket, a red cap, and brown shoes. My hair is blond, and I don't look at day over 20. (I'm just kidding.)

See you soon.

Your friend from long ago,

Lauren

EXERCISE 2: Present Progressive

(Grammar Notes 1–5)

Complete the conversation. Use the present progressive and the correct forms of the words in parentheses.

TIM: That's a funny picture. Who's that?

JESSICA: It's me. In high school. At a school picnic.

TIM: You _'re kidding_____.
              1. (kid)

JESSICA: No. Really! I _____ sunglasses and a funny hat. My hair is long, and I
                                2. (wear)

_____ makeup.
    3. (wear, not)

TIM: Oh. Well, what are you doing?

(continued on next page)

JESSICA: Lauren and I _____ cards.
          4. (play)

TIM: That's Lauren? She looks very unhappy.

JESSICA: She is. She _____ in the hot sun and _____ the game.
          5. (sit)   6. (lose)

Lauren hates picnics, and she hates to lose. She _____ the day. She
                                                  7. (enjoy, not)

_____ about her cool apartment.
8. (think)

EXERCISE 3: Affirmative and Negative   *(Grammar Notes 1–5)*

*Look at the picture. Write sentences. Use the present progressive and the words in
parentheses. Use the affirmative or negative.*

1. (Lauren / wear boots) _Lauren is not wearing boots._____

2. (Jessica / wear a brown jacket) _____

3. (Lauren and Jessica / stand near the baggage carousel) _____

   _____

4. (Jessica / sit)_____

5. (Jessica / look for someone)_____

6. (Lauren / call someone) _____

7. (Lauren and Jessica / smile) _____

EXERCISE 4: Editing

*There are eight mistakes in the sentences. The first mistake is already corrected. Find
and correct seven more mistakes. Use contractions.*

1. She ʼs wearing her new boots.

2. We no are looking for a taxi.

3. They're wait for a relative at the airport.

4. He watching a ball game. His team losing.

5. It no is raining today.

6. They're playing cards and are watching TV at the same time.

7. He's text me now.

STEP 4 COMMUNICATION PRACTICE

EXERCISE 5: Listening

A | *Listen and circle the correct letter to complete the sentence.*

Steve and Jessica are talking and looking at _____.

    a. photos of Lauren's visit   **b.** photos of Jessica's visit

B | *Listen again. Mark the sentences **T (True)** or **F (False)**.*

    1. In the first photo:

        _____ **a.** Lauren is wearing a new jacket.

        _____ **b.** Lauren is wearing Steve's jacket.

        _____ **c.** They're racing.

        _____ **d.** They're watching a race.

    2. In the second photo:

        _____ **a.** Lauren and Jeremy are talking about New York.

        _____ **b.** Lauren is talking to Jeremy about New York University.

        _____ **c.** Jeremy is not talking to his mom about college.

EXERCISE 6: Pronunciation

A | *Read and listen to the Pronunciation Note.*

> **Pronunciation Note**
>
> To make the /**l**/ sound, touch the tip of your tongue just behind the top teeth. (See Unit 14 for pronunciation of the /**r**/ sound.)

B | *Listen to the words. Then listen again and repeat.*

    race — lace   wrong — long   rate — late

C | *Listen and repeat each sentence.*

    1. Lauren is running in a race.   **3.** Lauren is late for the race.

    2. The race is long.   **4.** The officials won't let her run.

D | *Listen and check (✓) the sentence you hear.*

1. _____ **a.** He's right.

   _____ **b.** He's light.

2. _____ **a.** This race is good.

   _____ **b.** This lace is good.

3. _____ **a.** It's the wrong way home.

   _____ **b.** It's the long way home.

4. _____ **a.** What does *rate* mean?

   _____ **b.** What does *late* mean?

EXERCISE 7: True Statements

A | *Underline the correct words to make true sentences.*

1. The person on my right **is listening / isn't listening** to me.

2. The person on my left **is looking / isn't looking** at me.

3. Our teacher **is writing / isn't writing**.

4. **It's raining / It isn't raining** today.

5. The student near the door **is looking / is not looking** at his or her watch.

6. **I'm reading / I'm not reading** my sentences to my partner.

B | *PAIRS: Read your statements aloud. Compare them.*

EXERCISE 8: Picture Differences

PAIRS: Study the two pictures. Find five differences.

Picture A   Picture B

EXAMPLE: In Picture A the man is cooking hot dogs. He's not cooking hot dogs in Picture B. He's
cooking chicken.

EXERCISE 9: Writing

A | *Compare two photos of the same person. Write sentences with the present progressive. Answer the questions:*

- Where is the person in each photo?
- What is the person doing?
- What is the person wearing?

B | *Underline the present progressive.*

EXAMPLE: In this photo <u>I'm eating</u> at my favorite restaurant with two good friends. <u>I'm wearing</u> a new sweater. <u>I'm smiling</u> because it's my birthday and I'm happy.
In this photo <u>I'm</u> <u>playing</u> soccer. I'm with my family. <u>I'm wearing</u> shorts and a T-shirt. <u>I'm not smiling</u> because our team <u>is losing</u>.

C | *Check your work. Use the Editing Checklist.*

> ### Editing Checklist
>
> Did you use . . . ?
> ☐ the present progressive correctly
> ☐ correct spelling

EXERCISE A

Complete the conversation. Use the present progressive form of the words in parentheses.

A. Hey, Mike. What are you doing?

B: Me? I _____ on the phone with you.
1. (talk)

A: Very funny. Well, I _____ anything. How about your brother?
2. (not, do)

B: He _____ anything. He _____ TV. He's bored.
3. (not, do)   4. (watch)

A: Well, my friends _____ bored. They _____ soccer in the
5. (not, feel)   6. (play)

park. Do you and your brother want to play too?

B: Sure! Sounds like fun. I'll ask my brother.

EXERCISE B

Put the words in the correct order. Make sentences.

1. _____ .
   (Redmond / in / are / Jessica and her family / living)

2. _____ .
   (her parents / Jessica / standing / between / is)

3. _____ .
   (not / Jessica's / working / mother and father / are)

4. _____ .
   (watching / on TV / Tim and Steve / a game / are)

EXERCISE C

Correct the sentences. There are five mistakes. Use contractions.

1. He not standing.

2. She wearing glasses.

3. It isn't snow today.

4. They're listen to a CD.

5. We not playing cards.

Present Progressive: *Yes / No* Questions
BABYSITTING

Before You Read

Look at the pictures. Write **T (True)** *or* **F (False)**.

_____ Tim and Jessica are celebrating.

_____ Tim and Jessica are at home.

_____ The children's babysitter isn't watching them.

Read

Read the conversations.

TIM: Hi, hon. Happy anniversary!

JESSICA: Thanks! You too.

TIM: Everyone OK? **Is Jeremy watching** Ben and Annie?

JESSICA: No. Jeremy's at a basketball game with Steve.

TIM: Oh. **Is Mrs. Brown babysitting?**

JESSICA: No. Her granddaughter Kelly Brown is.

(Later—Jessica calls Kelly.)

KELLY: Hello?

JESSICA: Hi, Kelly. This is Mrs. Olson. How's everything? **Are the children listening** to you?

KELLY: Sure. Everything's great.

JESSICA: So **are you helping** Ben with his math? **Is he doing** his homework?

KELLY: No, not now. He's baking cookies. He says he's the family baker.

JESSICA: He is? Well, **is Annie studying** for her science test?

KELLY: I think so. Her friend Gail is here. They're in Annie's room. It's quiet. They're probably studying.

JESSICA: Hmm. Well, I'm sure they are, but can you check?

KELLY: OK, Mrs. Olson. Look. Don't worry. Everything's cool. Enjoy your anniversary.

JESSICA: Thanks, Kelly. We'll be back around 10:00.

KELLY: See you then. Bye.

After You Read

A | Practice GROUPS OF THREE: Practice the opening conversation.

B | Vocabulary Listen and repeat the words. Write new words in a notebook.

VOCABULARY

babysit

help someone with homework

get a haircut

cut someone's hair

make a mess

worry

celebrate an anniversary

around five o'clock

C | Vocabulary Complete the passage. Use the correct forms of the vocabulary words.

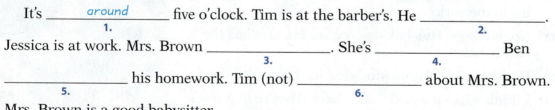

It's _____around_____ five o'clock. Tim is at the barber's. He _____.
       1.   2.

Jessica is at work. Mrs. Brown _____. She's _____ Ben
                                     3.   4.

_____ his homework. Tim (not) _____ about Mrs. Brown.
   5.   6.

Mrs. Brown is a good babysitter.

D | Comprehension *Look again at the opening conversation. Circle the correct letter.*

1. Are Tim and Jessica celebrating their anniversary?
   a. Yes, they are.
   b. No, they aren't.

2. Is Mrs. Brown babysitting?
   a. Yes, she is.
   b. No, she isn't.

3. Who is Kelly?
   a. Mrs. Brown's granddaughter.
   b. Mrs. Brown's daughter.

4. Is Kelly helping Ben with his math?
   a. No, she isn't.
   b. Yes, she is.

5. What is Ben doing?
   a. His homework.
   b. He's baking cookies.

6. Are Annie and Gail studying?
   a. Yes, they are.
   b. No, they aren't.

7. Is Gail cutting Annie's hair?
   a. Yes, she is.
   b. No, she isn't.

8. Is Annie cutting Gail's hair?
   a. Yes, she is.
   b. No, she isn't.

STEP 2 GRAMMAR PRESENTATION

PRESENT PROGRESSIVE: *YES / NO* QUESTIONS

Yes / No Questions	Short Answers			
Am I **making** a mess?	Yes, you **are**.	No, you**'re not**.	OR	No, you **aren't**.
Is he **studying**?	Yes, he **is**.	No, he**'s not**.	OR	No, he **isn't**.
Are they **playing**?	Yes, they **are**.	No, they**'re not**.	OR	No, they **aren't**.

GRAMMAR NOTES

1	In a *yes / no* question in the present progressive, put *am*, *is*, or *are* before the subject.	SUBJECT • Statement: You **are** working. SUBJECT • Question: **Are** you working?
2	We often use **short answers** in speaking and informal writing.	A: Are you doing your homework? B: **Yes, I am.** OR Yes. C: **No, I'm not.** OR No.
3	**Don't use contractions** in affirmative short answers.	A: Is he reading? B: Yes, **he is**. NOT: Yes, ~~he's~~.

STEP 3 FOCUSED PRACTICE

EXERCISE 1: Discover the Grammar

A | *Look at the questions. Check (✓) the questions in the present progressive. Match the questions and answers.*

   ✓   **1.** Are the parents leaving?   *1*   **a.** No, they aren't.

_____ **2.** Are the parents returning home?   _____ **b.** Yes, he is.

_____ **3.** Is the babysitter asleep?   _____ **c.** No, he isn't.

_____ **4.** Is the babysitter eating?   _____ **d.** Yes, they are.

_____ **5.** Is the little boy eating a   _____ **e.** No, she isn't.
             sandwich?   _____ **f.** Yes, she is.

_____ **6.** Is the little boy asleep?

B | *Look at the Dennis the Menace cartoon. Why does Dennis say, "Now you need to pay me. Right?"*

DENNIS THE MENACE

"The sitter is sleeping. Now you need to
pay me. Right?"

> Dennis the Menace is a cartoon character by
> Hank Ketcham. The cartoon is over 60 years old. It
> appears in 48 countries and in 1,000 newspapers
> all over the world.

EXERCISE 2: Present Progressive

(Grammar Notes 1–3)

A | *Write **yes** / **no** questions and answers. Use the present progressive and the correct forms of the words in parentheses.*

KELLY: Hello.

SUSAN: Kelly? It's me, Susan. So, tell me. Is Jeremy there?

KELLY: Uh . . . sure. Right here with me.

SUSAN: Oh, you're so lucky. <u>*Are you watching TV together*</u> ?
                                                  1. (you / watch TV together)

KELLY: _____ .
                                         2. (we / watch/ a DVD)

SUSAN: _____?
> **3. (you / watch a romance)**

KELLY: Uh-huh. _____ *Fifty First Dates*.
> **4. (We / watch)**

SUSAN: Awesome. _____?
> **5. (Jeremy / wear / his cool basketball jacket)**

KELLY: Sure. And he wants to take me to a concert.

SUSAN: Wow!

KELLY: Hey, Susan. _____ . _____

> **6. (I / kid)**   **7. (Jeremy / not / sit)**

here with me. _____ together. He isn't even
> **8. (We / not / watch a DVD)**

here. The Washington Huskies _____ the California
> **9. (play)**

Bears. Jeremy and his uncle are at the silly basketball game. And—Jeremy still

doesn't know I exist.

EXERCISE 3: Questions and Answers

(Grammar Notes 1–3)

Write questions and complete the answers. Use the present progressive and the correct forms of the words in parentheses. Use contractions when possible.

1. A: *Is Jeremy watching the game* _____?
> **(Jeremy / watch / the game)**

B: No, he _____ . _____ .
> **(He / wash / the car)**

2. A: _____?
> **(the kids / eat chips)**

B: No, _____ . They're eating sandwiches.

3. A: _____?
> **(it / rain)**

B: Yes, _____ . Take an umbrella.

4. A: _____?
> **(Uncle Steve / get a haircut)**

B: Yes, _____ . He's at the barbershop right now.

5. A: _____?
> **(Tim and Jessica / celebrate their anniversary)**

B. Yes, _____ . They're having a romantic dinner.

EXERCISE 4: Editing

There are seven mistakes in the conversations. The first mistake is already corrected.
Find and correct six more mistakes.

1. **A:** Are you ~~wear~~ *wearing* my watch?

   B: Yes, I am. Is that OK?

2. **A:** They celebrating Tim's birthday?

   B: No. They're celebrating Tim and Jessica's anniversary.

3. **A:** Is he gets a haircut now?

   B: Yes, he is. He likes his hair short.

4. **A:** Are the children eating chips?

   B: No, they not. They're eating sandwiches.

5. **A:** Is raining?

   B: Yes, it's.

6. **A:** Are you wash the dishes?

   B: Yes, I am.

STEP 4 COMMUNICATION PRACTICE

EXERCISE 5: Pronunciation

A | *Listen to the sound of the boldface letters. Then listen again and repeat.*

watch /tʃ/

wash /ʃ/

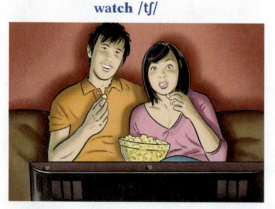

match — mash

ditch — dish

chip — ship

cheap — sheep

B | *Listen to the sentences. Underline the words you hear.*

1. Are you **watching** / <u>**washing**</u> them?

2. Please **match** / **mash** them.

3. What's a **ditch** / **dish**?

4. Are they buying **chips** / **ships**?

5. How do you spell ***cheap*** / ***sheep***?

C | *Listen again and repeat.*

D | *PAIRS: Say a sentence from Part B. Your partner writes the /tʃ/ or /ʃ/ word.*

EXERCISE 6: Listening

A | *Listen to the telephone conversation between Steve and his sister Jessica. Circle the correct letter.*

What is Steve doing when Jessica calls?

a. He's preparing for an online course.   **b.** He's taking an online course.

B | *Listen again. Answer the questions. Use short answers.*

1. Is Ben working on a model ship? ___Yes, he is._____

2. Is Ben eating chips? _____

3. Is Steve writing articles for the *Daily Times*? _____

4. Is Annie acting? _____

5. Is Annie playing basketball? _____

6. Is Annie writing for the *Daily Times*? _____

7. Is Annie writing for her school paper? _____

EXERCISE 7: Act Out Sentences

A | *Write a sentence in the present progressive. Use one of the verbs from the box.*

cook	**drink**	**help**	**read**	**wash**	**worry**
daydream	**eat**	**listen to**	**sleep**	**watch**	**write**

B | *Give your sentence to a classmate. That classmate acts out your sentence.*

EXAMPLE: You are watching TV.

(continued on next page)

C | *The class asks* **yes / no** *questions to guess the action.*

    EXAMPLE: **Class:** Are you watching TV?
                  You: Yes, I am. OR No, I'm not.

EXERCISE 8: Writing

A | *Look at the Dennis the Menace cartoon again. Label the items in the picture.*

a coat

a glass of milk

glasses

a sandwich

shoes

a sofa

DENNIS THE MENACE

"The sitter is sleeping. Now you need to pay me. Right?"

B | *Write five* **yes / no** *questions about the cartoon. Use the present progressive. Ask about the little boy, the parents, and the babysitter. Possible verbs:* drink, eat, hold, sit, wear, sleep.

1. _____

2. _____

3. _____

4. _____

5. _____

C | *Check your work. Use the Editing Checklist.*

Editing Checklist
Did you use . . . ? ☐ the present progressive correctly ☐ correct spelling

D | *Ask classmates your questions. Answer their questions.*

UNIT 16 Review

Check your answers on page UR-2.

Do you need to review anything?

EXERCISE A

Match the questions and answers.

_____ 1. Are you sleeping?   **a.** Yes, you are.

_____ 2. Are your classmates studying?   **b.** Yes, they are.

_____ 3. Is your sister babysitting?   **c.** No, he isn't.

_____ 4. Is your son watching TV?   **d.** Yes, she is.

_____ 5. Am I helping?   **e.** No, I'm not.

EXERCISE B

Write questions and complete the answers. Use the present progressive and the words in parentheses. Use contractions whenever possible.

1. A: _____?
   (Rob / go / to the movies)

   B: No, _____. He's going to a baseball game.

2. A: _____?
   (John and Eleanor / celebrate / an anniversary)

   B: No, _____. They're celebrating a birthday.

EXERCISE C

Correct the conversations. There are six mistakes.

1. A: Is snowing?

   B: Yes, it's.

2. A: Are you make a mess?

   B: No, I not.

3. A: Are the children to doing their homework?

   B: No, they not. They're watching TV.

Present Progressive: *Wh-* Questions
WAYS OF TRAVELING

STEP 1 GRAMMAR IN CONTEXT

Before You Read

PAIRS: Check (✓) the things that are true for you. Then compare your answers.

_____ I usually call friends.   _____ I usually email friends.

_____ I like to travel by car.   _____ I like to travel by plane.

_____ I get to school by car.   _____ I get to school by bus.

Read

Read the conversations.

MARK: Hello?

NICK: Hey, little brother . . . **what's happening**?

MARK: Nick? Is it really you?

NICK: Yep. This is your big brother.

MARK: I can't believe it. **Why are you calling** me? You hate phones.

NICK: I know . . . I emailed you, but you didn't answer.

MARK: **What are you doing?** Are you still in Kenya?

NICK: Nope. I'm back in the United States. I'm on my way to a job interview in Denver.

MARK: In Colorado? Wow! Are you planning to leave Kenya?

NICK: I don't know. It's possible.

MARK: **How are you traveling**? I think I hear a car engine.

NICK: By car. You still have good ears. Do you remember my old friend Jerry Gomez? He's driving me to Denver.

MARK: Sure I remember him. **What's Jerry doing** these days?

NICK: He's teaching at a college in Colorado.

MARK: Can you come to Seattle?

NICK: That's my plan. I'll be there next week.

＊　＊　＊　＊　＊

JUDY: **Why are you smiling?** Who was on the phone?

MARK: My brother Nick—the interesting one.

A | Practice *GROUPS OF THREE: Practice the opening conversations.*

B | Vocabulary *Listen and repeat the words. Write new words in a notebook.*

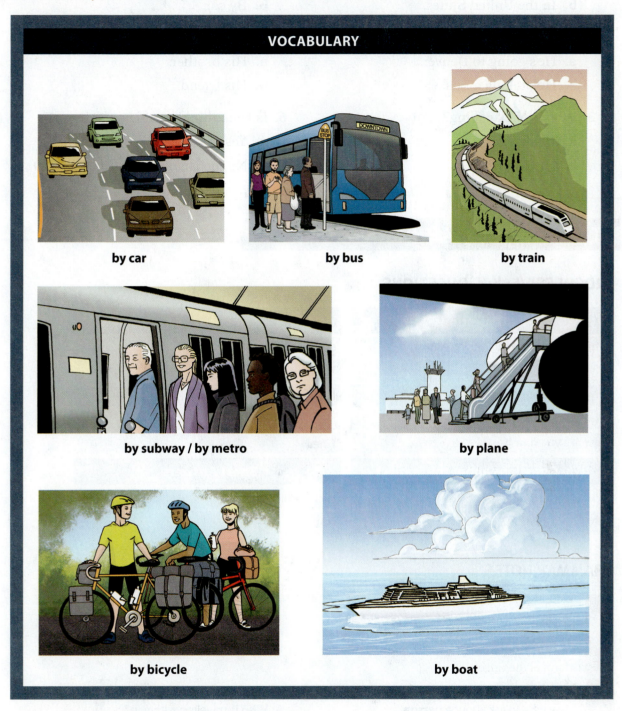

VOCABULARY

by car

by bus

by train

by subway / by metro

by plane

by bicycle

by boat

C | Vocabulary *PAIRS: Ask how your partner gets to school, work, friends' homes, and the supermarket. Use the vocabulary words.*

EXAMPLE: **A:** How do you get to school?
B: I get there by bus. OR Sometimes I get there by bicycle.

D | Comprehension *Look again at the opening conversations. Circle the correct letter.*

1. Where is Nick?
   a. In Kenya.
   (b.) In the United States.

2. What is he doing?
   a. He's going to Denver.
   b. He's taking a bus.

3. Who is Nick calling?
   a. His friend.
   b. His brother.

4. How is Nick traveling?
   a. By plane.
   b. By car.

5. Who is he traveling with?
   a. His brother.
   b. His friend.

6. Is Nick thinking of leaving Kenya?
   a. Yes, he is.
   b. No, he isn't.

STEP 2 GRAMMAR PRESENTATION

PROGRESSIVE: *WH-* QUESTIONS

Wh- Questions	Short Answers
What are you **making**?	Coffee.
Where are you **going**?	To an interview.
Why are you **smiling**?	I'm happy.
Who are you **talking** to?	Nick.
How are you **doing**?	Fine.

Wh- Questions about the Subject	Short Answers
Who is calling?	Nick. OR Nick is.
What's happening?	Nothing.

GRAMMAR NOTES

1	Begin *wh-* **questions** in the present progressive with a question word such as *what*, *where*, *why*, *who*, or *how*. Use *am*, *is*, or *are* + the *-ing* form of the verb.	WH- WORD + BE + SUBJECT + -ING FORM • **What** are you doing? • **Where** is he going?
2	Use *who* to ask about a **person**.	A: **Who** is traveling with you? B: My friend (is). A: **Who** are you talking to? B: My brother Nick.

3	Use *why* to ask for **reasons**.	**A: Why** are you calling me? **B:** You don't check your email.
4	In informal conversation, **answers** are often **short**. **BE CAREFUL!** Remember not to use contractions in affirmative short answers.	**A:** Where's Nick going? **B: To Denver.** **A:** Who's driving? **B: Jerry.** OR **Jerry is.** Not: ~~Jerry's.~~

STEP 3 FOCUSED PRACTICE

EXERCISE 1: Discover the Grammar

*Circle the **wh-** question word. Then match the questions and the answers.*

_e_ **1.** (How) are you traveling?   **a.** It's cheaper than flying.

____ **2.** Who are you talking to?   **b.** My friend Jerry Gomez.

____ **3.** How's it going?   **c.** To Denver. He has a job interview.

____ **4.** Where's Nick going?   **d.** Great. I love road trips.

____ **5.** Why are you driving there?   **e.** By car.

EXERCISE 2: *Wh-* Questions

(Grammar Notes 1–4)

Put the words in the correct order. Make questions. Then match the questions and answers.

Questions

1. wearing / you / a suit / are / Why /

_____?

2. Colorado / to / Who / him / taking / is /

_____?

3. Denver / Nick / to / traveling / is / How /

_____?

4. is / Where / teaching / Jerry /

_____?

Answers

____ **a.** At a college in Colorado.

____ **b.** This is a job interview, remember.

____ **c.** His friend Jerry Gomez.

____ **d.** In his friend's car.

EXERCISE 3: *Wh-* Questions

(Grammar Notes 1–3)

*Write Jerry's questions to Nick. Use **Where, How, What, Why,** or **Who**. Use the present progressive and the correct forms of the words in parentheses.*

1. **A:** ___Where are you staying___ ?
   (you / stay)

   B: At a Super 8 Motel.

2. **A:** _____ there?
   (you / stay)

   B: It's a good, inexpensive motel.

3. **A:** _____ now?
   (Mark / do)

   B: He's writing travel articles.

4. **A:** _____ now?
   (you / feel)

   B: Great! The job interview went well.

5. **A:** _____ ?
   (Mark / date)

   B: A woman named Kathy.

EXERCISE 4: Editing

There are eight mistakes in the conversations. The first mistake is already corrected. Find and correct seven more mistakes.

1. **A:** Why ~~Mark is~~ *is Mark* sleeping?

   B: He not feeling well.

2. **A:** Who driving Nick to Colorado?

   B: Jerry's.

3. **A:** Why you are studying, Judy?

   B: I have a history test tomorrow.

4. **A:** Why you wearing a suit today?

   B: I have a job interview.

5. **A:** Who you talking to?

   B: Nick. He's coming to Seattle.

6. **A:** What is he wear?

   B: A blue suit.

EXERCISE 5: Pronunciation

A | *Read and listen to the Pronunciation Note.*

Pronunciation Note
In **yes / no questions**, your voice goes up at the end of the question: *Are you using your cell phone?* In **wh- questions**, your voice goes up and then down at the end: *Who are you calling?*

B | *Listen to the questions. Write an up arrow (↑) if the voice goes up at the end. Write a down arrow (↓) if the voice goes down at the end.*

> EXAMPLES: What are you doing? ↓
> Do you have email? ↑

1. Is Mark taking the train to Seattle? ↑

2. Why is Mark taking the train?

3. Is Nick staying in Denver?

4. Where's he staying?

5. Is Jerry coming to Seattle with Nick?

6. What's Mark doing?

7. Why is he emailing?

8. Is he emailing his brother?

C | *PAIRS: Listen again and repeat. Then read the questions to your partner. Take turns.*

EXERCISE 6:   Listening

A | *Listen to the conversation. Check (✓) the one true sentence.*

_____ 1. Mark is alone.

_____ 2. Mark is listening to music.

_____ 3. The job interview was good.

_____ 4. Mark will see the caller on Thursday.

1. Who is calling Mark?

   Nick is calling Mark.

2. What is Mark doing now?

   _____

3. Which one is he watching?

   _____

4. Who is he with?

   _____

5. What is the caller planning to do?

   _____

6. In what city is the caller staying?

   _____

7. How is he planning to travel?

   _____

EXERCISE 7: Picture Discussion

PAIRS: Look at the pictures. Imagine you are visiting one of the countries. Your partner asks questions to identify the country. Answer your partner's questions. Take turns.

Possible questions:

What language are the people speaking?

What are you doing?

What country are you visiting?

The Empire State Building, U.S.A.

Kilimanjaro, Tanzania

Acapulco Beach, Mexico

Niagara Falls, Canada / U.S.A.

Sugar Loaf Mountain, Brazil

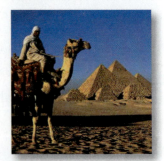
The Great Pyramid, Egypt

EXERCISE 8: Writing

A | *Imagine that a friend is visiting a foreign country. Write an email and ask questions about what the friend is doing. Include at least three **wh-** questions. Use the present progressive and suggestions from the box or your own questions.*

how / travel	what country / visit now	where / stay

EXAMPLE: Dear Mary,
What a great trip you're taking! What country are you visiting now?

B | *Check your work. Use the Editing Checklist.*

Editing Checklist

Did you . . . ?
☐ include three **wh-** questions
☐ use the present progressive correctly
☐ use correct spelling

EXERCISE A

Match the questions and answers.

_____ **1.** What are you doing?

_____ **2.** Where are you going?

_____ **3.** How are you getting to work?

_____ **4.** Who are you driving to work with?

_____ **5.** Why are you driving to work?

a. The bus is very slow.

b. By car.

c. Fixing my car.

d. My friend.

e. To work.

EXERCISE B

Put the words in the correct order. Make questions.

1. _____ ?
    (watching / TV / What / on / is / Steve)

2. _____ ?
    (are / me / now / calling / Why / you)

3. _____ ?
    (class / How / enjoying / the / you / are)

4. _____ ?
    (the bus / is / Who / work / taking / to)

5. _____ ?
    (with / Where / you / that book / going / are)

EXERCISE C

Correct the conversations. There are five mistakes. Use contractions if possible.

1. A: Who teaching the class?

   B: Mark's.

2. A: Why you are smiling?

   B: I'm watch a funny movie.

3. A: What is your sister wear?

   B: A blue sweatshirt and jeans.

PART VII

NOUNS; *THIS* / *THAT* / *THESE* / *THOSE*; *SOME* AND *ANY*; ARTICLES; *CAN* / *CAN'T*

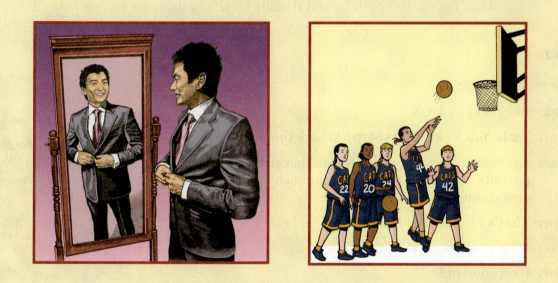

UNIT 18 Possessive Nouns; *This / That / These / Those*

CLOTHING

Before You Read

GROUPS: Tell your group the birthdays of five people you know. Then report to the class any of the same birthdays.

> EXAMPLES: My sister's birthday is on November 7. My dad's birthday is on May 23. My best friend's birthday is on . . .
> Ming Fen's sister's birthday and Hamid's friend's birthday are on September 8.

Read

Read the conversation.

MARK: Judy, do I look OK?

JUDY: Yeah. You look really sharp.[1] What's the occasion?

MARK: I'm having dinner with Kathy and her parents. It's her **parents'** anniversary. They're taking us to an expensive new restaurant, The Water Grill.

JUDY: **That's** nice. Is **that** a new sports jacket?

MARK: It's my **brother's** jacket.

JUDY: It's a good fit.[2]

MARK: Are **these** suspenders OK?

JUDY: Sure. They go well with **that** tie and **those** shoes.

MARK: Thanks. Actually they aren't mine. They're my **roommate's**. I almost never wear a tie or dress shoes.

JUDY: Oh yeah? Is *anything* yours?

MARK: Uh-huh. **This** new goatee. It's all mine.

JUDY: Oh. I see. You know, **that** goatee makes you look like an artist.

MARK: An artist? No kidding. I guess **that's** good. Now I need to remember— **Kathy's** mom is Bea Harlow, and her dad is Lee White.

JUDY: Relax, Mark. Just be yourself.[3] They're going to love you!

[1] *sharp:* really good
[2] *a good fit:* the right size
[3] *be yourself:* act as you always do

A | Practice *PAIRS: Practice the opening conversation.*

B | Vocabulary *Listen and repeat the words. Write new words in a notebook.*

VOCABULARY

| a tie | a sports jacket | slacks | dress shoes |

go well with = look good with

C | Vocabulary *PAIRS: Complete the conversations. Use the vocabulary words. Practice the conversations.*

1. **A:** What's he wearing?

   B: He's wearing a navy _____,
   a red tie, a pair of tan

   _____, and brown shoes.
   2.

2. **A:** You look sharp. The tie and shirt _____ the suit.
   3.

   B: Thanks.

3. **A:** I need a pair of _____. I'm going to a wedding, and I only
   4.

   have casual shoes.

   B: What size are you? Maybe you can wear mine.

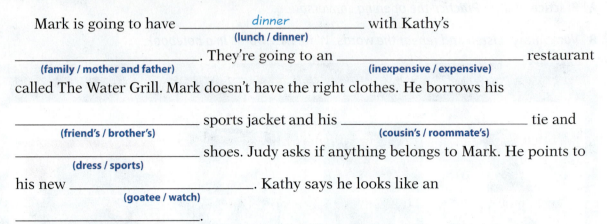

Mark is going to have _____*dinner*_____ with Kathy's
                (lunch / dinner)

_____. They're going to an _____ restaurant
(family / mother and father)   (inexpensive / expensive)

called The Water Grill. Mark doesn't have the right clothes. He borrows his

_____ sports jacket and his _____ tie and
(friend's / brother's)   (cousin's / roommate's)

_____ shoes. Judy asks if anything belongs to Mark. He points to
(dress / sports)

his new _____. Kathy says he looks like an
         (goatee / watch)

_____.
(actor / artist)

STEP 2 GRAMMAR PRESENTATION

POSSESSIVE NOUNS; *THIS / THAT / THESE / THOSE; THAT'S*

Possessive Nouns	
Singular	**Plural**
My **sister's** car is red.	My **parents'** car is blue.
The **actress's** first name is Rosa.	Her **daughters'** names are Tina and Marie.

This / That / These / Those	
Pronouns	**Adjectives**
This is my cell phone.	**This** cell phone is great.
That is your jacket.	**That** tie is Steve's.
These are my keys.	**These** keys don't work.
Those are your keys.	**Those** keys are Steve's.

That's
A: It's their 30th anniversary.
B: **That's** great.
A: He's in the hospital.
B: **That's** too bad.
A: I'm studying tonight. **That's** why I can't come to the party.

GRAMMAR NOTES

1	**Possessive nouns** show **belonging**.	• I'm wearing my **roommate's** dress shoes. *(The shoes belong to my roommate.)* • She's wearing **Joe's** sports jacket. *(The sports jacket belongs to Joe.)*
2	**To show belonging**, add an **apostrophe (')** + **-s** to a singular noun or an irregular plural noun. Add only an **apostrophe (')** to a plural noun ending in **-s**.	• That's my **father's** jacket. • Where's the **women's** restroom? • It's her **parents'** anniversary. • It's the **Becks'** house.
3	*This*, *that*, *these*, and *those* can be **pronouns** or **adjectives**. REMEMBER: *This* and *that* are **singular**; *these* and *those* are **plural**. Use *this* and *these* for things that are **near**. Use *that* and *those* for things that are **away** from you.	• **This** is my cell phone. *(pronoun)* • **This cell phone** is new. *(adjective)* • **These** are my sunglasses. *(pronoun)* • **Those sunglasses** on **that table** over there are Robert's. *(adjectives)*
4	*That's* is often used in speaking and informal writing. It refers to the idea that was just stated.	**A:** I really like her parents. **B: That's** great. **A:** I really don't like her brother. **B: That's** too bad. **A:** He's in Boston. **That's** why he's not here.

REFERENCE NOTE

For more practice with *this*, *that*, *these*, and *those* as **pronouns**, see Units 2 and 4.

STEP 3 FOCUSED PRACTICE

EXERCISE 1: Discover the Grammar

Read the sentences. Underline **this, that, these,** *and* **those.** *Circle the possessive nouns.*
Match the sentences.

_c_ **1.** Let's visit (Kathy's) grandmother.

____ **2.** Are those your father's slacks?

____ **3.** This is my sister's friend Melanie.

____ **4.** What color are your roommate's dress shoes?

____ **5.** Bob's son has a broken leg.

a. Nice to meet you. I'm Kathy's friend Mark.

b. They're black.

c. That's a good idea. She loves visitors.

d. That's too bad.

e. No, they're not. They're my brother's. These are my father's.

EXERCISE 2: *This / That / These / Those*

(Grammar Notes 2–3)

A | Complete the conversations with **this, that, these,** *or* **those.**

1.   **KATHY:** Mom, Dad, _____*this*_____ is

                    Mark. Mark, _____

                    are my parents.

      MARK: Nice to meet you.

  BEA HARLOW: Good to meet you.

2. **LEE WHITE:** Bea, is _____ your

                    phone over there?

       BEA: No, Lee. I think it's Kathy's.

    KATHY: It is, Dad.

3.   **MARK:** _____'s a beautiful ring. It's very unusual.

       BEA: Thanks. _____ ring is about 100 years old. It was my

                great-grandmother's ring.

4.   **BEA:** How do you like the food?

      MARK: _____ steak is delicious!

    KATHY: And _____ vegetables melt in your mouth. How's the chicken,

                Mom?

       BEA: Excellent, as always.

5.   **LEE:** Bea, do you see _____ men over there? I think the tall man is

               Adam Katz.

       BEA: You're right. What a small world! Let's go say hello.

B | Complete the conversations. Use the possessive form of the nouns in parentheses.

1.   **KATHY:** Excuse me. Where's the _____ restroom?
                               (women)

    WAITER: It's over there, next to the telephones.

2.   **LEE:** Mark, is your _____ home nearby?
                         (parents)

      MARK: Yes. They live in Redmond. It's just a few miles away.

3.   **BEA:** Lee, are these your car keys?

       LEE: No, they're _____.
                    (Kathy)

EXERCISE 3: Possessives

(Grammar Note 2)

Complete the reading. Use the possessive form of the words in parentheses.

Women in the United States are free to choose their family name when they marry.

Many women change their name to their _____*husband's family name*_____. For example,
1. (husband / family name)

before _____ married Bill Beck, she was Mary Meyers. After
2. (Steve Beck / mother)

her marriage, she became Mary Beck. But some women don't change their name.

_____, Bea Harlow, married Lee White. She is still Bea
3. (Kathy White / mother)

Harlow after 30 years of marriage. Today some women are keeping their name and adding

their _____. For example, _____
4. (husband / name)   **5. (Kathy / sister)**

Jill is married to Joe Smith. Her married name is Jill White-Smith. So a woman's last name

doesn't always match her husband's.

EXERCISE 4: *That's . . .*

(Grammar Note 4)

Complete the conversations. Write the correct phrases from the box.

That's a good idea.	That's great.	That's right.	That's too bad.

1. A: Her parents really like me.

    B: _____

2. A: My boss is impossible.

    B: _____

3. A: The Water Grill is that expensive restaurant on Third Street, right?

    B: _____

4. A: Let's watch that DVD.

    B: _____

EXERCISE 5: Editing

There are six mistakes in the reading. The first mistake is already corrected. Find and correct five more mistakes.

My family loves to eat out. On my ~~parents~~ parents' anniversary we go to a Chinese restaurant. That's because my parent's love Chinese food. On my brother birthday, we go to an Italian restaurant. My brother loves Italian food. On my sister birthday, we go to a Mexican restaurant. That because her favorite food comes from Mexico. And on my birthday, we go to a different restaurant every year because I like to try different places. These year I want to try a Brazilian restaurant.

STEP 4 COMMUNICATION PRACTICE

EXERCISE 6: Pronunciation

A | *Read and listen to the Pronunciation Note.*

Pronunciation Note

The 's in a possessive noun sounds like **/s/**, **/z/**, or **/ɪz/**.

/s/: This is my aunt's telephone number.

/z/: When is your uncle's birthday?

/ɪz/: Those are Ross's slacks. (Note that **/ɪz/** makes an extra syllable.)

B | *Listen to the sentences. Write the possessive noun. Then listen again. Check (✓) the sound you hear.*

Possessive Noun	/s/	/z/	/ɪz/
1. *mother's*		✓	
2.			
3.			
4.			
5.			
6.			

C | *PAIRS: Complete the sentences. Use the possessive form of the nouns in parentheses. Take turns saying each sentence.*

1. Her _____ sister's _____ (sister) name is Lauren.

2. Their _____ (parents) home is on Main Street.

3. My _____ (teacher) glasses are on the desk.

4. Our _____ (boss) home is on a lake.

5. His _____ (roommate) brother is staying with us.

6. My _____ (friend) birthday is tomorrow.

EXERCISE 7: Listening

A | *Listen to the conversation. What does Mark talk about? Circle the correct letter.*
   a. the food at the restaurant
   b. his conversation with Kathy's mom and dad
   c. his roommate

B | *Listen again. Circle the correct letter to complete the sentences.*

1. _____ has a boat.
   a. Kathy's dad
   b. Mark's dad
   c. Kathy's friend

2. _____ is worried about her sister.
   a. Kathy's mom
   b. Kathy
   c. Kathy's aunt

3. _____ doesn't like Mark's goatee.
   a. Kathy's mom
   b. Kathy's dad
   c. Kathy

4. _____ likes Mark's tie and suspenders.
   a. Kathy
   b. Mark's roommate
   c. Mark's friend

EXERCISE 8: Picture Differences

Picture A

Picture B

A | *PAIRS: Look at the pictures. What's different in Picture B?*

    EXAMPLE: In Picture B, Renee is wearing Amy's hat. Juan is wearing . . .

B | *GROUPS: One student leaves the room. The other students exchange glasses, backpacks, watches, shoes, and so on. The student returns and talks about the changes.*

    EXAMPLE: Yusuf is wearing José's hat.

EXERCISE 9: Writing

A | *Write a paragraph about how you celebrate the birthdays of four people you know. Use possessive nouns. Underline the possessive nouns and the nouns that follow them.*

    EXAMPLE: On my <u>niece's birthday</u>, my sister has a big party. My niece gets a lot of gifts, and she is always very happy. My niece is five years old. On my <u>father's birthday</u>, we usually have a barbecue. That's his favorite way to celebrate his birthday. On my <u>mother's birthday</u>, we go to a restaurant. My mother doesn't want to cook on her birthday, and she doesn't like my <u>dad's cooking</u>. And on my <u>brother's birthday</u>, he invites a few friends and relatives to his home. We always buy him something for his computer. That's his passion.

B | *Check your work. Use the Editing Checklist.*

> ### Editing Checklist
>
> Did you use . . . ?
> ☐ possessive nouns correctly
> ☐ correct spelling

UNIT 18 Review

Check your answers on page UR-2.

Do you need to review anything?

EXERCISE A

Complete the conversations. Choose the correct words in parentheses.

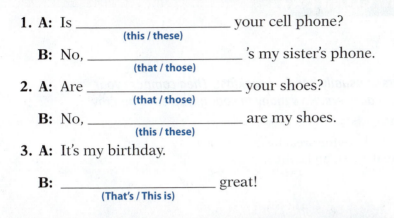

1. **A:** Is _____ your cell phone?
     (this / these)

   B: No, _____ 's my sister's phone.
          (that / those)

2. **A:** Are _____ your shoes?
          (that / those)

   B: No, _____ are my shoes.
          (this / these)

3. **A:** It's my birthday.

   B: _____ great!
          (That's / This is)

EXERCISE B

Complete the sentences. Use the possessive form of the nouns in parentheses.

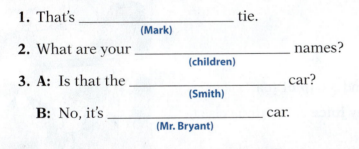

1. That's _____ tie.
           (Mark)

2. What are your _____ names?
                  (children)

3. **A:** Is that the _____ car?
                      (Smith)

   B: No, it's _____ car.
                   (Mr. Bryant)

EXERCISE C

Correct the conversations. There are six mistakes.

1. **A:** Is that a new dress?

   B: No, it's my sisters' dress.

2. **A:** Do you like this glasses on me?

   B: Yes, I really like that glasses. They make you look smart.

3. **A:** Why are you wearing your mom slacks?

   B: Because my jeans don't fit. That why.

4. **A:** Where are my keys?

   B: They're on this counter over there.

Count and Non-count Nouns; *Some* and *Any*
FOOD

Before You Read

GROUPS OF FIVE: Ask what each person usually has for breakfast. Then compare your group's answers with another group's answers. How many in your group eat a healthy breakfast?

> **EXAMPLE:** **A:** What do you usually have for breakfast?
> **B:** I usually have cereal, toast, and coffee.

Read

🎧 *Read the interviews.*

JESSICA: Hello, everyone. This morning we're interviewing people about their eating habits . . . Excuse me, sir, do you eat breakfast?

MAN: Yes, more or less.

JESSICA: What do you have?

MAN: I generally have **a bagel** and **a cup of tea**.

JESSICA: That's all? Do you have **any juice** or anything else to drink?

MAN: Not usually. Once in a while I have **coffee** instead of **tea**. I'm always in a hurry. Bye.

JESSICA: OK. Thanks. Bye.

JESSICA: Now, here's our next person. Ma'am, what do you have for breakfast?

WOMAN 1: I never eat breakfast.

JESSICA: Nothing at all?

WOMAN 1: No. I'm on **a diet**. I'm *always* on **a diet**.

JESSICA: OK. Thank you . . .

JESSICA: And what about you, ma'am? What do you have for breakfast?

WOMAN 2: Oh, I usually have **a bowl of cereal** and **some yogurt** with **fruit—a banana**, **a peach**, or **an orange**, or **some strawberries**. And I have **eggs** and **toast** and **a glass of juice**.

JESSICA: Hmm. That sounds healthy.

WOMAN 2: Yes, I always eat **a** good **breakfast**.

JESSICA: All right, thanks. Let's see what our next person says . . .

After You Read

A | Practice *GROUPS OF FOUR: Practice the opening interviews.*

B | Vocabulary *Listen and repeat the words. Write new words in a notebook.*

VOCABULARY

| a bagel | a cup of coffee | fruit | cereal |

| candy | yogurt | a sandwich | salad | a slice of toast |

C | Vocabulary *PAIRS: Look at the words in the box. Talk about which foods you like and which you don't like.*

| bagels | cereal | fruit | sandwiches | yogurt |
| candy | coffee | salad | toast | |

D | Comprehension *Look again at the opening interviews. Circle the correct letter to complete the sentences.*

1. It is _____.
   a. morning
   b. afternoon
   c. evening

2. The man has _____.
   a. a big breakfast
   b. a small breakfast
   c. no breakfast at all

3. He usually drinks _____.
   a. water
   b. coffee
   c. tea

4. The first woman _____ has breakfast.
   a. never
   b. rarely
   c. sometimes

5. The second woman has _____.
   a. a big breakfast
   b. a small breakfast
   c. no breakfast at all

6. Jessica thinks the _____ has a healthy meal.
   a. man
   b. first woman
   c. second woman

STEP 2 GRAMMAR PRESENTATION

COUNT AND NON-COUNT NOUNS; *SOME* AND *ANY*

Count Nouns		Non-count Nouns
Article + Singular Noun	**Plural Noun**	
a sandwich	sandwich**es**	yogurt
an orange	orange**s**	water

Quantifiers: *Some* and *Any*	
Count Nouns	**Non-count Nouns**
A: Do you have **any** oranges? **B:** Yes, I have **some**. OR No, I don't have **any**.	**A:** Do you have **any** bread? **B:** Yes, I have **some**. OR No, I don't have **any**.

Other Quantifiers

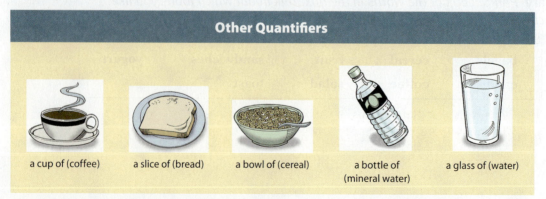

a cup of (coffee)   a slice of (bread)   a bowl of (cereal)   a bottle of (mineral water)   a glass of (water)

GRAMMAR NOTES

1	**Count nouns** refer to separate things. It is **easy to count** them. To form the plural of most count nouns, add **-s** or **-es**.	• **one** orange, **two** eggs, **three** bagels • orange orange**s** • sandwich sandwich**es**
2	**Non-count nouns** refer to things that are **difficult to count**. We use **quantifiers** to help us count non-count nouns. Some quantifiers are *a bag of*, *a bowl of*, *a slice of*, *a bottle of*, *a glass of*, and *a cup of*. *Some* and *any* are also quantifiers.	• I love **coffee**. • Bring me **a cup of coffee**. • Ben likes **bread**. • Please bring him **a slice of bread**. • I want **cereal**. • Please bring me **a bowl of cereal**. • I want **some cereal**. I don't want **any bread**.
3	Use **singular verbs** with **non-count nouns**.	• Rice **is** good for you. NOT: Rice ~~are~~ good for you.

4	Use *a* or *an* before **singular count nouns**. Use *a* before words that start with consonant sounds. Use *an* before words that start with vowel sounds.
	
	Use *some* (or no word) with **plural count nouns** and **non-count nouns**.
		• Steve wants **a banana**. *(starts with a consonant sound)*
		• I want **an orange.** *(starts with a vowel sound)*
		
		        PLURAL COUNT NOUN
		• We have **(some) oranges** in the refrigerator.
		
		        NON-COUNT NOUN
		• I drink **(some) juice** every morning.

5	Use *some* in **affirmative statements**. Use *any* in **negative statements** and in **questions**. **NOTE:** You can use *some* in a **question**, especially when you are offering something.	• I have **some** fruit. • I don't have **any** fruit. • Do you have **any** fruit? • Do you want **some** fruit? *(offer)*
6	Use **plural count nouns** or **non-count nouns** to talk about things you **like** or **dislike** in general. (Don't use *a*, *an*, or *some*.)	• I like **oranges**. I don't like **yogurt**. NOT: I like ~~an orange~~. I don't like ~~some~~ yogurt.

REFERENCE NOTES
For more information about **plural nouns**, see Appendix 3 on page A-3.
For a list of **non-count nouns and quantifiers**, see Appendix 4 on page A-3.

EXERCISE 1: Discover the Grammar

Read the paragraph. Find the foods and drinks. Write them in the correct column.

My favorite meal is lunch—my big meal of the day. I start with soup, and I usually have crackers with it. Next I have some meat. I also have vegetables: maybe carrots, peas, or beans. I almost always have rice. For dessert I sometimes have a cookie, and I usually have some fruit—an orange, or an apple, or a banana. Occasionally I have ice cream. I usually drink coffee, but once in a while I have tea. I'm never hungry after lunch.

Count Nouns

crackers

Non-count Nouns

soup

EXERCISE 2: Count and Non-count Nouns

(Grammar Notes 2, 4, 6)

Complete the conversation. Choose the correct words in parentheses.

WAITER: All right, folks. What would you like?

MARY: I'd like _____ some _____ chicken
　　　　　1. (a bag of / some)

and rice and _____ mixed
　　　　　　　2. (a / some)

vegetables. And I'll have

_____ hot tea to drink.
3. (a cup of / a bowl of)

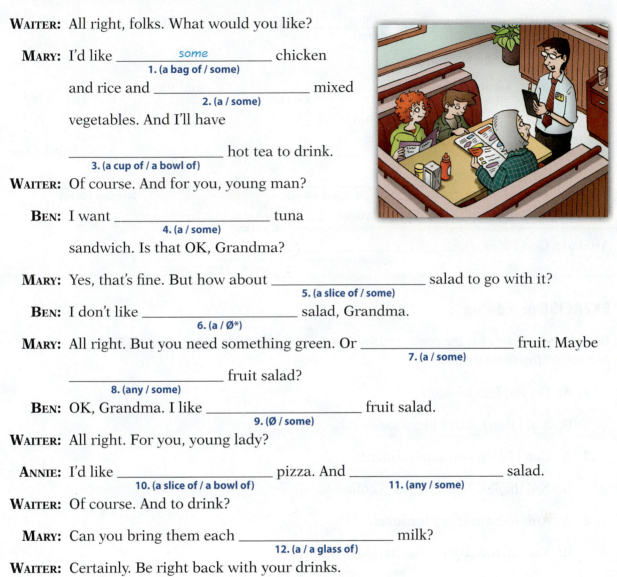

WAITER: Of course. And for you, young man?

BEN: I want _____ tuna
　　　　　4. (a / some)

sandwich. Is that OK, Grandma?

MARY: Yes, that's fine. But how about _____ salad to go with it?
　　　　　　　　　　　　　　　　　　5. (a slice of / some)

BEN: I don't like _____ salad, Grandma.
　　　　　　　　　　6. (a / Ø*)

MARY: All right. But you need something green. Or _____ fruit. Maybe
　　　　　　　　　　　　　　　　　　　　　　　　7. (a / some)

_____ fruit salad?
8. (any / some)

BEN: OK, Grandma. I like _____ fruit salad.
　　　　　　　　　　　　　9. (Ø / some)

WAITER: All right. For you, young lady?

ANNIE: I'd like _____ pizza. And _____ salad.
　　　　　　10. (a slice of / a bowl of)　　　　11. (any / some)

WAITER: Of course. And to drink?

MARY: Can you bring them each _____ milk?
　　　　　　　　　　　　　　　12. (a / a glass of)

WAITER: Certainly. Be right back with your drinks.

---

* Ø = no article or quantifier

EXERCISE 3: *Some* or *Any*

(Grammar Note 5)

Complete the conversation. Use **some** or **any** and the nouns in parentheses.

AMANDA: Josh, we need _____*some things*_____ for the party tonight. Can you go to the

1. (things)

store now?

JOSH: Sure. I know we don't have _____. And we don't have

2. (soda)

_____. What else?

3. (chips)

AMANDA: We need _____. And we need _____. But let me

4. (fruit)   5. (olives)

check . . . Oh, yes! Get _____. Don't get _____.

6. (black olives)   7. (green olives)

JOSH: OK. Anything else? Do you want _____?

8. (candy)

AMANDA: Good idea. Get _____.

9. (chocolate candy)

EXERCISE 4: Editing

There are six mistakes in the conversations. The first mistake is already corrected. Find
and correct five more mistakes.

1. **A:** Do you like a̶ ̶b̶a̶g̶e̶l̶ *bagels*?

   B: No, I don't. But I like a sandwich.

2. **A:** Can I bring you some coffee?

   B: No, thanks. I don't drink a coffee.

3. **A:** Are we having egg for lunch?

   B: Yes, we are. We're also having a yogurt.

4. **A:** Do we need milk?

   B: No, we don't need some milk.

EXERCISE 5: Listening

A | *Listen to Mark and Judy's conversation with a waiter. Check (✔) the two true statements.*

_____ **1.** It's late in the afternoon.

_____ **2.** Mark and Judy want to order lunch.

_____ **3.** Mark and Judy are having dinner.

_____ **4.** The coffee machine is broken.

B | *Listen again. Read the statements. Check (✔)* **T (True), F (False),** *or* **NI (No Information).** *Correct the false statements.*

	T	F	NI	
1. The restaurant is serving lunch now.	☐	✔	☐	*The restaurant isn't serving lunch now.*
2. Judy wants chips and salsa.	☐	☐	☐	_____
3. The restaurant has iced tea.	☐	☐	☐	_____
4. Mark likes tea.	☐	☐	☐	_____
5. The restaurant is out of salsa.	☐	☐	☐	_____
6. The restaurant has mineral water.	☐	☐	☐	_____
7. The soda is expensive.	☐	☐	☐	_____
8. Mark and Judy like the restaurant.	☐	☐	☐	_____

EXERCISE 6: Pronunciation

A | *Read and listen to the Pronunciation Note.*

Pronunciation Note
Plural nouns have three sounds: **/s/** fruits   **/z/** plums   **/ɪz/** peaches

B | *Listen to the sentences. Underline the plural nouns.*

1. We need some more bagels.

2. How many eggs do you want—one or two?

3. Do we need any oranges? They're on sale.

4. I really like black olives—but not green olives.

5. Mark had three slices of toast for breakfast.

6. I love chips and salsa.

7. Amy made some sandwiches for the picnic.

8. Bananas are very good on cereal.

9. Vegetables are also very healthy for you.

10. Blueberry pancakes are my favorite.

C | *Listen again. Write the plural nouns in the correct column.*

/s/	/z/	/ɪz/
	bagels	

D | *PAIRS: Practice the sentences. Take turns.*

EXERCISE 7: Discuss Foods

A | *GROUPS OF FOUR: Talk about the foods you really like and really don't like. Which things are the same for you and your partners? Which are different?*

> **EXAMPLE:** I really like . . .
> I really don't like . . .

B | *List the food each student really likes. Tell the class. Is there a favorite food in your class?*

EXERCISE 8: Writing

A | *Read Annie's composition and answer the question. Then check your answer on page P-1.*

> ### My Favorite Dish
>
> I love vegetables. This is about my favorite vegetable dish. The dish is usually green and red and orange. It has lettuce, tomatoes, and carrots. Sometimes it has cauliflower and broccoli. I always eat it with dressing. It's usually in a bowl, but it can also be on a plate. Can you guess what it is?

B | *Use Annie's composition as a model. Write a short composition (five or six sentences) about your favorite dish or your favorite food. Don't name the food. Read your composition to the class. Your classmates guess the food.*

C | *Check your work. Use the Editing Checklist.*

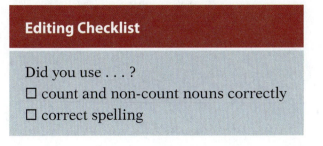

Editing Checklist

Did you use . . . ?
☐ count and non-count nouns correctly
☐ correct spelling

UNIT 19 Review

Check your answers on page UR-3.

Do you need to review anything?

EXERCISE A

Circle the correct words to complete the phrases.

1. a bag of **eggs / ice cream / salsa / chips**

2. a bowl of **bagels / sandwiches / cereal / pancakes**

3. a slice of **yogurt / candy / pizza / chocolate**

4. a bottle of **fruit / water / rice / chicken**

5. a glass of **milk / salad / olives / eggs**

EXERCISE B

Complete the conversation. Choose the correct words in parentheses.

A: What would you like to order?

B: I'd like _____ egg salad sandwich.
   1. (a / an)

A: Sorry, we don't have _____ eggs. How about _____
   2. (some / any)   3. (a / an)

   chicken sandwich?

B: No, I don't like _____ chicken. Just bring me a _____
   4. (some / Ø)   5. (bowl of / cup of)

   coffee.

EXERCISE C

Correct the sentences. There are five mistakes.

1. I always drink two cup of coffee for breakfast.

2. Usually I have an eggs and slice of toast.

3. Sometimes I have fruit, like a bananas.

4. I also like any milk and cereal.

A / An and *The*; *One / Ones*
SHOPPING FOR CLOTHES

STEP 1 GRAMMAR IN CONTEXT

Before You Read

A | *What clothing do you want? What clothing do you need? Write two sentences.*

    EXAMPLE: I want a new sweater. I need new socks.

B | *GROUPS OF FOUR: Talk about your answers. Compare your group's answers with another group's answers.*

Read

Read the conversation.

    CLERK: May I help you?

    KEN: Yes, I'm looking for **a** new sports jacket. I have **an** interview tomorrow.

    CLERK: Oh, you're in luck! We're having **a** sale on sports jackets.

    KEN: You are? Great!

    CLERK: What size?

    KEN: Forty-two.

    CLERK: OK. Be right back.

    CLERK: All right. Do you like any of these?

    KEN: Yes! I really like **the** blue **one**.

    CLERK: Do you want to try it on?

    KEN: Sure.

(continued on next page)

CLERK: How does it feel? Does it fit?

KEN: Perfectly. And it's really comfortable. How does it look, Laura?

LAURA: Well, it's pretty bright. And it's casual. How about that black **one**? It's more formal.

KEN: All **the** black **ones** are dull—really boring.

LAURA: OK. It's up to you.

After You Read

A | Practice *GROUPS OF THREE: Practice the opening conversation.*

B | Vocabulary *Listen and repeat the words. Write new words in a notebook.*

VOCABULARY

fit

a sale

try on

two sizes

bright / dull

formal / casual

C | Vocabulary *PAIRS: Underline the answers that are true for you. Then compare your answers.*

1. I (**sometimes / always**) try on clothes before I buy them.

2. I (**like / don't like**) bright clothes.

3. I usually wear (**formal / casual**) clothes.

4. I (**sometimes / never**) buy clothes on sale.

5. If my clothes don't fit, I (**always / sometimes**) return them to the store.

D | Comprehension *Look again at the opening conversation. Circle the correct letter to complete the sentences.*

1. Ken has an interview _____.
   - **a.** tomorrow
   - **b.** next week

2. Sports jackets are on sale. They will cost _____.
   - **a.** more than usual
   - **b.** less than usual

3. Ken likes clothes that are _____.
   - **a.** not bright
   - **b.** bright

4. Ken tries on a jacket that is _____.
   - **a.** the right size
   - **b.** too small

5. Laura thinks Ken needs to buy something _____.
   - **a.** more casual
   - **b.** more formal

STEP 2 GRAMMAR PRESENTATION

A / AN AND THE; ONE / ONES

Indefinite Articles (*A / An*)	
Singular Nouns	**Plural Nouns**
I'm looking for **a suit**.	**Suits** are expensive.
I have **an interview** tomorrow.	I don't like **interviews**.

The Definite Article (*The*)		One and Ones	
Singular Nouns	**Plural Nouns**	**Singular Pronouns**	**Plural Pronouns**
I like **the** blue **suit**.	I don't like **the** black **suits**.	I like **the** blue **one**.	I don't like **the** black **ones**.

GRAMMAR NOTES

1 Use *a* or *an* (**the indefinite articles**) before a **singular count noun** when you are talking about things in general. Use *a* before a **consonant** sound. Use *an* before a **vowel** sound.

- I'm looking for **a jacket**.
- I have **an interview** tomorrow.

BE CAREFUL! Don't put *a* or *an* before a non-count noun or a plural noun.

- **Meat** is expensive. (non-count)
  NOT: I like a meat.
- I usually wear **jackets**. (plural)
  NOT: I have a jackets.

(continued on next page)

2	Use *the* (the **definite article**) for **specific things** that the speaker and listener know about. You can use *the* before **singular count nouns**, **plural count nouns**, and **non-count nouns**.	**Salesperson:** Do you like **the** black suit? **Customer:** No, but I like **the** blue suit. • **The shirt** is too small. • **The apples** are green. • **The coffee** is delicious.

3	Use *the* when there is only one of something.	• I really like **the gray suit**.
		  (There is only one gray suit in the store.)
		• **The sun** is bright today.
		  (There is only one sun.)

4	Use *the* when you talk about something for the **second time** and afterwards.	• Jessica made pasta and meatballs. **The pasta** was delicious. **The meatballs** were spicy.
5	Use *one* to replace a **singular noun**. Use *ones* to replace a **plural noun**.	• They have three **suits** on sale. I like the blue **one**. I don't like the black **ones**.

STEP 3 FOCUSED PRACTICE

EXERCISE 1: Discover the Grammar

Read the conversations and look at the underlined words and expressions. Circle the correct explanation.

1. **A:** The sun is bright today!   (one / more than one) sun

   B: Yes. You need a hat.   (a hat in general / a specific hat)

2. **A:** Where's the cat?   (one / more than one) cat

   B: She's sleeping on the sofa.   (one / more than one) sofa

3. **A:** Do you have a car?   (a car in general / a specific car)

   B: No. I can't afford a car.   (a car in general / a specific car)

4. **A:** Do you want a jacket?   (a jacket in general / a specific jacket)

   B: Yes. I want the red one.   (a jacket in general / a specific jacket)

EXERCISE 2: Articles

(Grammar Notes 1–4)

Complete the conversation. Choose the correct words in parentheses. If no article or quantifier is needed, write Ø.

CLERK: Do you need anything else?

KEN: Yes, I need _____Ø_____ dress shoes.
1. (a / the / Ø)

CLERK: OK. _____ dress shoes are over here
2. (A / The)
. . . What size?

KEN: Ten medium.

LAURA: I like _____ black ones. What do
3. (a / the / Ø)
you think?

KEN: No. They're dark and formal. And I don't

like _____ style.
4. (a / the / Ø)

CLERK: What about these?

KEN: _____ tan ones? Cool! I like them.
5. (A / The / Ø)

CLERK: Do you want to try them on?

KEN: Yes, please.

CLERK: How do they feel?

KEN: Perfect. Laura, what do you think?

LAURA: Well, _____ shoes look nice. But they're casual. This is for _____
6. (a / the / Ø)   7. (a / an / Ø)
interview.

KEN: Don't worry. They're fine.

EXERCISE 3: *One* and *Ones*

(Grammar Note 5)

*Match the questions and answers. Complete the answers with **one** or **ones**.*

__c__ **1.** Which jacket do you like best?

____ **2.** I really like those orange socks.

____ **3.** Do you want those expensive
slacks?

____ **4.** Does this dress fit you?

____ **5.** Did you try on those formal shoes?

a. Yes. I hate the cheap
_____.

b. No, I need a larger _____.

c. I like the blue _____one_____ best.

d. No, I tried on the casual
_____.

e. I don't. They're too bright. I like the
gray _____.

EXERCISE 4: Editing

There are eight mistakes in the letter. The first mistake is already corrected. Find and correct seven more mistakes.

Dear Kathy,

    Josh and I have a great house! ~~The~~ House isn't very big,

and it's also a old one. It needs work. It has the nice

living room, but the colors are terrible. Each wall is the

different color. There's a orange wall, an yellow wall, a

blue wall, and the red wall. We need to repaint.

We want you to see house. Give me a call.

Love,

Amanda

STEP 4 COMMUNICATION PRACTICE

EXERCISE 5: Listening

A | *Listen to the conversation. Check (✔) the two false statements.*

____ **1.** Josh and Amanda are going out.

____ **2.** Amanda likes Latin music.

____ **3.** Amanda and Josh have three dogs.

____ **4.** They live in an apartment.

B | *Listen again. Complete the sentences. Circle the correct words.*

1. There is (one / (more than one)) concert.

2. Josh and Amanda have (one / more than one) dog.

3. They have (one / more than one) photograph.

4. They have (one / more than one) house.

5. They have (one / more than one) umbrella.

6. They have (one / more than one) car.

EXERCISE 6: Pronunciation

A | *Read and listen to the Pronunciation Note.*

Pronunciation Note
Use **a** before a noun that begins with a **consonant sound**. Use **an** before a noun that begins with a **vowel sound**.

B | *Read the conversations. Look at the word after each blank. Circle the words that begin with a vowel sound. Then write **a** or **an** in each blank.*

1. **A:** What do you want for your birthday, Mary?

   B: I want _____*a*_____ good novel. And I want _____ (umbrella) _____
   red one.

2. **A:** Annie, is someone at the door?

   B: Yes, there's _____ man outside. He's _____ old man.

3. **A:** Grandma, I have _____ interview tomorrow.

   B: Oh, good, Ken. I hope it's _____ good interview.

4. **A:** There's _____ college in our city.

   B: Yes, I know. I hear it's _____ expensive college.

C | *PAIRS: Listen and check your work. Then practice the conversations.*

EXERCISE 7: Picture Discussion

*PAIRS: Look at the pictures. Tell your partner about the clothes you like and don't like and why. Use **the** and **one / ones** in your statements.*

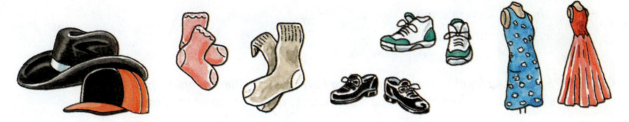

> **EXAMPLE:** **A:** I like the first hat. I like the color.
> **B:** I like the second one. It's red and black.
> OR I like the first one too.

EXERCISE 8: Writing

A | *What's wrong with the picture? Write several sentences about strange or unusual things. Use **a**, **an**, and **the**.*

EXAMPLE: I see a car in the mall . . .

B | *Check your work. Use the Editing Checklist.*

Editing Checklist

Did you use . . . ?
☐ *a*, *an*, and *the* correctly
☐ correct spelling

C | *GROUPS OF FOUR: Read your sentences from Part A aloud. Then compare your group's sentences with another group's sentences. Which group has the most?*

Check your answers on page UR-3.

Do you need to review anything?

EXERCISE A

Match the questions and answers.

_____ 1. Which is your jacket?

_____ 2. Do you like that orange tie?

_____ 3. Which are your shoes?

_____ 4. Do those shoes fit?

a. The white ones.

b. No, I need larger ones.

c. No, I like the green one.

d. The brown one.

EXERCISE B

Circle the correct explanation for the underlined words and phrases.

1. **A:** Where's the dog?

   (one / more than one) dog

   B: It's in the park.

   (one / more than one) park

2. **A:** Do you want an umbrella?

   (an umbrella in general / a specific umbrella)

   B: Yes. I want the black one.

   (an umbrella in general / a specific umbrella)

3. **A:** What's he doing at the library?

   (one / more than one) library

   B: He's returning a book.

   (a book in general / a specific book)

EXERCISE C

Correct the sentences. There are five mistakes.

1. Bozo's suit is a very bright ones.

2. Each shoe is the different color.

3. He's wearing a orange shoe and an yellow one.

4. He's wearing the funny hat too.

5. He looks like a clown!

21 Can / Can't
ABILITIES

Before You Read

A | *How do you rate your skills in English? Check (✓) the correct box.*

	Reading	Writing	Speaking	Listening Comprehension
I'm pretty good at				
I'm not so good at				

B | *GROUPS: Talk about your ratings.*

    EXAMPLE: I think I'm pretty good at reading. I'm not so good at writing.

Read

Read the conversation.

JESSICA: What's the matter, Jeremy? You look really down.

JEREMY: I **can't understand** my Spanish teacher. She speaks too fast. And no one **can understand** my Spanish. My pronunciation is pretty bad. I have to give a presentation Friday. I **can't do** it.

JESSICA: But last year you were so good in Spanish.

JEREMY: It wasn't a conversation class. I **can read**. I just **can't speak**.

JESSICA: **Can** someone in the class **help**?

JEREMY: No. I don't know anyone that well . . . But that gives me an idea. You know Jorge, the star of our basketball team?

JESSICA: Uh-huh.

JEREMY: Well, Jorge's in my math class. He's not doing well. The coach says he has to pass math or he **can't stay** on the team.

JESSICA: Oh?

JEREMY: But he's fluent in Spanish. Maybe he **can help** me with Spanish and I **can teach** him math.

JESSICA: Well, that sounds like a plan.

A | Practice *PAIRS: Practice the opening conversation.*

B | Vocabulary *Listen and repeat the words. Write new words in a notebook.*

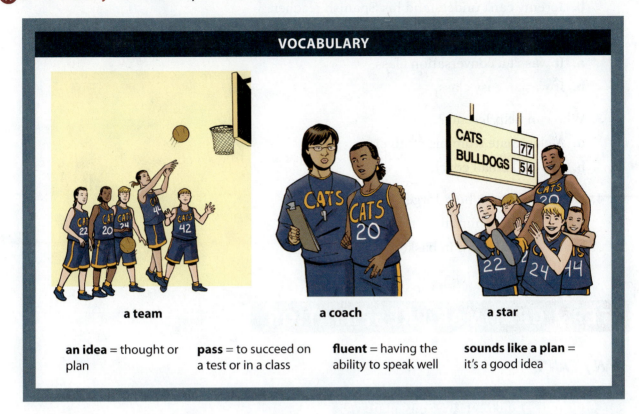

VOCABULARY

a team   a coach   a star

an idea = thought or plan   **pass** = to succeed on a test or in a class   **fluent** = having the ability to speak well   **sounds like a plan** = it's a good idea

C | Vocabulary *Complete the conversations. Use the correct forms of the vocabulary words.*

1. A: She has a lot of good _____ideas_____.

   B: I know. We always ask her what she thinks.

2. A: Who's the _____ of the team?

   B: Jorge is. He scores a lot of points.

3. A: What grade do I need to _____ the test?

   B: Sixty-five or above.

4. A: Does Marco speak Portuguese?

   B: Yes, he does. He lived in Brazil for six years. He's _____ in

   Portuguese.

5. A: What does he do?

   B: He's a gym teacher and the _____ of the girls' soccer team.

D | Comprehension *Look again at the opening conversation. Circle the correct letter.*

1. Why is Jeremy unhappy?
   a. His Spanish teacher can't speak Spanish.
   b. Jeremy can't understand his Spanish teacher.

2. Why was Jeremy good in Spanish last year?
   a. It wasn't a conversation class.
   b. It was an easy class.

3. Who can help Jeremy?
   a. A classmate from his math class.
   b. His basketball coach.

4. How can Jeremy help Jorge?
   a. He can help him in math.
   b. He can help him in basketball.

STEP 2 GRAMMAR PRESENTATION

CAN / CAN'T

Affirmative and Negative Statements		
Subject	Can / Can't	Base Form of Verb
I You He / She / It We You They	can can't	speak Russian.

Yes / No Questions	Short Answers	Wh- Questions
Can you **do** me a favor?	**Yes**, I **can**.	**What can** I **do**?
Can he **understand** French?	**No**, he **can't**.	**Who can help**?

GRAMMAR NOTES

1	Can is a modal. A modal changes the meaning of the verb that follows. Can has different meanings, including ability, possibility, and request.	• I can understand Korean. (ability) • I can meet you at 4:00. (possibility) • Can you do me a favor? (request)
2	Use the base form of the verb after can. BE CAREFUL! Do not use to after can. Do not add -s or -ing to verbs that follow can.	• I can speak Spanish. • You can get there by bus or by train. Not: He can to speak English. Not: He can speaks English. Not: He can speaking English.
3	Cannot is the negative form. Can't is the contraction. We usually use can't in speaking and informal writing.	• I cannot help you. • I can't help you.
4	For questions (yes / no questions or wh-questions), put can before the subject (unless the subject is who or what).	• Can she speak English? • How can we help? • Who can help?

STEP 3 FOCUSED PRACTICE

EXERCISE 1: Discover the Grammar

Underline **can** *and* **can't**. *Circle the verb that goes with* **can** *or* **can't**. *Then match the questions and answers.*

__d__ 1. Can you do the problems in Part I, Jorge?

____ 2. I can't understand this Spanish idiom. What does it mean?

____ 3. How can I remember new words?

____ 4. I can meet you on Tuesday, but not until 6:00.

____ 5. We can do an hour of Spanish and an hour of math.

a. *Con mucho gusto?* It means *with pleasure.*

b. Say them. Write them down. Use them in sentences. You need to hear a new word seven times to remember it.

c. That's fine. I'm free all evening.

d. Yes, I can. They're easy. But I can't do the ones in Part II.

e. How about an hour of basketball too?

EXERCISE 2: *Can* or *Can't* (Grammar Notes 1–4)

*Complete the conversations. Use **can** or **can't** and the verbs in parentheses.*

1. **JEREMY:** OK. Jorge. I have to prepare a talk about computers. (help)

   _____*Can*_____ you _____*help*_____ me?

   JORGE: Well, I don't know much about computers. I (help) _____ you

   with technical stuff, but I (try) _____ to help you with your

   pronunciation.

2. **JORGE:** Jeremy, I (do) _____ this math problem. (explain)

   _____ you _____ it to me?

   JEREMY: (understand) _____ you _____ the problem?

   JORGE: Yes, I _____, but I (get) _____ the right answer.

3. **JEREMY:** Jorge, there are so many Spanish words. I (remember) _____

   all of them.

   JORGE: Well, you (keep) _____ a notebook of new words. Then we

   (review) _____ the new words each week.

   JEREMY: Good idea.

4. **JEREMY:** OK. That's enough schoolwork. Let's play some ball.

   JORGE: Great. We (play) _____ in East Park.

   JEREMY: No, we _____. There's a game there now. But we (play)

   _____ at the junior high. Those courts are usually empty.

   JORGE: Sounds like a plan.

EXERCISE 3: *Can* or *Can't*

(Grammar Notes 1–4)

Complete the sentences. Use **can** *or* **can't** *and the correct verbs from the box.*

change	~~open~~	open	see	show	speak	understand	work

1. Our classroom is locked. We _____ *can't open* _____ the door.

   _____ you please _____ it for us?

2. I _____ the blackboard. _____ I _____ my

   seat?

3. We _____ this printer. _____ you _____ us how

   it works?

4. She's fluent in Italian, but she _____ Portuguese.

5. They _____ you. Please speak more slowly.

EXERCISE 4: Editing

There are seven mistakes in the sentences. The first mistake is already corrected. Find and correct six more mistakes.

1. Erika ^*can* understand English, but she can't speak it well.

2. Mei Liang can't speaks English. She can to speak Mandarin Chinese.

3. Can they working this weekend?

4. How I can get to the library?

5. Can she teaches us Portuguese?

6. He speak Spanish fluently.

EXERCISE 5: Pronunciation

A | *Read and listen to the Pronunciation Note.*

> **Pronunciation Note**
>
> When **can** is followed by a base form verb, we usually pronounce it /kən/ or /kn/ and stress the base form verb: I can SPEAK Spanish.
>
> In sentences with **can't** followed by a base form verb, we stress both *can't* and the base form verb: I CAN'T SPEAK French.

B | *Listen to the sentences. Then listen again. Check (✓) the words you hear.*

	1.	2.	3.	4.	5.	6.
can						
can't	✓					

C | *Complete the conversations. Use* **can** *or* **can't.**

1. **A:** We _____can't_____ understand you.

   B: Sorry. I'll speak slowly.

2. **A:** We _____ understand you now.

   B: That's good.

3. **A:** I _____ pronounce that word.

   B: I can't either. It's hard for me to say words that begin with "S-C-R."

4. **A:** I _____ pronounce that word.

   B: I can too. It's easy to pronounce.

5. **A:** I _____ see the letters.

   B: Maybe you need glasses.

6. **A:** I _____ see the letters.

   B: Good. Please read them to me.

D | *PAIRS: One partner chooses a conversation from 1–6 above. Read A's line. Your partner reads the correct response from B. Then switch roles.*

EXERCISE 6: Listening

A | *Listen to the conversation. Complete the sentence. Circle the correct letter.*

Jeremy and his mother are talking about _____.

   a. Spanish and math class

   b. Jeremy's homework

   c. the soccer team

| *Listen again. Underline the correct words to complete the sentences.*

1. Jeremy **can / can't** understand his teacher's Spanish.

2. Jeremy's pronunciation is **good / not so good**.

3. Jeremy **is improving / isn't improving**.

4. Jorge **can do / can't do** math well.

5. Jorge **can stay / can't stay** on the team.

6. Jeremy **can tutor / can't tutor** in math.

EXERCISE 7: Find Someone Who . . .

A | *Go around the classroom. Find someone who can . . .*

- stand on his or her head
- do a martial art well
- fix a computer
- lift 50-pound weights
- write poetry
- cook well
- say "yes" in five languages

B | *Report to the class.*

EXAMPLE: Glenda can stand on her head. Kilsun is good at tae kwon do. Shohei can prepare sushi. Camilla can say "yes" in five languages.

EXERCISE 8: Find Someone Who . . .

Look at the pictures on the next page. Then walk around the class. Find someone who can do each activity. Write the name of the student below the picture. When you have three names in any direction, you win.

EXAMPLE: MARIA: Can you water ski?
            KEIKO: Yes, I can. *(Maria writes Keiko's name in the box with "water ski.")*

water ski

1. *Keiko*
2. _____
3. _____

speak Mandarin

1. _____
2. _____
3. _____

change a tire

1. _____
2. _____
3. _____

play the guitar

1. _____
2. _____
3. _____

speak Italian

Buona sera

1. _____
2. _____
3. _____

play tennis

1. _____
2. _____
3. _____

play golf

1. _____
2. _____
3. _____

dance well

1. _____
2. _____
3. _____

play chess

1. _____
2. _____
3. _____

EXERCISE 9: Writing

A | *Write about some special abilities of a person you know well. Include at least two examples of* **can** *or* **can't**.

EXAMPLE: My friend Ali can play soccer very well. He's the star of his team. Ali plays soccer every
weekend. I can't play soccer, but I love to watch the game. Ali and I often watch soccer
on TV together. Our favorite team is the L.A. Galaxy.

B | *Check your work. Use the Editing Checklist.*

> ### Editing Checklist
>
> Did you use . . . ?
> ☐ *can* and *can't* correctly
> ☐ correct spelling

Check your answers on page UR-3.

Do you need to review anything?

EXERCISE A

Circle the correct words to complete the conversation.

A: I'm sorry. I <u>can / can't</u> remember your name. <u>Can / Can't</u> you repeat it?
                              1.   **2.**

B: It's Elmer.

A: I'm sorry. I <u>can / can't</u> hear you. <u>Can / Cannot</u> you speak a bit louder?
                              3.   **4.**

B: OK. It's ELMER!

EXERCISE B

Complete the conversations. Use **can** *or* **can't** *and the verbs in parentheses.*

1. A: _____ you _____ (explain) this email to me?

    B: No, it's in French, and I _____ (not, read) French.

    A: Maybe Marie _____ (help). She knows French.

2. A: Do you want to watch TV this evening?

    B: Sorry, we _____ (not, watch) TV. The TV isn't working.

    A: That's too bad. What _____ we _____ (do) this evening?

    B: Well, we _____ (go) to the movies.

    A: That's a good idea!

EXERCISE C

Correct the sentences. There are five mistakes.

A: Pietro can't speaks Chinese. He can to speak Italian.

B: Can he speaking Spanish?

A: No, he not can, but I can't.

VIII

SIMPLE PAST

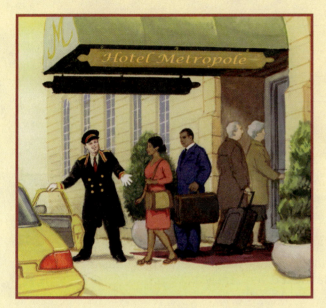

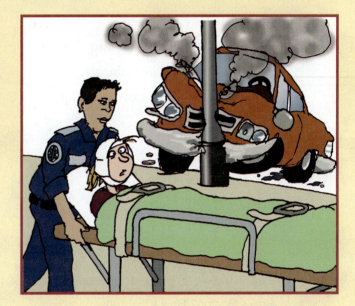

UNIT	GRAMMAR FOCUS	THEME
22	Simple Past: Regular Verbs (Statements)	Business Trips
23	Simple Past: Regular and Irregular Verbs; *Yes / No* Questions	A Biography
24	Simple Past: *Wh-* Questions	A Car Accident

22 Simple Past: Regular Verbs (Statements)
BUSINESS TRIPS

STEP 1 GRAMMAR IN CONTEXT

Before You Read

GROUPS: Check (✓) what is true for you. Then talk about it.

____ Yesterday I worked.	____ Yesterday I didn't work.
____ I stayed home last Sunday.	____ I didn't stay home last Sunday.
____ I watched TV last night.	____ I didn't watch TV last night.
____ Last weekend I visited a friend.	____ Last weekend I didn't visit a friend.

Read

Read the email messages.

Kathy,

Thanks for the delicious chocolates. Everyone at the party **enjoyed** them. The party was a blast *, but we all **missed** you, especially Mark. He **looked** very lonely. :>(

How's Boston? How's the convention?

Judy

Judy,

Once again, happy birthday!

Boston is terrific :)! But the convention was a lot of work.

I **arrived** here late Monday night. Tuesday I **worked** from 7:00 in the morning until 10:00 at night. Wednesday I **started** at 7:00 and **didn't finish** until 9:00 at night. The convention finally **ended** last night.

This morning I **checked out** of my hotel. I'm staying with my cousin Ted for a couple of days. He's a really nice guy, and he has a great apartment. I'd like you to meet him.

Again, I'm so sorry I **missed** your party.

Kathy

---

* *a blast:* a lot of fun

Hi Kathy,

Who's this cousin? I'd love to meet him.

Judy

After You Read

A | Practice *PAIRS: Practice the opening reading. Take turns reading the messages.*

 B | Vocabulary *Listen and repeat the words. Write new words in a notebook.*

VOCABULARY

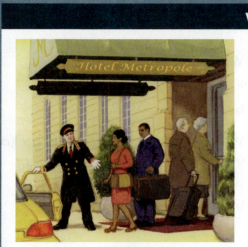

a hotel

check in   **check out**

a convention

a presentation

arrive =
to get to a place

enjoy =
to get pleasure and happiness from
something

stay =
1. to live in a place as a guest for a short
   time
2. to continue to be in a place (to stay
   home)

miss =
1. to feel sad someone isn't there.
2. to not be somewhere or not hear or see
   something.

C | Vocabulary *Complete the passage. Write the correct words from the box.*

checked in	enjoyed	presentations
convention	~~Hotel~~	stayed

We arrived at the Marriott _____*Hotel*_____ last Wednesday. We were there for

a sales _____. We _____ at the front desk. We attended a

welcome party that evening. For the next two days we listened to _____. We

_____ for three nights. Some of the presentations were boring. Some were

interesting. But we _____ meeting salespeople from all over the country.

D | Comprehension *Look again at the opening email messages. Circle the letters of the correct answers.*

1. Where was Kathy?
   a. At a convention in Boston.
   b. At a party in Boston.

2. Why was Kathy there?
   a. She was there for work.
   b. To celebrate Judy's birthday.

3. Who missed Kathy a lot?
   a. Ted did.
   b. Mark did.

4. Where did Kathy go after she checked out of her hotel?
   a. Home.
   b. To her cousin's home.

STEP 2 GRAMMAR PRESENTATION

SIMPLE PAST: REGULAR VERBS (STATEMENTS)

Affirmative			Negative			
Subject	**Past Form of Verb**		**Subject**	**Did not**	**Base Form of Verb**	
I You He She It We You They	**arrived**	at 2:00 P.M.	I You He She It We You They	**did not (didn't)**	**arrive**	at 3:00 P.M.

PAST TIME EXPRESSIONS

Past Time Expressions		
Yesterday	*Ago*	*Last*
yesterday	two days **ago**	**last** night
yesterday morning	a week **ago**	**last** week
yesterday evening	a month **ago**	**last** Monday

March

12	13	(14)

two days ago   yesterday   today

GRAMMAR NOTES

1   Use the **simple past** to talk about an event that happened in the past.

Now

Past ◄——X—————► Future

I arrived last night.

- I **arrived** last night.
- I **stayed** at the Grand Hotel.

2   **Regular verbs** in the simple past **end in -*ed***. If the base form ends in -*e*, add only -*d*. If the base form ends in -*y* after a consonant, change the *y* to *i* and add -*ed*.

BASE FORM
- I stay**ed** at a hotel.   (stay)
- I arriv**ed** yesterday.   (arriv**e**)
- I stud**ied** all night.   (stu**dy**)

3   Use ***did not*** + the **base form** of the verb for a **negative statement** in the simple past.

We usually use ***didn't*** for speaking and informal writing.

BE CAREFUL! Do not add -*ed* to sentences with ***did***.

- She **did not stay** at the hotel.
- She **didn't stay** at the hotel.

Nᴏᴛ: She ~~didn't stayed~~ at the hotel.

4   **Time expressions** come at the **beginning** or the **end** of a sentence.

- **Last night** I arrived in Boston.
- I arrived in Boston **last night**.

REFERENCE NOTES

For the **past of *be***, see Unit 7.
For **irregular past verbs**, see Unit 23.
For information about the **pronunciation of the simple past of regular verbs**, see Appendix 6 on page A-4.

EXERCISE 1: Discover the Grammar

A | *Read about Kathy's cousin. Find and underline the simple past verbs.*

Ten years ago Ted Geller <u>graduated</u> from college. He was smart, and he finished college in three years. A year after graduation, Ted and four friends started an online business. For three years they worked very hard. They hired and fired a lot of people. They improved their business. In their third year, a big company offered to buy their company. The five partners agreed. At the age of 26, Ted ended up without a job but with a lot of money. He used half his money to help poor children. Ted's an unusual man.

B | *Write the base form of the underlined words in Part A.*

_____*graduate*_____ _____ _____ _____

_____ _____ _____ _____

EXERCISE 2: Simple Past   *(Grammar Notes 1–2)*

Complete the sentences. Write the past form of the verbs from the box.

graduate	~~help~~	learn	open	stay	work

Jane loves flowers. As a child she always _____*helped*_____ her mother in their garden.
                                            1.
Six years ago she _____ from art school. She _____ in a flower
                    2.   **3.**
shop after graduation. She _____ at the flower shop for three years. She
                            4.
_____ a lot about flowers and about the flower business. Three years ago she
5.
_____ her own flower shop. Today her flower shop is doing very well.
6.

EXERCISE 3: Affirmative or Negative

(Grammar Notes 1–3)

Look at the pictures. Complete the sentences. Write correct forms of the verbs from the box. Use the affirmative or negative. Use some verbs more than once.

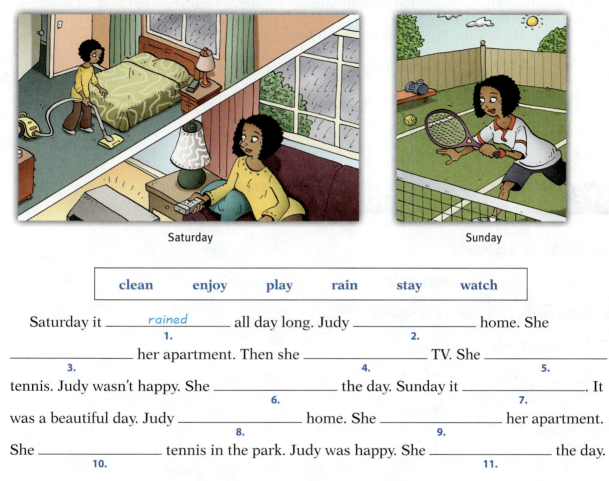

Saturday	Sunday

clean	enjoy	play	rain	stay	watch

Saturday it _____rained_____ all day long. Judy _____ home. She
                 1.   **2.**

_____ her apartment. Then she _____ TV. She _____
       3.   **4.**   **5.**

tennis. Judy wasn't happy. She _____ the day. Sunday it _____. It
                                        6.   **7.**

was a beautiful day. Judy _____ home. She _____ her apartment.
                                8.   **9.**

She _____ tennis in the park. Judy was happy. She _____ the day.
          10.   **11.**

EXERCISE 4: Editing

There are seven mistakes in the messages. The first mistake is already corrected. Find and correct six more mistakes.

                          missed

1. I'm sorry I ~~did missed~~ your call. Please leave your name and a short message.

2. Hi, Ted. This is Al. I am arrived at the hotel this morning. My phone number is

   555-9090.

3. Hello, Ted. This is Melissa. I yesterday talked to Ellen. She loved your presentation.

4. Hi, Ted. This is Judy. Sorry I was missed your call. Call me. I have some exciting

   news.

(continued on next page)

5. Hi, Uncle Ted. This is Mickey. I received this morning your gift. It's awesome. Thank you so much. I love the game.

6. Hi, Teddy. This is Mom. I arrived in Miami last night. I didn't stayed at Aunt Sophie's house. She has the flu. I'm staying with Sara.

7. Hi, Ted. This is Justino. Warren did checked in at the Grand Hotel today. His presentation is tomorrow. He wants to have lunch with us after his presentation. Call me.

STEP 4 COMMUNICATION PRACTICE

EXERCISE 5: Listening

A | *Listen to three phone messages. Who are the messages from?*

B | *Listen again. Complete the messages.*

Message from

1. _____ Thanks for the _____ *flowers* _____. They _____ yesterday.

2. _____ I'm still _____. Let's meet at _____, not _____.

3. _____ I _____ a really good _____ a couple of _____ _____. It's on tonight on Channel _____ at _____ o'clock.

EXERCISE 6: Pronunciation

A | *Read and listen to the Pronunciation Note.*

> **Pronunciation Note**
>
> The regular simple past verb ending has three sounds: **/t/, /d/,** and **/ɪd/.**
> The sound of the past ending depends on the last sound of the base form of the verb.
>
> *I miss**ed** you.* **/t/**   *She arriv**ed** at 7 P.M.* **/d/**   *He graduat**ed**.* **/ɪd/** *(= extra syllable)*

B | Complete the sentences with **last, ago,** or **yesterday.** *Then read the sentences. Underline the past verb forms. Write the base forms of the verbs.*

Sentence	Base Form of Verb	/t/	/d/	/ɪd/
1. He <u>graduated</u> from college _____*last*_____ year.	*graduate*			✓
2. They started a business 10 years _____.				
3. They worked for 10 hours _____.				
4. They hired many people _____ month.				
5. They learned a lot _____ year.				
6. A company wanted to buy their business three years _____.				
7. They agreed to the sale _____ afternoon.				

C | *Listen and check your answers. Check (✓) the **-ed** sound you hear.*

EXERCISE 7: True or False?

A | *Write four true sentences and one false sentence about yourself in the past. Use the ideas from the box or your own ideas.*

graduate from _____	listen to a kind of music	travel to a place
like a food	play a sport	watch _____ on TV _____

B | *GROUPS: Read your sentences aloud. The group guesses the false sentence.*

EXAMPLES: **A:** I played soccer in high school.
I didn't like candy as a child.
I listened to classical music in high school.
I traveled to Kenya five years ago.
I watched *Star Trek* on TV last night.
B: You didn't really travel to Kenya five years ago.
C: You didn't really listen to a lot of classical music in high school.
D: You liked candy as a child.
A: I really traveled to Kenya five years ago. I listened to a lot of classical music in high school. D's right. I liked candy as a child.

EXERCISE 8: Writing

A | *Write sentences about yourself as a child. Use five verbs from the box. Use the simple past affirmative or negative.*

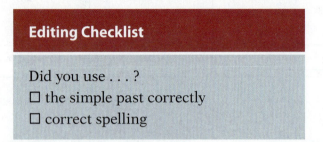

| enjoy | like | listen to | look | play | want | watch |

B | *Check your work. Use the Editing Checklist.*

Editing Checklist

Did you use . . . ?
☐ the simple past correctly
☐ correct spelling

C | *The teacher collects the papers and reads the sentences. The class guesses who it is.*

EXAMPLES: I liked chocolate ice cream. I didn't like green vegetables.
I listened to rock and roll. I didn't listen to classical music.
I played with my brother. I didn't play with my younger sister.
I wanted to be an astronaut. I didn't want to go to school.
I enjoyed science fiction books and movies. I didn't enjoy romances. WHO AM I?

EXERCISE A

Complete the sentences. Use the simple past form of the words in parentheses. Use the affirmative or negative.

1. We _____ (check in) four days ago. We

   _____ (not, check out) until yesterday.

2. I _____ (study) last night. I _____

   (not, watch TV).

3. We _____ (start) our presentation at 9:00 in the morning, but

   we _____ (not, finish) it until 2:00 in the afternoon.

EXERCISE B

Complete the paragraph. Write the past forms of the verbs from the box.

end up	fail	graduate	not, work	start

Last year my cousin Louis _____ from college. He

_____ a business. He _____ hard, and it

_____. But then he started another business. This time he worked

very hard. He _____ with a great business and a lot of money.

EXERCISE C

Correct the sentences. There are four mistakes.

1. We didn't stayed with our friends.

2. The guests are arrived at the hotel.

3. I call you this morning.

4. She was enjoy her trip.

Simple Past: Regular and Irregular Verbs; *Yes / No* Questions

A BIOGRAPHY

STEP 1 GRAMMAR IN CONTEXT

Before You Read

A | *GROUPS OF FOUR: Think of a person you admire. Who is the person? Why do you admire him or her? Discuss your answers.*

B | *PAIRS: Who is this famous movie character? What is the actor's name? What do you know about him?*

Read

Read the conversation and the biography.

JEREMY: Dad? I **wrote** this paper for my drama class. Can you read what I have so far?

TIM: Sure, Jeremy. What's the assignment?

JEREMY: We have to write about an actor we admire. I **picked** Christopher Reeve.

Jeremy Beck
Drama 201
Ms. Gomez

Christopher Reeve, An Admirable Actor

Christopher Reeve **was born** on September 25, 1952, in New York City. He **began** to act at the age of nine when he **got** a part in his first play. He **acted** in a lot of plays during his teenage years and many more when he **went** to Cornell University. After college he **moved** to New York City and **worked** in theater.

Christopher **had** his first role in a Hollywood movie in 1978. Today he is most famous as the star of the *Superman* movies. Christopher **made** four *Superman* films.

A sad thing happened to Christopher on May 27, 1995. He **was** in a horseback riding competition and **fell** off his horse. He **was** paralyzed below his neck and **had** to spend the rest of his life in a wheelchair. But he **didn't give up**. He **started** an organization to help people who are paralyzed. His organization **gave** a lot of money for research.

In 2004 Christopher Reeve **died** of a heart attack. He **didn't have** a long life, but he **did** a lot of good things. We will remember him for a long time.

TIM: This is really good, Jeremy. **Did** you **use** the Internet to get your information?

JEREMY: Yes, I **did**.

TIM: Well, I think people will like your paper.

After You Read

A | Practice *PAIRS: Practice the opening conversation and reading. Each person reads a paragraph from the reading.*

B | Vocabulary *Listen and repeat the words. Write new words in a notebook.*

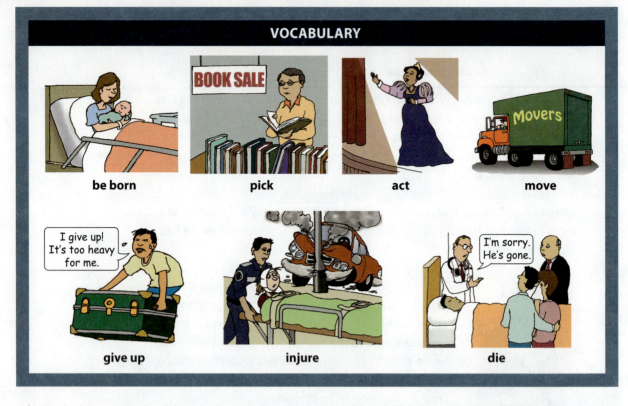

C | Vocabulary *Complete the sentences. Use the correct forms of the vocabulary words.*

1. On my birthday, I always _____ *pick* _____ my favorite restaurant for dinner.

2. She was very tired, but she didn't _____, and she won the race.

3. He danced and _____ in many movies.

4. They got married in 2004, and their baby _____ in 2006.

5. The fire _____ several people, but no one _____.

6. We lived in Mexico City before we _____ to Los Angeles.

D | Comprehension *Look again at the opening conversation and reading. Complete the sentences. Circle the correct letter.*

1. Christopher Reeve was _____.
　　a. a teacher
　　b. an actor

2. His first acting experience was in _____.
　　a. a play
　　b. a movie

3. Christopher Reeve _____ to college.
　　a. went
　　b. didn't go

4. Reeve was injured in _____.
　　a. a car accident
　　b. a horseback riding accident

5. Jeremy used _____ to write his biography.
　　a. the Internet
　　b. an encyclopedia

SIMPLE PAST: IRREGULAR VERBS (STATEMENTS)

Statements	
Affirmative	**Negative**
He **ate** chocolate bars.	He **did not eat** regular meals.
You **had** the chocolate.	You **didn't have** the cookies.
She **drank** coffee.	She **didn't drink** water.
He **went** to Cornell University.	He **didn't go** to Harvard.

SIMPLE PAST: REGULAR AND IRREGULAR VERBS (*YES / NO* QUESTIONS)

Yes / No Questions				Short Answers	
Did	Subject	Base Form		**Affirmative**	**Negative**
	I	**wake**	you up?	Yes, you **did**.	No, you **didn't**.
	you	**sleep**	late?	Yes, I **did**. Yes, we **did**.	No, I **didn't**. No, we **didn't**.
Did	he	**stay**	home?	Yes, he **did**.	No, he **didn't**.
	it	**rain?**		Yes, it **did**.	No, it **didn't**.
	we	**eat**	all the cookies?	Yes, you **did**.	No, you **didn't**.
	they	**take**	a vacation?	Yes, they **did**.	No, they **didn't**.

GRAMMAR NOTES

1	Remember that **regular verbs** end in **-ed** in the simple past.	• It **started** to rain. **start**
	Irregular verbs have **different forms** in the simple past. (*See the verbs in Note 5.*)	• I **ate** my sandwich. **eat** • We **went** out of town. **go**
	REMEMBER: The past forms of *be* are *was* and *were*. See Unit 7.	
2	For a **negative sentence** in the simple past, use *did not* + the **base form** of the verb. Use the contraction *didn't* + the **base form** in conversation and informal writing.	• He **did not eat** much. • He **didn't eat** much.
	BE CAREFUL! Don't use *did* or *didn't* with the past tense form of the verb.	NOT: He ~~didn't ate~~ much.

3	To make a **yes / no question** in the simple past, use **did** + the **subject** + the **base form** of the verb.	• **Did** you **stop**? • **Did** he **eat** anything?	

4	You can use **did** or **didn't** in the **short answer** in the simple past.	**A:** Did it rain? **B:** Yes, it **did**. OR Yes. No, it **didn't**. OR No.

5   Here are some common **irregular verbs** and their simple past forms.

BASE FORM	SIMPLE PAST	BASE FORM	SIMPLE PAST	BASE FORM	SIMPLE PAST
become	**became**	fall	**fell**	make	**made**
come	**came**	get	**got**	see	**saw**
do	**did**	give	**gave**	take	**took**
drink	**drank**	go	**went**	tell	**told**
eat	**ate**	have	**had**	write	**wrote**

REFERENCE NOTE

For more about **irregular verbs and their simple past forms**, see Appendix 7 on page A-5.

STEP 3 FOCUSED PRACTICE

EXERCISE 1: Discover the Grammar

*Read the conversation. Underline the three **yes / no** questions in the simple past. Then circle the irregular verbs in the simple past.*

YOSHIO: Wow! I'm starved. Let's go have lunch. I (didn't) have breakfast.

JEREMY: Why? <u>Did you get up late?</u>

YOSHIO: Yeah, I got up at 8:15. I just drank a glass of orange juice. That's all I had time for.

JEREMY: Did you stay up late last night?

YOSHIO: I sure did.

JEREMY: Why?

YOSHIO: Well, I had a lot of homework to do. It took about three hours. After that I watched two *Superman* movies. It was 2 A.M. when I went to bed.

JEREMY: Did you write your paper for drama class?

YOSHIO: Yeah. I wrote it on Christopher Reeve.

JEREMY: Oh no! You too?

EXERCISE 2: Simple Past

(Grammar Notes 1–2, 5)

Complete the paragraph. Use the simple past form of the verbs in parentheses.

Christopher Reeve _____ *graduated* _____ from Cornell University in 1974. After
1. (graduate)

that he _____ to work in theater. In 1978 he _____ a
2. (go)   3. (have)

theater audition. The famous actress Katharine Hepburn _____ him and
4. (see)

_____ him a part in a play. They _____ good friends.
5. (give)   6. (become)

But Christopher _____ so busy he _____ enough.
7. (get)   8. (not eat)

In fact, he mostly _____ chocolate bars and _____
9. (eat)   10. (drink)

coffee. One day he _____ so weak he _____. But he
11. (be)   12. (faint)

_____ and soon became famous.
13. (not give up)

EXERCISE 3: *Yes / No* Questions

(Grammar Note 3)

Complete the conversations. Write **yes** */* **no** *questions with the words from the chart.*

Subjects	Reeve	it	Reeve	Reeve	she	~~you~~
Verbs	go	~~have~~	have	play	take	write

1. **A:** _____ *Did you have* _____ breakfast this morning, Yoshio?

   B: No. All I had was a glass of juice.

2. **A:** _____ her paper on Christopher Reeve?

   B: No, she didn't. She wrote it on Heath Ledger.

3. **A:** _____ you a long time to write your paper?

   B: Yes, it took me about three hours.

4. **A:** _____ to Columbia University?

   B: No, he didn't. He went to Cornell University. He acted in a lot of student plays there.

5. **A:** _____ the role of Superman?

   B: Yes, he did. He also played the role of Clark Kent.

6. **A:** _____ a long life?

   B: No, he didn't, but he did a lot of good things.

EXERCISE 4: Editing

There are eight mistakes in the conversations. The first mistake is already corrected.
Find and correct seven more mistakes.

1. **A:** Yoshio, did you ~~stayed~~ *stay* up late last night?

   B: Yes, I do. I stayed up until 2 A.M.

2. **A:** Tim, Jeremy finished his drama paper?

   B: Yes, and he does a good job.

3. **A:** How many *Superman* movies did Reeve make?

   B: He maked four of them.

4. **A:** Christopher Reeve had a long life?

   B: No, he doesn't. He dead at the age of 52.

STEP 4 COMMUNICATION PRACTICE

EXERCISE 5: Listening

A | *Listen to the school interview with Jeremy's classmate and friend Yoshio. Does Yoshio like or not like the Seattle area?*

B | *Listen again. Check (✓) T (True), F (False), or NI (No Information).*

	T	F	NI
1. Yoshio came to the United States four months ago.	✓	☐	☐
2. Yoshio was born in Hamamatsu.	☐	☐	☐
3. Yoshio has two sisters and one brother.	☐	☐	☐
4. Yoshio played soccer in high school.	☐	☐	☐
5. Yoshio has a black belt in karate.	☐	☐	☐
6. Yoshio climbed Mount Everest when he was 14.	☐	☐	☐
7. Yoshio's family took a trip to the United States when he was a teenager.	☐	☐	☐
8. Yoshio went to Universal Studios in Los Angeles.	☐	☐	☐
9. They went to Seattle on that trip.	☐	☐	☐

EXERCISE 6: Pronunciation

🎧 **A** | *Read and listen to the Pronunciation Note.*

Pronunciation Note
In the simple past, the last "d" in **did** + a **/y/** sound is often pronounced **/dʒ/**.

🎧 **B** | *Read and listen to the sentences. Circle* **did** *where the last "d" is pronounced as /dʒ/.*

1. (Did) you go to the movies last night?

2. Did she go with you?

3. Did your friends pick the movie?

4. Did Josh come to the party?

5. Did he injure his back?

6. Did you eat breakfast this morning?

7. Did your brother visit New York?

8. Did they go with you?

9. Did you visit Florida too?

10. Did he finish his assignment?

C | *PAIRS: Practice the sentences. Take turns. Be sure to pronounce* did you *correctly.*

EXERCISE 7: Did You . . . ?

You have five minutes to ask your classmates seven **yes** / **no** *questions. Use the question phrases from the box and a past time expression. Report interesting answers.*

Question Phrases			
drink tea for breakfast	go out of town	see a movie	get up after 10 A.M.
eat at a fast-food restaurant	go to bed after midnight	make a new friend	visit a new city

Past Time Expressions			
last month	last weekend	this morning	last summer
last night	on Monday	yesterday	last year

EXAMPLE: **A:** Did you go to bed after midnight last night?
B: Yes, I did. I studied until 3 A.M.

EXERCISE 8: Writing

A | *Write a short biography (6 to 10 sentences) of a famous person you admire. Use simple past verbs.*

B | *Check your work. Use the Editing Checklist.*

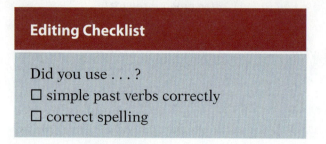

Editing Checklist

Did you use . . . ?
- ☐ simple past verbs correctly
- ☐ correct spelling

C | *Read your biography to the class, but don't say who the person is. The class guesses the person.*

EXAMPLE: **A:** This person was born in Transkei, South Africa, in 1918. He worked against the policy of apartheid there. Because of that, he was in prison for 27 years. After prison he became president of the new South Africa. . . .
B: Is the person Nelson Mandela?
A: Yes, it is.

EXERCISE A

Complete the passage. Use the simple past form of the verbs in parentheses.

Yesterday after school, I _____ (go) home. Then I

_____ (make) some soup, and I _____ (eat) dinner. Then I

_____ (see) a movie on TV. After that, I _____ (drink) a glass of

milk. Finally, I _____ (fall) asleep.

EXERCISE B

*Complete the conversations. Write past **yes** / **no** questions with the words from the box.*

play	snow	stay up	take

1. **A:** _____ Christopher _____ soccer on Saturday?

   B: No, he played baseball.

2. **A:** _____ the children _____ late last night?

   B: No, they didn't. They went to bed early.

3. **A:** _____ it _____ last night?

   B: No, it didn't. It rained.

4. **A:** _____ you _____ a vacation this year?

   B: Yes, I took a vacation in February. It was great!

EXERCISE C

Correct the conversations. There are five mistakes.

1. **A:** You moved to this city in 2009?

   B: No, I don't. I moved here in 2010.

2. **A:** Did Katharine took her keys?

   B: No, she didn't.

3. **A:** Do your parents go out of town?

   B: Yes, they are went on vacation.

Simple Past: *Wh-* Questions
A CAR ACCIDENT

STEP 1 GRAMMAR IN CONTEXT

Before You Read

PAIRS: Tell about a time when you or people you know were in a car accident.

Read

Amanda talks to her brother Rob on the phone then speaks with her husband, Josh. Read the conversations.

AMANDA: Hi, Rob. What's up? . . . Are you OK? . . . Well, that's good. **When did it happen? . . . Where did it happen?** . . . Are you there now? . . . **Why did you *drive*?** . . . Does Dad know?

(AMANDA hangs up.)

JOSH: **What happened?**

AMANDA: Rob had a car accident this morning.

JOSH: How is he?

AMANDA: He's fine, but the car is damaged. He didn't want to walk to the supermarket in the rain, so he took Dad's car.

JOSH: **What happened to the car?**

AMANDA: One of the headlights is broken, and there's a big dent in the bumper.

JOSH: **How did it happen?**

AMANDA: I guess the road was slippery. The car skidded on some leaves and hit a pole.

JOSH: That's too bad.

AMANDA: And Rob drove Dad's car without his OK.

JOSH: Uh-oh.

AMANDA: He's at Charlie's Auto Repair Shop now. It will cost $600 to fix the car.

JOSH: Six hundred dollars? Poor Dad.

AMANDA: **What do you mean** "poor Dad"? Poor Rob.

After You Read

A | Practice *PAIRS: Practice the opening conversation.*

B | Vocabulary *Listen and repeat the words. Write new words in a notebook.*

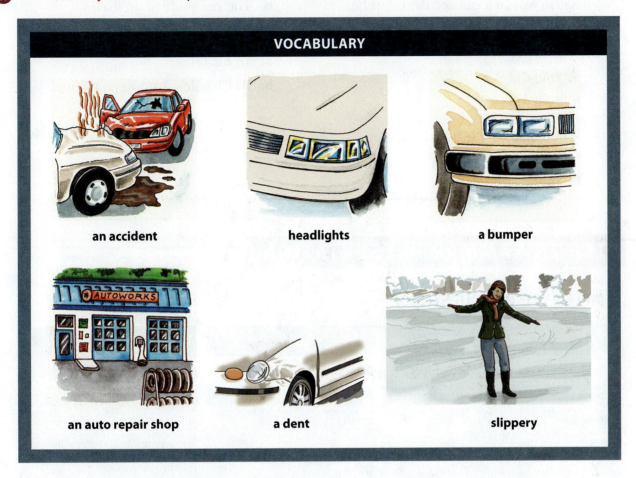

VOCABULARY

an accident

headlights

a bumper

an auto repair shop

a dent

slippery

C | Vocabulary *PAIRS: Complete the conversations. Use the correct forms of the vocabulary words. Practice the conversations.*

1. **A:** There was an _____accident_____ on the highway. A truck hit a car.

   B: Was anyone hurt?

2. **A:** There's a _____ on the driver's side of your car.

   B: I know. My uncle will fix it. He has _____.

3. **A:** Your _____ doesn't work.

   B: Really? Thanks for telling me. I guess I need a new bulb.

4. **A:** How did the accident happen?

   B: The street was _____. She fell and hurt her arm.

D | Comprehension *Look again at the opening conversations. Circle the correct letter.*

1. What happened to Rob?

   a. He was hurt in an accident.

   b. He was in a car accident, but he wasn't hurt.

2. Who drove the car?

   a. Dad did.

   b. Rob did.

3. When did it happen?

   a. In the morning.

   b. In the afternoon.

4. How did it happen?

   a. The car hit another car.

   b. The car skidded on leaves.

5. Where did Rob take the car?

   a. To his father.

   b. To Charlie's Auto Repair Shop.

STEP 2 GRAMMAR PRESENTATION

SIMPLE PAST: *WH-* QUESTIONS

Questions					Answers
Wh- Question Word	*Did*	Subject	Base Form of Verb		
Where		the accident	happen?		In front of the store.
When		it	occur?		In the morning.
Why	did	he	go	there?	He wanted to get some food.
Who		he	drive	with?	He drove alone.
How		it	happen?		The car skidded.
How long		it	take	to fix?	Three hours.

Questions about the Subject	Answers
Who drove?	Rob (did).
What happened?	He had a car accident.

More Irregular Verbs

Base Form	Simple Past
break	broke
drive	drove
hit	hit
say	said
teach	taught
wear	wore
win	won

GRAMMAR NOTES

1	Most *wh-* questions **in the simple past** use a *wh-* word + *did* + the **subject** + the **base form** of the verb.	**A: When did** he **call**? **B:** At 11:00 in the morning.
2	*Wh-* questions **about the subject** use a *wh-* word + the **simple past form** of the verb. **BE CAREFUL!** Do not use *did* with questions about the subject.	**A: Who called?** **B:** My brother called. Noт: Who ~~did~~ call?

REFERENCE NOTE
For a list of **common irregular past forms**, see Appendix 7 on page A-5.

STEP 3 FOCUSED PRACTICE

EXERCISE 1: Discover the Grammar

Read the conversation. Underline the **wh-** *questions.*

A: Guess what? I saw Josh Beckett.

B: Really? Where did you see him?

A: On Pike Street.

B: What time did you see him?

A: It was about 3:00 in the afternoon.

B: What did he look like?

A: Like Josh Beckett, of course.

B: Did you ask for his autograph?

A: Yes, I did.

B: What did he say?

A: He said, "Here you go" and wrote his name on a piece of paper.

EXERCISE 2: *Wh-* Questions

(Grammar Notes 1–2)

Put the words in the correct order. Make questions.

JOSH: You know, I once drove without a license.

AMANDA: <u>_When did you do that_</u>?
　　　　　　1. (you / When / do / did / that)

JOSH: Oh, about 10 years ago. I was 15, and I went to my grandmother's house.

AMANDA: _____?
　　　　　　2. (you / Why / there / did / drive)

JOSH: It was impossible to get to her home by bus. She called and said she was sick. My parents were away for the day.

AMANDA: So _____?
　　　　　　3. (happened / what)

JOSH: Well, I drove to her house. She was really sick. I took her to the hospital.

AMANDA: _____?
　　　　　　4. (How long / the drive / did / take)

JOSH: About 30 minutes.

AMANDA: _____?
　　　　　　5. (your / parents / What / say / did)

JOSH: They said I did the right thing. I got my license the next month.

EXERCISE 3: Questions with *Who*

(Grammar Note 2)

*Write questions beginning with **Who**. Use the simple past form of the words in parentheses.*

1. (go to an auto repair shop last week) <u>_Who went to an auto repair shop last week_</u>?

2. (eat kimchee last night) _____?

3. (teach you to drive) _____?

4. (come late today) _____?

5. (visit you last weekend) _____?

6. (give you a special gift last year) _____?

EXERCISE 4: Editing

There are six mistakes in the conversations. The first mistake is already corrected. Find and correct five more mistakes.

A: Hello. This is Rob Peck. I'd like to report an accident.

B: Thank you, Mr. Peck. What time $\overset{did}{\wedge}$ the accident occur?

A: At 9:30 this morning.

B: Where did it happened?

A: It did happen on Oak Street between First and Second Avenues.

B: How it did happen?

A: A cat ran into the street. The car ahead of me stop suddenly. The road was slippery, and

    I hit the car. My headlights are broken. There's a dent in the other car's bumper.

B: Thank you for reporting the accident.

* * *

C: What the insurance company say?

A: Just "Thank you for reporting the accident."

STEP 4 COMMUNICATION PRACTICE

EXERCISE 5: Pronunciation

A | *Read and listen to the Pronunciation Note.*

> **Pronunciation Note**
>
> In speaking, we often contract *did* after *wh-* question words.

B | *Listen to the conversation. Then listen again and repeat B's lines.*

    A: Sorry I'm late. There was an accident on the highway. I couldn't move for 20 minutes.

    B: **Where'd** it happen?

    A: Near exit 6.

    B: **When'd** it happen?

    A: About 20 minutes ago.

    B: **How'd** it happen?

    A: A driver got sick, and his car went into the wrong lane and hit another car.

    B: Was anyone hurt?

(continued on next page)

A: I think so. A police car and an ambulance arrived.

B: What'd the police do?

A: They wrote a report, and they sent the drivers to the hospital.

B: How'd the drivers look?

A: I didn't see them.

C | *Now listen and write the questions. Write the full form. Then say the contracted form.*

1. *Where did it happen?* _____   4. _____

2. _____   5. _____

3. _____

EXERCISE 6: Listening

A | *Listen to the telephone conversation between Amanda and Rob. Circle the correct letter to complete the sentence.*

Amanda and Rob are talking about _____.

    a. paying for the damage to his father's car

    b. how the accident happened

B | *Listen again. Answer the questions.*

1. What did Rob promise to pay for? _____

2. When did he start work? _____

3. How many hours did he work yesterday? _____

4. How many hours did he work the day before? _____

EXERCISE 7: Interview

Work with a partner. Interview your partner about his or her past. Student A, write five things that were the same for both of you. Student B, write five things that were different.

EXAMPLES: **1. A:** What sports did you play in high school?
               B: I played soccer.
               A: I played soccer too.
                 We both played soccer in high school.

           2. B: Where did you go on your last vacation?
               A: I went to the beach.
               B: I went to the mountains.
                 On my last vacation, I went to the beach. Juan went to the mountains.

EXERCISE 8: Discuss Childhood

Ask three classmates three questions about their childhood. Use the suggestions from the box or your own ideas.

cook in your family	help you with homework	teach you to drive
give you nice gifts	read stories to you	teach you to ride a bike

EXAMPLE: **A:** Who taught you to ride a bike?
                B: Nobody did. I can't ride a bike.
                C: My father.
                D: My friend did.

EXERCISE 9: Writing

A | *Complete the sentence: "On my way to school I saw* _____.*"*

B | *GROUPS: Read your sentence to each person in your group. Each person asks you two* wh- *questions. Respond to your classmates' statements.*

C | *Write a conversation that begins, "On my way to school I saw . . . " Include three* **wh-** *questions.*

EXAMPLE: **A:** On my way to school I saw a beautiful bird.
                B: Where did you see it?
                A: I saw it in East Park.
                B: When did you see it?
                A: At 8:30 A.M.
                B: What did it look like?
                A: It had beautiful red feathers.

D | *Check your work. Use the Editing Checklist.*

Editing Checklist

Did you use . . . ?
☐ past **wh-** questions correctly
☐ correct spelling

UNIT 24 Review

Check your answers on page UR-3.

Do you need to review anything?

EXERCISE A

Match the questions and answers.

_____ 1. Who got angry at Rob?

_____ 2. Where did Rob get a part-time job?

_____ 3. Why did he get a part-time job there?

_____ 4. When did he start his job?

_____ 5. How many hours did he work yesterday?

a. A couple of days ago.

b. He worked for seven hours.

c. His father.

d. At BQ Drugstore.

e. To pay for the damage.

EXERCISE B

Put the words in the correct order. Make questions about Rob's accident.

1. _____?
   (the accident / happen / did / When)

2. _____?
   (happen / did / How / the accident)

3. _____?
   (Rob / Why / to the supermarket / drive / did)

4. _____?
   (did / Who / with / Rob / drive there)

5. _____?
   (take / Rob / Where / the car / did)

EXERCISE C

Correct the conversation. There are five mistakes.

A: Where did the accident happened?

B: It did happen in front of the library.

A: When it was occur?

B: It occurred at 10:00 this morning.

A: How it happened?

B: A car hit another car.

A: How long did it takes the police to come?

B: It took 20 minutes.

PRONOUNS; QUANTITY EXPRESSIONS; *THERE IS / THERE ARE*

UNIT	GRAMMAR FOCUS	THEME
25	Subject and Object Pronouns	Gifts and Favors
26	*How much / How many*; Quantity Expressions	A Trip to the Galápagos Islands
27	*There is / There are*	Describing Places

Subject and Object Pronouns
GIFTS AND FAVORS

STEP 1 GRAMMAR IN CONTEXT

Before You Read

GROUPS OF FOUR: Ask what three gifts each person would like to get. Is there a most popular gift in your group?

> **EXAMPLE:** I would like to get tickets for a concert, a DVD, and a tennis racquet.

Read

Read the conversation.

CARLOS: Kathy, **you**'re an American. What's a good gift?

KATHY: For what?

CARLOS: For the party at Bill's house on Saturday. I want to get **him** a gift.

KATHY: Right. Let **me** think.

CARLOS: How about flowers?

KATHY: Well, **I** suppose so. But **you** don't usually give flowers to a man.

CARLOS: **He** has a wife. Can I give **them** to **her**?

KATHY: Hmm. **I**'m not sure.

CARLOS: What about tickets for a concert? **I** know **he** likes music.

KATHY: No. Not appropriate. **You** don't give your boss tickets.

CARLOS: Well, what do **you** suggest?

KATHY: Why don't **you** give **him** some chocolates? **He**'s always eating **them** at his desk.

CARLOS: OK, good idea. A box of chocolates. Now, can you do **me** a favor?

KATHY: What?

CARLOS: Tomiko and **I** need a ride to the party. Can you take **us**?

KATHY: For a price.

CARLOS: For a price? What do **you** mean?

KATHY: Get **me** a box of chocolates too.

CARLOS: I don't believe **you**. **You**'re not serious, are **you**?

KATHY: No, just kidding! **I**'ll pick **you** up at 6:30 on Saturday.

After You Read

A | Practice *PAIRS: Practice the opening conversation.*

B | Vocabulary *Listen and repeat the words. Write new words in a notebook.*

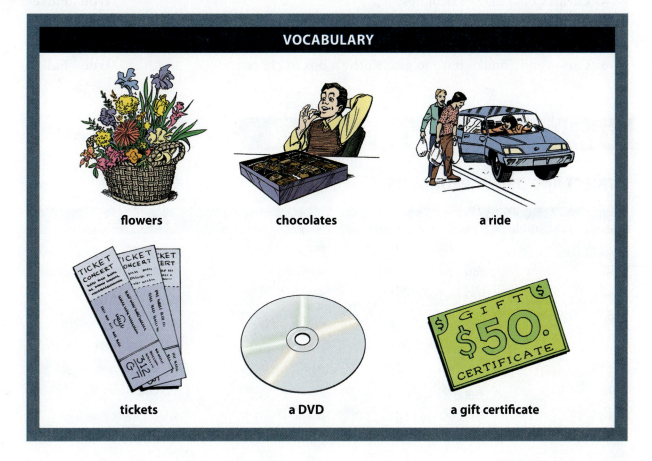

VOCABULARY

flowers   chocolates   a ride

tickets   a DVD   a gift certificate

C | Vocabulary *Complete the sentences. Use the correct forms of the vocabulary words.*

1. I got _____*tickets*_____ to the play on Saturday.

2. My friend gave me _____ for Macy's in the amount of $75.

3. I missed the bus this morning, but a friend gave me _____ to work.

4. My favorite _____ is *Star Wars*.

5. When I give _____, I cut them from my own garden.

6. My problem with getting _____ as a gift is that I eat the whole box.

D | Comprehension *Look again at the opening conversation. Circle* **True** *or* **False**.

1. Bill is Carlos's boss.	**True**	**False**
2. According to Kathy, people often give flowers to a man.	**True**	**False**
3. According to Kathy, tickets are a good gift for a boss.	**True**	**False**
4. Carlos's boss likes chocolates.	**True**	**False**
5. Kathy will drive to the party.	**True**	**False**
6. Carlos and Tomiko have to give Kathy a box of chocolates.	**True**	**False**

(Item 1: **True** is circled.)

STEP 2 GRAMMAR PRESENTATION

SUBJECT AND OBJECT PRONOUNS

Subject Pronouns	Example Sentences	Object Pronouns	Example Sentences
I	**I** like flowers.	me	Maria called **me**.
you	**You** have the tickets	you	Yusuf knows **you**.
he	**He**'s my boss.	him	Please ask **him**.
she	**She** needs a ride.	her	Kei met **her** yesterday.
it	**It**'s for a party.	it	Bring **it** to the party.
we	**We** don't know Bill.	us	Call **us** tomorrow.
you	**You** will be happy.	you	I saw **you** last night.
they	**They**'re a good gift.	them	The boss loves **them**.

GRAMMAR NOTES

1	*I*, *you*, *he*, *she*, *it*, *we*, and *they* are **subject pronouns**. They replace a subject noun.	• **The boys** need a ride to the party. **They** don't have a car.
2	*Me*, *you*, *him*, *her*, *it*, *us*, and *them* are **object pronouns**. They replace an object noun.	SUBJECT NOUN OBJECT NOUN • **Bill** loves **chocolates**. SUBJECT PRONOUN OBJECT PRONOUN • **He** loves **them**.
	Object pronouns come **after prepositions** like *to* or *for*.	• Give them **to him**. • The chocolates are **for him**.
3	**NOTE:** *You* and *it* are both subject and object pronouns.	SUBJECT OBJECT • **You**'re kidding. I don't believe **you**. SUBJECT OBJECT • **It**'s Latin music. He likes **it**.
4	The pronoun *you* is the same for singular and plural. When *you* is **plural**, we sometimes add the word *both* to make the sentence clearer.	• I don't believe **you**. (*you* = Kathy) • See **you** at 6:30. (*you* = you and Tomiko) • See **you both** at 6:30.

STEP 3 FOCUSED PRACTICE

EXERCISE 1: Discover the Grammar

Read the conversation. Underline the subject pronouns. Circle the object pronouns.

STEVE: You like parties. Right?

AMANDA: I love them. Why?

STEVE: Well, we're having a party on Sunday at my apartment. You and Josh are both invited. Are you free at three o'clock?

AMANDA: I think so. What's the occasion?

STEVE: It's Jessica's birthday, but I don't know what to get her. What's a good gift? Any ideas?

AMANDA: How about tickets for a concert? Does she like music?

(continued on next page)

STEVE: Yes. She listens to it all the time.

AMANDA: Good. Get her some tickets. Or else get her a gift certificate. Now, tell me again. What's your new address?

STEVE: Fourteen Vine Street, Apartment 202.

AMANDA: OK. See you then.

EXERCISE 2: Subject and Object Pronouns

(Grammar Notes 1–2)

Complete the conversations. Use subject and object pronouns.

1. **A:** It's Jessica's birthday on Sunday. What's a good gift for _____ *her* _____?

   B: How about a book? _____ loves to read.

2. **A:** It's Mark's birthday next week. What's a good present?

   B: Well, _____ likes music. Get _____ some concert tickets.

3. **A:** Our car is in the shop. Can _____ give _____ a ride to the party?

   B: Sure. I'll pick _____ up at 5:00.

4. **A:** The Johnsons are having a party on Saturday. What's a good gift for _____?

   B: _____ love flowers.

5. **A:** Hello? Steve? Is _____ raining there? Do I need my umbrella?

   B: Yes, bring _____. It's raining hard.

6. **A:** My friends are visiting from Portland. _____'re a lot of fun.

   B: Well, bring _____ on Saturday. We have plenty of food.

EXERCISE 3: Object Pronouns

(Grammar Note 2)

Write a suggestion for each picture. Use **Why don't you get** *+ object noun +* **for** *+ object pronoun.*

1. a travel book

2. a tennis racquet

3. a vest

4. a DVD

1. _____

2. _____

3. _____

4. _____

EXERCISE 4: Editing

There are six mistakes in the invitation. The first mistake is already corrected. Find and correct five more mistakes.

Dear Sarah,

Jim and ~~me~~ I are having a party on Saturday, June 10, at 3:00. Is for our son, Bob, and our daughter, Sally. Them both have birthdays in June. You and Stan are invited. Please don't bring they any presents. Us are just having a band and lots of food, but no gifts. Please come! Give Jim and I a call if you can come.

See both you soon,

Doris

EXERCISE 5: Listening

A | *Listen to Tim and Jessica's conversation. Who wrapped the gifts?*

B | *Listen again. Complete the chart with the words from the box.*

Colors				
blue	green	orange	~~red~~	white
Gifts				
a DVD	a game	something special	~~a tennis racquet~~	tickets

Color of Package	Who is it for?	Gift
red	Cousin Martha	a tennis racquet
	Mom and Dad	
	Jeremy	
	Ben and Annie	
	Jessica	

EXERCISE 6: Pronunciation

A | *Read and listen to the Pronunciation Note.*

> **Pronunciation Note**
>
> When we correct a speaker's mistake, we use stress to indicate what we are correcting.
>
> **EXAMPLES:** **A:** Is that your CD?   **A:** Is that your CD?
>   **B:** No, it's **Amy's** CD. [It's not <u>my</u> CD.]   **B:** No, it's my **DVD**. [It's not a <u>CD</u>.]

B | *Listen to the conversations. In Sentence B, circle the word that shows the correction.*

1. **A:** The blue box is a present for Mark, right?

   B: No, the (red) box is Mark's present.

2. **A:** You gave your boss flowers, didn't you?

   B: No, I gave his wife flowers.

3. **A:** Did you get Mark a new necktie for his birthday?

   B: No, I got Josh a new necktie.

4. **A:** You're giving Elena flowers, aren't you?

   B: No, I'm giving her chocolates.

5. **A:** You bought the Wangs a painting, right?

   B: No, I bought the Grants a painting.

C | *PAIRS: Practice the conversations.*

244   UNIT 25

EXERCISE 7: Choose Gifts

PAIRS: Write the names of five people. Talk about a good gift for each person. Then tell the class.

EXAMPLES: **A:** It's my brother's birthday tomorrow. What's a good gift for him?
                 B: Hmm. How old is he?
                 A: Ten.
                 B: Maybe a DVD?
                 A: I don't think so.
                 B: OK, then why don't you get him a soccer ball?
                 A: Good idea.

OR

                 A: It's my brother's birthday tomorrow. What's a good gift for him?
                 B: What does he like?
                 A: He loves sports.
                 B: How about a tennis racquet?
                 A: I don't think so.
                 B: OK, then how about a soccer ball?
                 A: Good idea.

EXERCISE 8: Writing

A | Write six or seven sentences about a time when you gave a gift that made someone happy. Use subject and object pronouns.

EXAMPLE: My sister had her 17th birthday last July. I didn't have much money to get her a gift, but she loves flowers. I only had $10 to spend, so I bought her . . .

B | Check your work. Use the Editing Checklist.

Editing Checklist

Did you use . . . ?
☐ subject and object pronouns
   correctly
☐ correct spelling

25 Review

Check your answers on page UR-4.

Do you need to review anything?

EXERCISE A

Circle the correct subject or object pronouns to complete the conversations.

1. A: It's Steve's birthday on Sunday. What's a good gift for **he / him**?

   B: How about a gift certificate to a movie theater? **He / Him** really likes movies.

2. A: What's a good gift for the children? Do **they / them** like games?

   B: Yes, bring **they / them** games. **We / Us** all love games!

EXERCISE B

Complete the suggestions. Use the correct object pronouns. Refer to the nouns in parentheses.

1. Why don't you get flowers for _____ (your wife)?

2. Why don't you get a tie for _____ (Uncle Toshi)?

3. Why don't you take chocolates to _____ (your cousins)?

4. Why don't we give a ride to _____ (John's sister).

5. Why don't you buy a new TV for _____ (Grandma and Grandpa)!

EXERCISE C

Correct the note. There are five mistakes.

Dear Doris and Jim,

Thank you for inviting we to the party on June 10. Us will bring some cookies for dessert. It are really good, and we hope you like they. I don't have your address. Could you please email its to us?

See you on Saturday!

Sarah and Stan

How much / How many; Quantity Expressions

A TRIP TO THE GALÁPAGOS ISLANDS

STEP 1 GRAMMAR IN CONTEXT

Before You Read

GROUPS: The Galápagos Islands are known for their unusual animal and plant life. Look at the map. Where are the Galápagos Islands? How many students in your group would like to visit them?

Read

🎧 *Read the conversation.*

STEVE: So how was Ecuador?

JESSICA: Great.

STEVE: **How many days** were you away?

JESSICA: Ten. We were in the capital, Quito, and on the Galápagos Islands.

MARK: The Galápagos Islands? That sounds exciting. **How much time** did you spend there?

TIM: Not much. Only four days. But it was fantastic. We took hundreds of photos of the plants and animals. We ate and slept on a boat.

MARK: Really? **How many people** were on the boat?

JESSICA: Twelve including us.

STEVE: **How much** did the trip cost?

JESSICA: It was expensive, but we used our frequent flier miles for the flight.

MARK: Well, nothing beats travel.*

TIM: I agree.

---

* ***nothing beats travel:*** traveling is great

A | Practice *GROUPS OF FOUR: Practice the opening conversation.*

B | Vocabulary *Listen and repeat the words. Write new words in a notebook.*

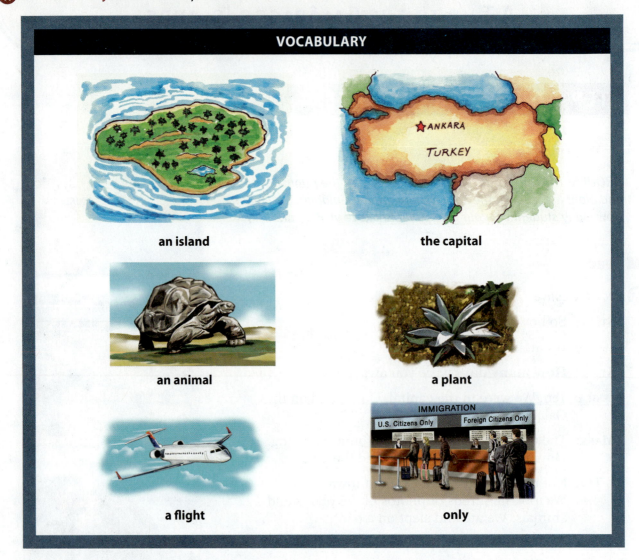

VOCABULARY

an island

the capital

an animal

a plant

a flight

only

C | Vocabulary *Complete the conversations. Write the correct forms of the vocabulary words.*

1. **A:** Is Seoul _____*the capital*_____ of Korea?

   B: Yes, it is.

2. **A:** Which continent is an _____?

   B: Australia.

3. **A:** How was your _____ home?

   B: OK, but the plane was full. There were no empty seats.

4. A: He has beautiful _____ in his garden.

   B: I know. Some come from Hawaii.

5. A: How many weeks of vacation do you have?

   B: _____ one week a year.

6. A: Are any of the _____ on the Galápagos Islands dangerous?

   B: I don't think so.

D | Comprehension *Look again at the opening conversation. Answer the questions. Use the words from the box.*

A lot	~~hundreds~~	Two—Quito and the Galápagos Islands
10 days	12 people	

1. How many photos did they take? *hundreds.* _____

2. How much time did they spend in Ecuador? _____

3. How much money did they spend? _____

4. How many people were on the boat to the Galápagos Islands? _____

5. How many places did they visit? _____

STEP 2 GRAMMAR PRESENTATION

HOW MUCH / HOW MANY

Count Nouns
A: How many photos did you take?
B: A lot. (I took a lot of photos.)
Not many. (I didn't take many photos.)
A few. (I took a few photos.)
Sixty. (I took 60 photos.)

Non-count Nouns
A: How much time did you spend there?
B: A lot. (We spent a lot of time there.)
Not much. (We didn't spend much time there.)
A little. (We spent a little time there.)

GRAMMAR NOTES

1	Use *how many* + a **plural count noun** to ask about a quantity of something.	**PLURAL COUNT NOUN** **A: How many days** were you there? **B:** Fifteen.
	Use *how much* + a **non-count noun** to ask about an amount.	**NON-COUNT NOUN** **A: How much time** did you spend there? **B:** A lot.
2	*A lot*, *a few*, *a little*, *not many*, and *not much* are **general** expressions. *A lot* tells that an amount is large. *A few*, *not many*, and *not much* tell that amounts are small. **BE CAREFUL!** *Much* is not usually used in affirmative statements. We usually use *a lot* instead.	**A:** How many people were on the boat? **B: Not many.** (a small quantity) **A:** How much time did you spend in Quito? **B: Not much.** (a small amount) • I spent a lot of money. Not: I spent ~~much money~~.
3	**Numbers** also answer questions with *how many*. Numbers give an **exact** amount.	**A:** How many days were you there? **B: Ten days.**
4	Use *how much* to ask about the **cost** of something. We often use *how much* **without a noun**.	• **How much** was the trip? • **How much** did the trip cost? • **How much (money)** did it cost?

REFERENCE NOTE
For more about **count and non-count nouns**, see Unit 19.

STEP 3 FOCUSED PRACTICE

EXERCISE 1: Discover the Grammar

Read the conversations. Underline **how much** *and* **how many,** *and circle the nouns they go with. Draw two lines under each quantifier.*

1. **A:** How many flights go to the Galápagos Islands from Guayaquil?

   B: A few each day.

2. **A:** How many seats are available on Flight 1 to Quito?

   B: Not many. You need to make a reservation now.

3. **A:** How much time does it take to get to the airport?

   B: Not much. Only about 30 minutes.

4. A: How much money does the flight cost?

   B: About $360.

5. A: How many tourists visit the Galápagos Islands in May?

   B: A lot. Most tourists go there in April, May, and November.

6. A: Is there a lot of rain in July?

   B: No, there isn't, just a little mist called "garua."

EXERCISE 2: *How much / How many*

(Grammar Notes 1, 3–4)

Read about the trip to Washington, D.C. Match the questions and answers.

Come to Washington, D.C.!
See the beautiful cherry blossoms.
Visit the White House. See the Capitol.
INCLUDES:
- round-trip airfare from Seattle
- 2 nights, 3 days at the Best Eastern
- double rooms
- lunch and dinner for 3 days
- sightseeing tour of Washington, D.C.
- free bus from airport to hotel

All this for only $650!

_b_ **1.** How many days is the trip?	**a.**	Two.
___ **2.** How many meals does the trip include?	**b.**	Three.
___ **3.** How much does the trip cost?	**c.**	Six.
___ **4.** How many people share a room?	**d.**	Nothing.
___ **5.** How much is the bus ride from the airport?	**e.**	$650 from Seattle (flights included)

EXERCISE 3: *How much / How many*

(Grammar Notes 1, 3–4)

*Read the ad for a trip to Boston. Write questions with **how much** or **how many**.*

VISIT BOSTON!

Includes:

• **Round-trip airfare from Seattle**
• **5 days and 4 nights at Motel 9**
• **4 to a room**
• **Delicious breakfast every day**
• **3-hour sightseeing tour of Boston**

ONLY $800!

Visit the Freedom Trail, Faneuil Hall,
Quincy Market, and Old North Church

JUDY: I'm thinking of visiting New York or Boston.

MARK: Well, here's an ad for a trip to Boston.

JUDY: _____ ?
　　　　　　　　　　　　1.

MARK: Eight hundred dollars.

JUDY: _____ ?
　　　　　　　　　　　　2.

MARK: Five days.

JUDY: Do they include meals?

MARK: Some.

JUDY: _____ ?
　　　　　　　　　　　　3.

MARK: Five breakfasts.

JUDY: Do you have your own room?

MARK: Uh, no.

JUDY: _____ ?
　　　　　　　　　　　　4.

MARK: They put four people in a room.

JUDY: That's not for me.

MARK: Oh, well. It's a good price.

EXERCISE 4: Editing

There are six mistakes in the conversations. The first mistake is already corrected. Find and correct five more mistakes.

1. **A:** How ~~much~~ *many* people did you travel with?

   B: Only one other person, but we met a little people on the trip.

2. **A:** How many day were you away?

   B: Not much, only three days. But we were on a small island.

3. **A:** How much time did you spend in your hotel room?

   B: Not many time. We left early and returned late.

4. **A:** How much trips do you usually take in a year?

   B: Two or three. I love to travel.

STEP 4 COMMUNICATION PRACTICE

EXERCISE 5: Listening

A | *Listen to Steve and Jessica's conversation and the news that follows. Circle the correct letter to complete the sentence.*

The news is about _____.

a. a travel writer who talks about his new book

b. a travel writer who died last Monday

B | *Listen again. Complete the questions with **how much** or **how many**.*

1. _____*How many*_____ books did John Phillips write? _____*more than 30*_____

2. _____ children did he have? _____

3. _____ grandchildren did he have? _____

4. _____ money did John Phillips have? _____

5. _____ people did he leave his money to? _____

6. _____ time did his children spend with him? _____

C | *Listen to the conversation and news broadcast again and answer the questions in Part B.*

EXERCISE 6: Pronunciation

A | *Listen and repeat the words:*

Jell-o—yellow   jail—Yale

Jess—yes   jams—yams

juice—use

B | *Underline the above words in the sentences. Then listen and repeat each sentence.*

1. I drank a lot of <u>juice</u> yesterday.

2. I ate a lot of yams.

3. I bought a lot of yellow sweaters.

4. Jess has a lot of friends at Yale.

5. She met a lot of people in jail.

6. They served a lot of jams.

7. He ate a lot of Jell-o.

C | *Take turns. Say a sentence from Part B. Your partner asks a question that begins with "How much" or "How many." Give an answer with an exact amount.*

> EXAMPLE: **A:** I drank a lot of juice yesterday.
>   **B:** How much did you drink?
>   **A:** Four glasses.

EXERCISE 7: Ask and Answer

A | *GROUPS: Take turns. Ask questions with* **how much** *and* **how many**. *Your classmates answer with* **a lot, a little, a few, not much, not many, some,** *or* **none,** *or give an exact amount. Use the ideas from the box or your own ideas.*

> time / spend online
>
> clothes / buy in a month
>
> different animals / see in an average day
>
> email messages / get in a week
>
> money / give to charity in a year
>
> movies / watch in a month
>
> people / help in a week
>
> plants / have in your home
>
> time / spend on the telephone in a day

> EXAMPLE: **A:** How much time do you spend online?
>   **B:** Not much. About 10 minutes a day.

B | *On a separate sheet of paper, write four of your questions and your classmates' answers. Report the results.*

EXAMPLE: Juan doesn't spend much time online: about 10 minutes a day.

EXERCISE 8: Writing

A | *Tell your partner about an interesting place you visited. Use quantifiers to answer the questions:*

How much time did you spend there?

How many people did you go with?

How many photos did you take?

How much did it cost to go there?

B | *Write about your trip.*

EXAMPLE: Last year I went to Philadelphia. I was there for three days. I traveled with my two friends. We took a lot of photos—over 140. We went by bus and stayed with friends. The trip only cost us $100.

C | *Check your work. Use the Editing Checklist.*

> ### Editing Checklist
>
> Did you use . . . ?
> ☐ quantifiers correctly
> ☐ correct spelling

Check your answers on page UR-4.

Do you need to review anything?

EXERCISE A

Complete the conversations with **much** *or* **many**.

1. A: How _____ students are in this class?   **B:** Twenty.

2. A: How _____ weeks does this class last?   **B:** It lasts eight weeks.

3. A: How _____ does the class cost?   **B:** It's $200.

4. A: How _____ textbooks do we use?   **B:** Two.

5. A: How _____ are the textbooks?   **B:** About $50.

EXERCISE B

Circle the correct words to complete the conversations.

1. A: How much time did you spend at work?   **B:** **A lot / Much**. About 10 hours.

2. A: How many mistakes did you make?   **B:** **Not many / Not much**. Just two.

3. A: How much coffee do you drink each day?   **B:** Just **a little / a few**.

4. A: How many people came?   **B:** **A lot / Much**. Almost 30.

5. A: How much money do you have?   **B:** **Not much / Not many**.

EXERCISE C

Correct the conversations. There are five mistakes.

1. A: How much time do you spend on the phone each week?

   B: Not many time. Only a couple of hours.

2. A: How many movies do you see each year?

   B: Not much. Only two or three.

3. A: How much email messages do you send each day?

   B: Each day? Only one or two. But I send a little of text messages—maybe 20 or 30.

4. A: How much time do you spend surfing the Internet?

   B: I spend many time. Maybe six hours a day!

There is / There are
DESCRIBING PLACES

Before You Read

GROUPS OF FOUR: Name an interesting or a beautiful place in or near your hometown. Say one thing about it. Then report to the class.

There's an interesting _____ near my hometown.

OR

There's a beautiful _____ near my hometown.

Read

Read the conversation.

JUDY: OK. So where did you guys go on your vacation?

JOSH: South Dakota. We went there especially to see Mount Rushmore.

ELENA: **Isn't there** something famous about Mount Rushmore?

AMANDA: Yes, **there is. There are** four presidents' heads carved* into the mountain. Here's a picture of them.

Mount Rushmore

JOSH: Do you know who they are?

JUDY: Sure. Washington, Jefferson, Theodore Roosevelt, and Lincoln.

ELENA: Wow! It looks like a fantastic place. What else **is there** to see in the area?

---

* *carved:* cut out of stone or wood

(continued on next page)

JOSH: Well, **there's** a great national park called The Badlands. It's only about 60 miles away, and it's beautiful.

AMANDA: And **there are** two interesting old mining towns called Lead and Deadwood.

JOSH: And **there are** a lot of caves in the area.

AMANDA: And **there's** a little town called Wall. It has an amazing drugstore—maybe the biggest one in the world.

JUDY: Do you want to go back next year? Elena and I will go with you. Show us more.

Badlands National Park

After You Read

A | Practice *GROUPS OF FOUR: Practice the opening conversation.*

B | Vocabulary *Listen and repeat the words. Write new words in a notebook.*

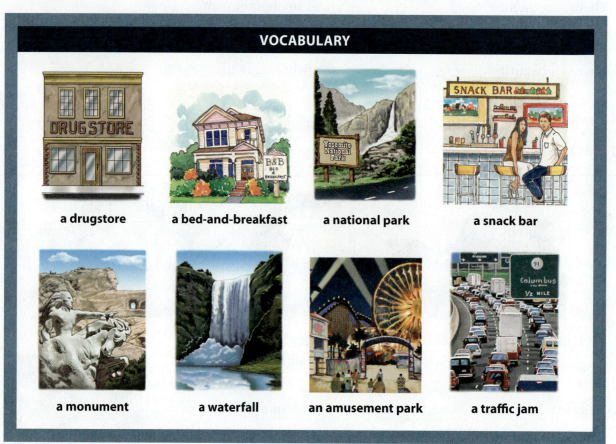

VOCABULARY

a drugstore   a bed-and-breakfast   a national park   a snack bar

a monument   a waterfall   an amusement park   a traffic jam

C | Vocabulary *GROUPS: Use the vocabulary to ask about your partners' city, neighborhood, or area.*

EXAMPLE: A: Is there a drugstore in your neighborhood?
           B: No, there isn't.
             OR
             Yes, there is. Are there any national parks in your state?
           C: Yes, there are. There are two.
             OR
             No, there aren't.

D | Comprehension *Look again at the opening conversation. Write* **T (True)** *or* **F (False).**
Correct the false statements.

__T__ **1.** Mount Rushmore is famous.

_____ **2.** There are statues of five presidents on Mount Rushmore.

_____ **3.** Two of the presidents are Washington and Lincoln.

_____ **4.** Josh thinks the Badlands are beautiful.

_____ **5.** Wall is a drugstore.

STEP 2 GRAMMAR PRESENTATION

THERE IS / THERE ARE

Statements	
Singular	**Plural**
There is a bank on this block. **There isn't a bank** near here.	**There are** three **banks** on this block. **There aren't** any **banks** around here.

Questions and Answers	
Singular	**Plural**
A: **Is there a drugstore** around here? B: Yes, **there is**. OR No, **there isn't**.	A: **Are there** any **national parks** in the area? B: Yes, **there are**. OR No, **there aren't**.

GRAMMAR NOTES

1	Use **there is** or **there's** to state facts about a person or thing.	• **There is** a message for you. OR • **There's** a message for you.
	Use **there are** if the noun is plural.	• **There are** two postcards from Mount Rushmore.
	We often use **there is** or **there are** to tell the location of things or people.	• **There is** a snack bar over there. • **There are** two snack bars over there. • **There's** someone at the door.
2	To state a **negative fact**, you can use **there isn't a / an** or **there aren't any**.	• **There isn't a** subway in this city. • **There aren't any** theaters near here.
3	To make a **question**, put **is** or **are** before **there**.	• **Is there** a bank near here? • **Are there** any caves in this area?

(continued on next page)

4	Use *there* both in **questions** and in **short answers**.	**A:** **Is there** a pool in our hotel? **B:** Yes, **there is**. OR No, **there isn't**. OR No, **there's not**. **A:** How many rooms **are there** on this floor? **B:** **There are** eight.
5	Use *there's* in speaking and informal writing. (*There's = There is*) **BE CAREFUL!** Don't use a plural noun after *there's*.	• **There's** a mall two miles from here. • **There are** some beautiful paintings in this museum. NOT: ~~There's~~ some beautiful paintings in this museum.
6	Use *there* the **first time** you talk about something. Use *it* or *they* after that.	**A:** Is **there** a bank around here? **B:** Yes, **there is**. **It**'s on the corner of First Avenue and Barton Street. **A:** Are **there** any theaters near here? **B:** Yes, **there are** several. **They**'re in the mall.

STEP 3 FOCUSED PRACTICE

EXERCISE 1: Discover the Grammar

Read the conversation about a bed and breakfast. Underline **there is** *and* **there are**.
Draw an arrow between **there** *and the noun or nouns it refers to.*

MRS. GRANT: Hello. You must be Josh and Amanda Wang. I'm Amy Grant. Welcome. Can you please sign the guest book? There's a pen right over there.

JOSH: Thank you. We're glad there's a room for us.

MRS. GRANT: Actually, there are two rooms to choose from, one on the second floor and one on the third. The one on the third floor has a nice view of the waterfall, but there isn't an elevator, unfortunately.

AMANDA: Oh, that's fine. We'd like the one with the nice view. Is there a bath in the room?

MRS. GRANT: No. Sorry about that. There's just one bathroom per floor. But we don't have many guests. So, let's see . . . breakfast is from 7:00 until 9:00. There's coffee in your room, and there are also crackers and cookies. Your room is up that stairway over there. We'll see you in the morning.

JOSH: Thanks a lot. See you then.

EXERCISE 2: *There is / There are / They are*

(Grammar Notes 1–6)

Complete the conversation. Choose the correct words in parentheses.

MAN: What are your plans for today?

AMANDA: We're going to the Mount Rushmore Monument. _____*Is there*_____ a bus we
1. (Is there / There's)
can take? We don't want to drive.

MAN: Yes, _____.
2. (there is / it is)
The number 10 bus will get you there. And

_____ a bus stop just a block
3. (there's / there are)
down the street from the bed and breakfast.

JOSH: Great . . . Hmm. What about lunch? _____ any places to eat at
4. (Is there / Are there)
the park?

MAN: Yes, _____ a good park restaurant, and _____
5. (there's / it's)   **6. (they are / there are)**
a couple of snack bars. _____ a town a couple of miles
7. (There's / It's)
away called Keystone. _____ a lot of restaurants there, and
8. (There are / They are)
_____ pretty reasonable in price. So have a great day. See you
9. (there are / they're)
this evening.

EXERCISE 3: *There / It / They*

(Grammar Note 6)

Complete the conversations with **there**, **it**, *or* **they**.

1. **A:** Why are you in such a hurry? Where are you going?

   B: _____*There*_____'s a concert downtown that starts in 15 minutes.

1.

   A: What kind of concert is _____?

2.

   B: _____'s an indie rock concert.

3.

2. **A:** What is _____ to do around here?

4.

   B: Well, _____ are a lot of beautiful national parks to see.

5.

   A: Are _____ nearby?

6.

   B: Yes, _____ are all within 50 miles from here.

7.

EXERCISE 4: Editing

There are five mistakes in the letter. The first mistake is already corrected. Find and correct four more mistakes.

Calamity Jane's Bed-and-Breakfast

Dear Kathy,

    Greetings from South Dakota. We're having a wonderful time. ~~It is~~ *There are* so many interesting things to see and do here! Right now we're in Deadwood, an old mining town. Are interesting little shops on every street, and is a lot of fun stuff to buy. I hope my suitcase is big enough. Are also a lot of beautiful landmarks to see; we went to Mount Rushmore yesterday, and we're going to the Crazy Horse monument today. We're staying at a really nice bed-and-breakfast called Calamity Jane's. Is a nice, comfortable place, and there are lots of interesting people from different places staying here.

I have to sign off now; we're ready to go to Crazy Horse.
Say hi to Mark and everyone else.

Love,

Amanda

STEP 4 COMMUNICATION PRACTICE

EXERCISE 5: Listening

A | *Listen to Josh and Amanda's conversation with some people they meet at breakfast.*

What country are the people from? _____

B | *Listen again. Check (✓) T (True), F (False), or NI (No Information).*

	T	F	NI
1. At breakfast, there are no free tables.	✓	☐	☐
2. Josh and Amanda like the British accent.	☐	☐	☐
3. Martin and Helen are from Manchester.	☐	☐	☐
4. Martin and Helen arrived by train.	☐	☐	☐
5. They will go to Mount Rushmore with 20 other people.	☐	☐	☐
6. Josh says to visit Wall Drug Store.	☐	☐	☐
7. Wall is about 60 miles west.	☐	☐	☐
8. There are restaurants inside Wall Drug Store.	☐	☐	☐
9. There are a lot of animals in Badlands National Park.	☐	☐	☐
10. Helen and Martin will visit Wall and the Badlands.	☐	☐	☐

EXERCISE 6: Pronunciation

A | *Listen to the conversations. Then circle* **there are** *or* **they are, there aren't,** *or* **they aren't.**

1. (there are)   they are

2. there are   they are

3. there are   they are

4. there are   they are

5. there aren't   they aren't

6. there aren't   they aren't

B | PAIRS: Practice the conversations. Take turns.

1. A: What can we see in this area?

   B: There are caves nearby.

2. A: How are the people at your bed-and-breakfast?

   B: They're great.

3. A: Are there any good hotels in this town?

   B: Yes, there are several.

4. A: What are Lead and Deadwood?

   B: They're old mining towns.

5. A: Where are Judy and Elena?

   B: They aren't here yet.

6. A: Let's go to a movie.

   B: There aren't any theaters nearby.

EXERCISE 7: Game

GROUPS: Form two teams. Everyone is going on a trip. Everyone has a suitcase with something special in it. Each person describes his or her special item:

I have a _____.

The other team must repeat all the items in sentences with **there, it,** *and* **they.** *The team that remembers the most items wins.*

EXAMPLE: **Team A:** I have a cheap DVD player in my suitcase.
   Team B: There's a DVD player in Alicia's suitcase. It's cheap.
   Team A: I have two blue soccer balls in my suitcase.
   Team B: There's a DVD player in Alicia's suitcase. It's cheap. There are two soccer balls in Kam Wa's suitcase. They're blue . . .

EXERCISE 8: Writing

A | *Write a short description (6 to 10 sentences) of one of your favorite places. Use* **there is, there are, it is,** *and* **they are.**

EXAMPLE: One of my favorite places is the Los Angeles area. There are lots of interesting things to see around L.A. There's Hollywood, for example. It's a fascinating place. Sometimes you can see movie stars in Hollywood. There are several amusement parks, and they're a lot of fun. There's Disneyland . . .

B | *Check your work. Use the Editing Checklist.*

Editing Checklist

Did you use . . . ?
- [ ] *there is*, *there are*, *it is*, and *they are* correctly
- [ ] correct spelling

Check your answers on page UR-4.

Do you need to review anything?

EXERCISE A

Complete the conversation. Choose the correct words in parentheses.

A: _____ a bed-and-breakfast near here?
1. (Is there / There's)

B: Yes, _____. It's just a few block from here.
2. (there is / it is)

A: And _____ any restaurants around here?
3. (is there / are there)

B: Yes, _____ a great Chinese restaurant on Second Street, and
4. (there's / it's)

_____ two good pizza places on Mina Street.
5. (they are / there are)

EXERCISE B

Complete the conversation with **there** *or* **they**.

A: Good afternoon. Betty's Bed-and-Breakfast.

B: Hi, are _____ any rooms?

A: Yes, _____ are two rooms. _____'re both on the third floor.

B: Do _____ have TVs?

A: Yes. _____'s a TV in every room.

EXERCISE C

Correct the conversation. There are five mistakes.

A: What is the West Edmonton Mall?

B: There's a gigantic shopping center in Edmonton, Canada.

A: What is they to see in the mall?

B: Well, there is probably the biggest mall in North America. There has 800 stores, and

it is even a skating rink.

MODIFIERS; COMPARISONS; PREPOSITIONS OF TIME

Before You Read

A | *You are looking for a new friend. What's most important for you? Rank the characteristics from* **1** *(least important) to* **6** *(most important)*

____ artistic ____ honest ____ rich

____ fun-loving ____ kind ____ smart

B | *Circle the two things you like best:*

action films   bird-watching   computer science   modern art   science museums

art museums   computer games   jazz bands   romantic films

C | *GROUPS: Compare your answers.*

Read

Read the personal ads from the Seattle Daily's *online list www.sdo.gom.*

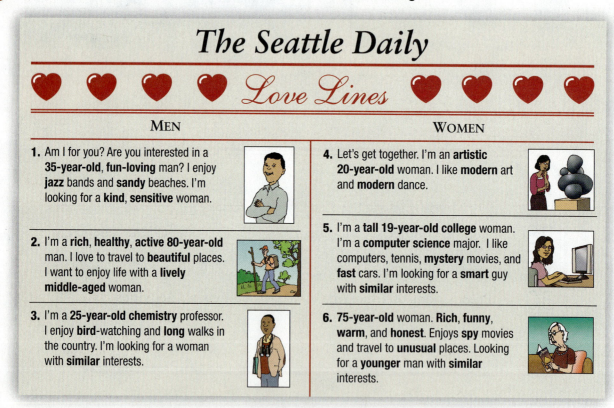

The Seattle Daily

♥ ♥ ♥ ♥ *Love Lines* ♥ ♥ ♥ ♥

MEN

1. Am I for you? Are you interested in a **35-year-old**, **fun-loving** man? I enjoy **jazz** bands and **sandy** beaches. I'm looking for a **kind**, **sensitive** woman.

2. I'm a **rich**, **healthy**, **active 80-year-old** man. I love to travel to **beautiful** places. I want to enjoy life with a **lively middle-aged** woman.

3. I'm a **25-year-old chemistry** professor. I enjoy **bird**-watching and **long** walks in the country. I'm looking for a woman with **similar** interests.

WOMEN

4. Let's get together. I'm an **artistic 20-year-old** woman. I like **modern** art and **modern** dance.

5. I'm a **tall 19-year-old college** woman. I'm a **computer science** major. I like computers, tennis, **mystery** movies, and **fast** cars. I'm looking for a **smart** guy with **similar** interests.

6. **75-year-old** woman. **Rich**, **funny**, **warm**, and **honest**. Enjoys **spy** movies and travel to **unusual** places. Looking for a **younger** man with **similar** interests.

After You Read

A | Practice *PAIRS: Practice the opening reading. Take turns reading the ads.*

B | Vocabulary *Listen and repeat the words. Write new words in a notebook.*

VOCABULARY

ADJECTIVE + NOUN

fun-loving man

honest man

artistic woman

NOUN + NOUN

WOMEN

A. Let's get together. Artistic 20-year-old woman looking for an artistic man.

B. 19-year-old computer science major. Enjoys tennis, mysteries, and fast cars. Looking for a smart guy with similar interests.

personal ads

spy movies

chemistry professor

computer science major

C | Vocabulary *Complete the sentences. Write the correct vocabulary words.*

1. Do you think online _____personal ads_____ are a good way to meet someone?

2. She's a _____. She wants to write computer programs after college.

3. We always have fun when we're with him. He's a _____.

4. My grandfather likes _____, especially the James Bond series.

5. After class, I can ask my _____ about that chemistry problem.

6. She's an _____. You can see her artwork in the library this month.

7. I always believe him. He's an _____.

D | Comprehension *Match the events with the ads in the opening reading.*

WEEKEND EVENTS

West Park

_3_ 9 A.M. Walk in the park with Dr. John Brook. Learn about the interesting plants, animals, and birds in West Park.

_____ 8 P.M.—Jazz concert—The King Trio

Cineplex

_____ 6 P.M.—*The Spy from Alaska*

_____ 8 P.M.—*Who Killed Sammy Singer?*

Art Museum

_____ The Art of Jackson Pollack

Trip to Westville Falls in Montana

_____ Take a trip to the beautiful waterfall. Sign up today.

STEP 2 GRAMMAR PRESENTATION

DESCRIPTIVE ADJECTIVES

Subject	*Be*	Adjective		Subject	*Be*		Adjective	Noun
This woman	is	artistic.		She	is	an	artistic	woman.
These women	are			They	are			women.

NOUN MODIFIERS

		Noun	Noun
We saw	a	spy	film.
	two		films.

DESCRIPTIVE ADJECTIVE + NOUN MODIFIER

		Adjective	Noun	Noun
He's	a	**young**	**computer**	scientist.
She's	an	**excellent**	**tennis**	player.

GRAMMAR NOTES

1	Adjectives can **modify (describe) nouns**. They give more information about a noun. Nouns can also **modify nouns**.	ADJECTIVE NOUN • I like **romantic** music. NOUN NOUN • He's a **tennis** player.
2	Adjectives can come **after the verb be** or **before a noun**.	• She is **artistic**. • She's an **artistic** woman.
3	**BE CAREFUL!** Adjectives can end in *-ing*, *-ly*, and *-ed*.	• She's an **interesting** woman. • She's **lively** and **friendly**. • She's never **bored**.
4	Some adjectives contain **two or more words**.	• She's **fun-loving**.

5	**Do not add *-s*** to an adjective or a noun modifier.	• He's looking for a **fast** car.
		• He likes **fast** cars.
		• He wants a **leather** jacket.
		• He likes **leather** jackets.
		  NOT: He likes ~~fasts~~ cars.
		       He likes ~~leathers~~ jackets.

6	Before a singular count noun: Use *a* before a modifier that begins with a **consonant sound**. Use *an* before a modifier that begins with a **vowel sound**.	• She's **a young** woman. • It's **a travel** magazine. • She's **an artistic** woman. • It's **an art** school.
7	When both an **adjective** and a **noun modify a noun**, the **adjective** comes **first**.	• I have a **new leather** jacket. • He's a **good tennis** player.

EXERCISE 1: Discover the Grammar

Underline the adjective modifiers. Circle the noun modifiers. Then match the sentence beginnings and endings.

<u>c</u>   1. He's a (biology)   **a.** walks.

____   2. He likes to take <u>long</u>   **b.** interests.

____   3. We are listening to a jazz   **c.** major.

____   4. They like the same things.   **d.** books.
          They have similar   **e.** shop.

____   5. He likes to read grammar   **f.** band.

____   6. Let's meet in front of the gift   **g.** salad.

____   7. She's a famous movie   **h.** shirts.

____   8. My favorite dish is chicken   **i.** star.

____   9. They both like spy   **j.** movies.

____ 10. He always wears cotton

EXERCISE 2: Modifiers   *(Grammar Notes 1–6)*

Complete the conversation. Put the words in the correct order.

A: How does he dress?

B: He usually wears an _____*old leather jacket*_____,
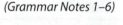
          1. (old / jacket / leather)

_____, and _____.
   2. (cotton / black / T-shirts)   **3. (jeans / baggy)**

A: What does he drive?

B: He drives a _____
          4. (sports / black / car)

A: Where does he live?

B: He lives in a _____
          5. (house / brick / small)

with a _____
   6. (garden / beautiful / rock)

in front.

A: What does he like?

B: _____
      7. (spy / old / movies)

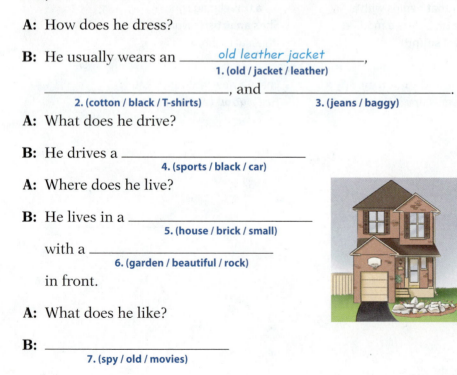

EXERCISE 3: Modifiers

(Grammar Notes 1–6)

Complete the conversation. Write the correct words from the box.

blue	~~coffee~~	delicious	juice	nice	pancakes	shop
blueberry	computer science	hungry	major	orange	polite	

JUDY: So, Elena, How was your date?

ELENA: OK. We met at 11:00 in front of the _____coffee_____ _____. I
   1.   **2.**

had _____ _____. They were _____. He
   3.   **4.**   **5.**

just drank a glass of _____ _____. I guess he wasn't
                      6.   **7.**

_____.
   8.

JUDY: What did you talk about?

ELENA: School mostly. He's a _____ _____. He plans to teach. He
                           9.   **10.**

wants to be a professor.

JUDY: What did he wear?

ELENA: He wore a light _____ shirt and jeans.
                         11.

JUDY: Are you going to go out again?

ELENA: I don't know. He was _____ and _____ but nothing more.
                             12.   **13.**

EXERCISE 4: Editing

*There are six mistakes in the letter to advice columnist Dahlia. The first mistake is
already corrected. Find and correct five more mistakes.*

Dear Dahlia,

   My boyfriend, Joe, is wonderful. He's a kind, honest, and intelligent. He has

an job good and a heart kind. There's only one problem. He doesn't like to

spend money. We always watch TV at his house, and he doesn't even have

TV cable. Sometimes we go to frees concerts and picnics. I have fun with

Joe, but I want to do differents things. Do you have any suggestions?

                           Sincerely,

                           Rosa

EXERCISE 5: Listening

A | *Listen to the conversation between Ken and his friend Brian. Circle the correct letter to complete the sentence.*

Mia and Ken are in the same _____.

a. history class   **b.** music class

B | *Listen again. Find Brian's friend Mia. Draw a circle around Mia.*

EXERCISE 6: Pronunciation

A | *Read and listen to the Pronunciation Note.*

> **Pronunciation Note**
>
> *And* is usually a weak word. It sounds like *'n'*. Join *and* to the word before it.

B | *Listen to the sentences and repeat.*

1. He's kind and honest.
2. She's young and fun-loving.
3. They're rich and famous.
4. He enjoys math and computer science.

C | *PAIRS: Tell your partner the following information. Use "and" in your statements.*

- two school subjects you like
- two colors you like
- two kinds of movies you like
- two kinds of music you like

EXAMPLES: I like history and geography.
          I like blue and green.

EXERCISE 7: Describe People

A | *Match the words and their opposites. Use your dictionary if you need to.*

   _b_   **1.** friendly   **a.** stingy

   _____   **2.** kind   **b.** unfriendly

   _____   **3.** generous   **c.** serious

   _____   **4.** honest   **d.** dishonest

   _____   **5.** fun-loving   **e.** cold

   _____   **6.** warm   **f.** mean

B | *Use adjectives to describe six people. For example, describe your neighbor, sister or brother, cousin, aunt or uncle, a friend, boss, or doctor. Write six sentences. Begin three sentences with* **I have a / an** _____. *Begin three sentences with* **My** _____ **is** _____.

    EXAMPLES: I have a generous uncle.
                 My doctor is serious and kind.

C | *GROUPS: Read your sentences to the group.*

EXERCISE 8: Describe Things

A | *Do you know the words? If not, look them up in your dictionary.*

brick	cotton	denim	glass	leather	nylon	paper	wool

B | *PAIRS: Look around your classroom. Describe 10 things by their material or fabric.*

    EXAMPLES: a leather belt, a nylon jacket

C | *Add an adjective to each item in Part B.*

    EXAMPLES: an interesting leather belt, a colorful nylon jacket

D | *Write five sentences using the items in Part B.*

    EXAMPLE: Won Il is wearing an interesting leather belt.

EXERCISE 9: Writing

A | *Write an answer to one of the personal ads on page 268. Use adjectives and noun modifiers. Post your answer on the wall. Read your classmates' answers.*

EXAMPLE:

Dear Am I for You,

I think you are for me. I'm easygoing, and I love jazz bands and walks on the beach.

I'm an artist. I love to read and write and talk. I'm 26 years old. There's one other thing. I love cats. I have six cats. Is that OK? Please email me at catlovers@qol.com.

Sincerely,

You're for Me

B | *Check your work. Use the Editing Checklist.*

Editing Checklist

Did you use . . . ?
- [ ] adjectives and noun modifiers correctly
- [ ] correct spelling

EXERCISE A

Complete the sentences. Write the correct words from the box.

| artistic | fun-loving | honest | personal | spy |

1. She used a _____ ad to find a new friend.

2. I love _____ movies with James Bond.

3. My brother is _____; he paints beautiful pictures.

4. Roberto loves parties; he's a _____ guy.

5. Mei-ling is very _____ and never tells lies.

EXERCISE B

Complete the sentences. Put the words in parentheses in the correct order.

1. Do you have _____?
   (running / new / shoes)

2. Those are _____!
   (sandwiches / chicken / big)

3. That's _____.
   (expensive / suit / an / wool)

4. Dino's is _____.
   (a / restaurant / pizza / popular)

5. They live in _____.
   (apartment / building / a / brick)

EXERCISE C

Correct the personal ad. There are five mistakes.

I'm an smart, lively, 35-year-old woman. I like to cook, and I enjoy longs walks on the beach. I'm not a tennis great player, but I love to play tennis! I'm looking for a educated, man sensitive. Do you have similar interests? Let's get together!

29 Comparative Adjectives
PLANNING A GET-TOGETHER

STEP 1 GRAMMAR IN CONTEXT

Before You Read

PAIRS: Write the names of two types of music. Which is better for listening? Which is better for dancing? Then report to the class.

> **EXAMPLE:**   I think rock is better for listening. . . .

Read

🎧 *Read the conversation.*

KEN: So when's the party?

LAURA: Saturday night about 8:00.

MARTY: How many people are coming? Did you send invitations?

LAURA: Yeah. I've got 15 on the list.

MARTY: What about music? I can bring my rap and heavy metal CDs.

KEN: Get real! We want to dance, right? Rap is bad for dancing, and heavy metal is **worse**. Any other kind of pop music is **better** for dancing.

MI YOUNG: Let's have hip-hop then.

LAURA: OK. My **older** brother has a lot of hip-hop CDs. Now, what about food and snacks?

KEN: How about steak? We can barbecue some steak. And chips are fine for a snack.

MI YOUNG: Let's get pizza. It's **easier** and **quicker than** steak. And it's **cheaper**.

LAURA: OK. What about desserts and beverages?

MI YOUNG: We've got ice cream, and we've got soda and juice.

KEN: What about entertainment? Besides dancing, I mean.

MARTY: How about watching some DVDs?

LAURA: Well . . . I'm tired of them. Games are **more interesting** than DVDs, at a party.

KEN: Hey, I know a really funny new game. It's called, "Who's **faster**? Who's **smarter**? Who's **funnier**?" We can play that.

After You Read

A | **Practice** *GROUPS OF FOUR: Practice the opening conversation.*

B | **Vocabulary** *Listen and repeat the words. Write new words in a notebook.*

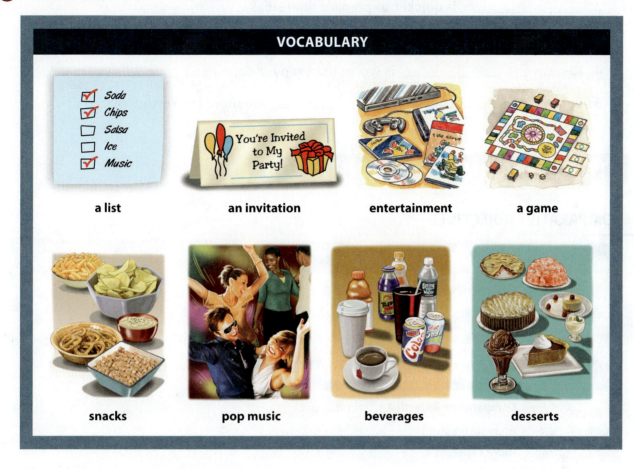

VOCABULARY

a list **an invitation** **entertainment** **a game**

snacks **pop music** **beverages** **desserts**

C | **Vocabulary** *Complete the sentences. Use the correct forms of the vocabulary words.*

1. Rock, rap, hip-hop, and heavy metal are all types of _____*pop music*_____.

2. When you are planning a party, you usually make _____ of the

   people you want to invite.

3. Sometimes you send people _____ to the party.

4. _____ are foods, usually sweet, that people eat after a meal.

5. We usually play that _____ when we get together.

6. Things to drink are called _____.

7. Games, movies, and dancing are all types of _____.

8. _____ are foods that people eat between meals or at parties.

D | Comprehension *Look again at the opening conversation and complete the sentences.*

1. Mi Young thinks _____hip-hop_____ is better for dancing.

2. _____ is quicker to prepare than steak.

3. _____ is more expensive than pizza.

4. Ken says _____ is worse than rap for dancing.

5. Laura thinks that, at a party, _____ are more interesting than DVDs.

STEP 2 GRAMMAR PRESENTATION

COMPARATIVE ADJECTIVES

Comparative Adjectives with *-er*				
		Comparative Adjective	*than*	
The train	is	**quicker**	**than**	the bus.
The bus	is	**cheaper**.		

Comparative Adjectives with *more*				
		Comparative Adjective	*than*	
Movies	are	**more interesting**	**than**	television.
They	're	**more expensive**		too.

GRAMMAR NOTES

1	Use the comparative form of an adjective + *than* to compare **two** people, places, or things. We **can omit** *than* when the context is clear.	• Ken is **taller than** Laura. • Pizza **is quicker than** steak. • It's **cheaper**. (cheaper than steak)
2	To form the comparative of **short (one-syllable)** adjectives, **add -er** to the adjective. If the adjective **ends in -e**, just add **-r**.	YOUNG → YOUNGER • Laura is **younger than** Ken. LARGE → LARGER • New York is **larger than** Chicago.
3	To form the comparative of **two-syllable** adjectives that **end in -y**, change the **y** to **i** and add **-er**.	EASY → EASIER • Pizza is **easier than** steak.

4	To form the comparative of most adjectives of **two or more syllables**, use *more* before the adjective.	CROWDED → MORE CROWDED • New York is **more crowded than** Chicago. INTERESTING → MORE INTERESTING • This book is **more interesting than** that one.
5	The adjectives **good** and **bad** have **irregular** comparative forms.	GOOD → BETTER • Rock is **better than** metal for dancing. BAD → WORSE • Rap is **worse than** metal for dancing.
6	Use **which** to ask about a comparison of things or places. Use **who** to ask about people.	**A: Which** is **better**, rock or rap? **B:** I think rock is **better** (**than** rap). **A: Who**'s **older**, you or your cousin? **B:** I am. I'm 25, and he's 23.

STEP 3 FOCUSED PRACTICE

EXERCISE 1: Discover the Grammar

A | *Look at the opening conversation. Write the adjectives in bold in the correct category.*

Short Adjectives	Adjectives That End in -y	Long Adjectives	Irregular Adjective Forms
			worse

B | *Match the sentence beginnings and endings.*

1. Nuts are a healthier snack ___f___   **a.** the movies than at the supermarket.

2. My shopping list is longer _____   **b.** than pie.

3. Beverages are more expensive at _____   **c.** than yours.

4. Level 1 is easier _____   **d.** than the weather on Tuesday.

5. For dessert, fruit is better _____   **e.** than level 2.

6. The weather on Friday was worse _____   **f.** than candy.

EXERCISE 2: Comparative Adjectives

(Grammar Notes 1–5)

Look at the picture. Compare the people. Use the words in parentheses.

1. (Marty / Ken / tall) <u>*Ken is taller than Marty.*</u>

2. (Marty / Ken / old) _____

3. (Marty's clothes / Ken's clothes / colorful) _____

4. (Mi Young / Laura / short) _____

5. (Mi Young's hair / Laura's hair / dark) _____

6. (Lisa / David / good) _____ at dancing.

7. (Jason / Maia / bad) _____ at singing.

EXERCISE 3: Comparative Adjectives

(Grammar Notes 1–6)

Put the words in the correct order. Make conversations.

1. **A:** worse, / cafeteria food / is / Which / restaurant food / or

    <u>*Which is worse, cafeteria food or restaurant food*</u>_____?

   B: is / worse / cafeteria food / think / I

    _____.

2. **A:** father / you / taller / Are / your / than

    _____?

   B: heavier / he's / but / Yes,

    _____.

3. A: fun / than DVDs / Are / more / games

_____?

B: fun / Yes, games / more / than DVDs / are

_____.

4. A: for a party, / better / is / Which / pop music or jazz

_____?

B: think / pop music / better / I / is

_____.

EXERCISE 4: Editing

There are seven mistakes in the composition. The first mistake is already corrected. Find and correct six more mistakes.

Ben Olson

Dogs Rule

In my opinion, a dog is a ~~gooder~~ *better* pet than a cat. I know because we have a dog and a cat at home. Here are my reasons. First, a dog is friendly than a cat. My dog is more happy to see me when I come home. My cat just doesn't care. Second, a dog is activer. I always take my dog for a walk. I can't do that with my cat. She only wants to sleep. Third, a dog is interesting than a cat. My dog is playfuler than my cat. He knows a lot of tricks. My cat doesn't know any tricks at all. She's boring. Last, a dog is more protectiver than a cat. My dog barks if anyone comes to the house. The cat just runs and hides. I think dogs rule.

EXERCISE 5: Listening

A | *Listen to Ken's conversation with his grandmother. What two new subjects is Ken taking this semester?*

_____

B | *Read the statements. Listen again. Check (✓)* **T (True), F (False),** *or* **NI (No Information).**

	T	F	NI
1. Ken's classes are easier than they were last semester.	☐	☑	☐
2. Ken is taking a Spanish class this semester.	☐	☐	☐
3. Ken is better at music than he is at art.	☐	☐	☐
4. The music teacher is harder than the art teacher.	☐	☐	☐
5. The art teacher's tests are easier than the music teacher's tests.	☐	☐	☐
6. The art teacher gives lower grades than the music teacher.	☐	☐	☐
7. Ken's grandmother thinks he should take the music class.	☐	☐	☐
8. Ken's grandmother is making raspberry cheesecake.	☐	☐	☐

EXERCISE 6: Pronunciation

A | *Read and listen to the Pronunciation Note.*

> **Pronunciation Note**
>
> There are two "th" sounds in English: the voiced sound /ð/ and the voiceless sound /θ/. Voiced means that the vocal cords make a vibration. Voiceless means that the vocal cords do not make a vibration. The "th" sound in **this**, **that**, **these**, and **those** is voiced. The "th" sound in **think**, **tooth**, and **thing** is voiceless.

B | *Listen and repeat the sentences. Circle the voiced **"th"** sounds you hear. Underline the voiceless **"th"** sounds.*

1. I think this path is longer than that one.

2. The weather is better this month than last month.

3. The exercise on page thirty-two is easier than the exercise on page thirty-one.

4. Beth is thinner than my mother.

5. Their brothers are older than our brothers.

6. Let's go to another movie that's more interesting.

7. They're luckier than we are.

8. Kathy's toothache is getting worse, and it's bothering her a lot.

C | *PAIRS: Practice the sentences.*

EXERCISE 7: Compare People and Things

A | *GROUPS OF FOUR: On the chart, write two examples of each topic. Then write the question for that topic. Use the comparative of the adjective given.*

> **EXAMPLE:** algebra, psychology
> Which is harder, algebra or psychology?

Topic / Adjective	Example 1	Number	Example 2	Number
School subject / hard	algebra		psychology	
Actor / funny				
Music / good for dancing				
Activities / interesting				

B | *GROUPS OF FOUR: Take turns asking and answering until everyone has given an opinion on the topic.*

> **EXAMPLE:** **A:** Which is harder, algebra or psychology?
> **B:** I think algebra is harder.

C | *GROUPS OF FOUR: Record the numbers for each opinion. Report your answers to the class.*

> **EXAMPLE:** Three people in our group think algebra is harder than psychology, but one person thinks psychology is harder.

EXERCISE 8: Writing

A | *Write a paragraph (6 to 10 sentences) that compares two people. Use comparative adjectives in your paragraph.*

EXAMPLE: I have two good friends, Tomás and Luís. I like them both very much, but they're very different. Tomás is serious—a lot more serious than Luís. Luís is funnier than Tomás . . .

B | *Check your work. Use the Editing Checklist.*

Editing Checklist

Did you use . . . ?
☐ comparative adjectives correctly
☐ correct spelling

EXERCISE A

Complete the sentences. Use the comparative forms of the words in parentheses.

1. Trains are _____ (fast) than buses.

2. Planes are _____ (expensive) than trains.

3. Apples are _____ (healthy) than donuts.

4. The book was _____ (good) than the movie.

5. My math grades are _____ (bad) than my science grades.

EXERCISE B

On a separate sheet of paper, put the words in the correct order. Make conversations.

1. **A:** Is Miami / hotter / than / Los Angeles

   B: is / hotter / Miami / think / I

2. **A:** than / Are amusement parks / interesting / more / museums

   B: amusement parks / I / are / interesting / think / more

3. **A:** sister / older / your / you / Are / than

   B: taller / she's / but / Yes,

EXERCISE C

Correct the description. There are four mistakes.

I met two interesting men through personal ads—Ken and John. Ken is smarter and funny than John. But John is more richer and more handsome. Ken is more nice, so I think Ken is much good.

Prepositions of Time: *In, On, At*
LEISURE ACTIVITIES

Before You Read

GROUPS OF FOUR: Ask each other, "Where do you expect to be on the weekend? Where do you want to be in 2015?" Then report to the class.

> **EXAMPLE:** I expect to be in Mexico City on the weekend.
> I want to be in college in 2015.

Read

🎧 *Read the conversations.*

TIM: Tim Olson.

FELIX: Hello, Tim! This is Felix Maxa. Do you remember me? We met **in June** on the train to Seattle.

TIM: Felix! Of course! It's great to hear from you. How are you doing?

FELIX: Wonderful. Say, I called to invite you and your wife to our house for a barbecue.

TIM: That sounds like fun. We'd really like that. When is it?

FELIX: **On Saturday**, the 20th, **in the afternoon**.

TIM: I think we're free. But I need to check with Jessica. Can I call you back?

FELIX: Sure.

> (*LATER — phone rings*)

FELIX: Hello?

TIM: Hi, Felix. This is Tim. We're free **on the 20th**. We can come to the barbecue.

FELIX: Great!

TIM: What's the address?

FELIX: We're at 819 40th Avenue. From 45th, turn left on Stone Way and then right on 40th. It's the third house on the right, a light blue two-story.

TIM: OK. What time?

FELIX: We're going to eat about 2:00. Why don't you come **at 1:00**? We can talk for a while.

Tim: Great. Can we bring anything?

Felix: Maybe your sneakers. We're going to play volleyball.

Tim: OK. Thanks a lot. I'm looking forward to it. See you **on Saturday at 1:00**. Bye.

Felix: Good-bye.

After You Read

A | Practice *PAIRS: Practice the opening conversations.*

B | Vocabulary *Listen and repeat the words. Write new words in a notebook.*

VOCABULARY

have a barbecue   **play volleyball**   **go shopping**

go to a play   **a two-story house**

be free = to have open time without anything planned

of course = certainly, naturally

look forward to = to expect to enjoy something

C | Vocabulary *GROUPS: Look at the vocabulary again. What activity do you like the most? What activity do you like the least? Tell the group.*

D | Comprehension *Look again at the opening conversations. Write* **T** *(True)* or **F** *(False).*
Correct the false statements.

    _F_   **1.** Tim met Felix on a ~~plane~~. *train*

    _____   **2.** They met in June.

    _____   **3.** The barbecue is on Saturday evening.

    _____   **4.** Felix and his wife live on 50th Avenue.

    _____   **5.** They live in a house with two floors.

    _____   **6.** They're going to eat at 2:00.

    _____   **7.** They're going to play baseball at the barbecue.

STEP 2 GRAMMAR PRESENTATION

PREPOSITIONS OF TIME: *IN, ON, AT*

In		On		At
in 2012	**in** the afternoon	**on** Saturday	**on** holidays	**at** 2:30 P.M.
in January	**in** the evening	**on** January 20	**on** weekdays	**at** dinnertime
in the morning		**on** weekends	**on** the 10th	**at** night

GRAMMAR NOTES

1	Use *in* with **years**, **months**, and **parts of the day**, and in expressions like *in a few minutes*.	• I was born **in 1988**. • We were in Japan **in August**. • The barbecue is **in the afternoon**. • Can I call you back **in a few minutes**?
	BE CAREFUL! Don't use *in the* with **night**. Use *at*.	• The game is **at night**. Nот: The game is ~~in the~~ night
2	Use *on* with **days of the week** and **dates**, and in expressions like *on weekdays*, *on weekends*, and *on weeknights*.	• The barbecue is **on Saturday**. • It's **on January 21**. • I often go to the movies **on weekends**.
3	Use *at* with **times** and in expressions such as *at night* and *at dinnertime*.	• The party starts **at 7:00 at night**. • We always have good conversations **at dinnertime**.

EXERCISE 1: Discover the Grammar

*Read Tim's email to Jessica. Find and underline all time expressions with **in, on,** and **at.***

Hi Honey, I couldn't reach you on the phone. Do you remember Felix Maxa? I met him on the train in June. Felix called and invited us to a barbecue at their house near the university. The barbecue is on the 20th, at 1:00. I know we're going to a play on Sunday afternoon, but I think we're free on Saturday. Are we free? Please get back to me right away. Love, Tim

EXERCISE 2: *In, On,* and *At*

(Grammar Notes 1–3)

*Complete the conversation with **in, on,** or **at**.*

TIM: This is a nice big meal. Is lunch the biggest meal in Romania?

FELIX: Yes, it is. We don't eat much for dinner.

JESSICA: Are mealtimes the same as here? Do you eat lunch ___*at*___ noon like we do?
1.

DANIELA: No, we usually have lunch later _____ the afternoon—_____ 2:00 or 2:30.
2.   3.

TIM: What about breakfast? I usually have breakfast _____ 6:45 or 7:00. Is it similar in Romania?
4.

FELIX: Well, we usually have breakfast a bit later —_____ 7:30 or so.
5.

JESSICA: So it's a long time between breakfast and lunch. You must get hungry.

DANIELA: Well, people usually have a snack, like a sandwich, _____ the late morning—_____ 11:30 or so.
6.   7.

FELIX: It's different _____ weekends, of course. We get up later.
8.

TIM: I'd like to visit Romania sometime.

DANIELA: Well, Felix and I are going back to Romania _____ a few weeks—on separate flights, unfortunately. But we'll send you a postcard.
9.

EXERCISE 3: *In, On,* and *At*

(Grammar Notes 1–3)

Write questions and answers. Add necessary words.

1. **A:** What time / be / dinner

    What time is dinner _____?

   B: Dinner / be / usually / 7:00 or 7:30

    _____.

2. **A:** What time / people / start work / morning

    _____?

   B: People / usually / start work / 8:00

    _____.

3. **A:** What / people / do / evening

    _____?

   B: They / often / watch TV / evening

    _____.

4. **A:** What / people / do / weekends

    _____?

   B: They / often / go shopping / weekends

    _____.

EXERCISE 4: Editing

There are eight mistakes in the statements. The first mistake is already corrected. Find and correct seven more mistakes.

1. Daniela is leaving Seattle ~~in~~ Monday, January 25, on 12:00 noon.
   on

2. Her flight arrives in Chicago at 6:00 at the evening.

3. Her flight to London leaves at 7:30 in night.

4. Flight 774 arrives in London in 11:30 in the morning.

5. Her flight to Bucharest leaves in 2:00 P.M. in January 26.

6. It arrives in Bucharest at 6:05 at the evening.

EXERCISE 5: Listening

🎧 A | *Listen to the telephone conversation. Where is Felix going on his trip?*

🎧 B | *Listen again. Complete the chart. Use **in**, **on**, or **at**.*

Day, month, and date Felix leaves Seattle	Time first flight leaves Seattle	Time second flight leaves Seattle	Day, month, and date Felix returns to Seattle
on Thursday, January 30th			

EXERCISE 6: Pronunciation

🎧 A | *Read and listen to the Pronunciation Note.*

> **Pronunciation Note**
>
> Two important vowels in English are /æ/, as in the word *hat*, and /ɑ/, as in the word *hot*.
>
> **EXAMPLES:** How do you spell "pat"? /æ/
> How do you spell "pot"? /ɑ/

🎧 B | *Listen to the sentences. Circle the /æ/ sounds. Underline the /ɑ/ sounds.*

1. Saturday, October 30th, is Stan's birthday.

2. Bob has a snack every morning at eleven o'clock.

3. Nancy usually has a sandwich in the early afternoon.

4. The party starts at 6:30 and will be at Robert's house.

5. John and I plan to watch the play after we go shopping.

6. Alice can't be here at 6:00, but Margaret can.

C | *PAIRS: Practice the sentences. Make the /æ/ and /ɑ/ sounds different from each other.*

EXERCISE 7: Ask and Answer

GROUPS OF FOUR: Ask questions. Complete the chart. Then tell the other groups one thing you learned.

EXAMPLE: **A:** What do you never do on Sundays?
                 B: I never study on Sundays.

	You	Student 1	Student 2	Student 3
never / on Sundays				
rarely / in July				
usually / on weekdays				
almost never / in the evening				
almost always / at night				

EXERCISE 8: Writing

A | *Write a short letter (6 to 10 sentences) describing a party. Say what type of party it was, where it was, and when it was. Use **in**, **on**, and **at** in your letter.*

EXAMPLE: Dear Mom and Dad,
                 I had a great birthday party on Saturday, August 17, in the evening. The party started at 6:00. We played volleyball for an hour. At 7:00 we ate pizza and all kinds of desserts. I got some really nice presents . . .

B | *Check your work. Use the Editing Checklist.*

Editing Checklist

Did you use . . . ?
☐ *in*, *on*, and *at* correctly
☐ correct spelling

EXERCISE A

Complete the sentences with **in, on,** or **at.**

1. My birthday is _____ September.

2. What do you usually do _____ weekends?

3. This class starts _____ 9 A.M.

4. They usually do their homework _____ the evening.

5. Our anniversary is _____ Friday.

EXERCISE B

Write questions and answers. Add necessary words.

1. **A:** What / your children / do / afternoon

   _____?

   B: They / often / watch TV / afternoon

   _____.

2. **A:** What time / be / breakfast

   _____?

   B: Breakfast / be / usually / 8:00

   _____.

3. **A:** Where / you / go / holidays

   _____?

   B: We / usually / go to the beach / holidays

   _____.

EXERCISE C

Correct the passage. There are four mistakes.

On weekdays, my life is a little boring. I usually leave the house at 6:00 the morning. I start work at 8:00, and I go home at 6 P.M. On dinnertime, I surf the Internet. Then I make phone calls at the evening. I go to bed at 11:00 at the night.

FUTURE WITH *BE GOING TO*

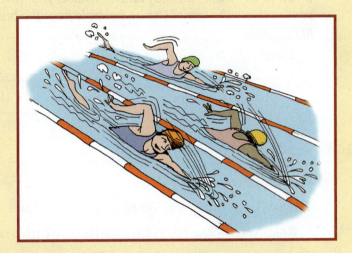

Future with *Be going to*: Statements
SPORTING EVENTS

STEP 1 GRAMMAR IN CONTEXT

Before You Read

GROUPS OF FOUR: Ask each other, "What is your favorite sporting event?" Are any of your answers the same? Use an example from the box or your own example. Then report to the class.

> **EXAMPLE:** My favorite sporting event is the Super Bowl.

> the Olympics   the Super Bowl   the World Cup   the World Series

Read

🎧 *Read the conversation.*

LAURA: Ken, hurry up! We**'re going to be** late!

KEN: What's the hurry? It's just a silly little soccer game!

LAURA: It's not silly, and it's not little. Sam's on the team! It's a big game. I think they**'re going to win**.

KEN: I know. That's what you told me. Is your brother a good player?

LAURA: He's really good.

KEN: Do I need an umbrella?

LAURA: No. It**'s not going to rain** . . . Come on.

(LATER)

LAURA: Can you drive any faster?

KEN: I'm already doing the speed limit. But how come you like soccer so much?

LAURA: It's a great game. A lot of people can play it. You don't have to be a giant.

KEN: But is it a real sport? Take baseball or basketball or football. Those are sports.

LAURA: Soccer is the most popular sport in the world.

KEN: Well, it's not the most popular sport in *my* world.

LAURA: Oh, no! A traffic jam! The game**'s going to start** soon.

KEN: Laura, chill out! We**'re going to make** it on time.

A | Practice *PAIRS: Practice the opening conversation.*

B | Vocabulary *Listen and repeat the words. Write new words in a notebook.*

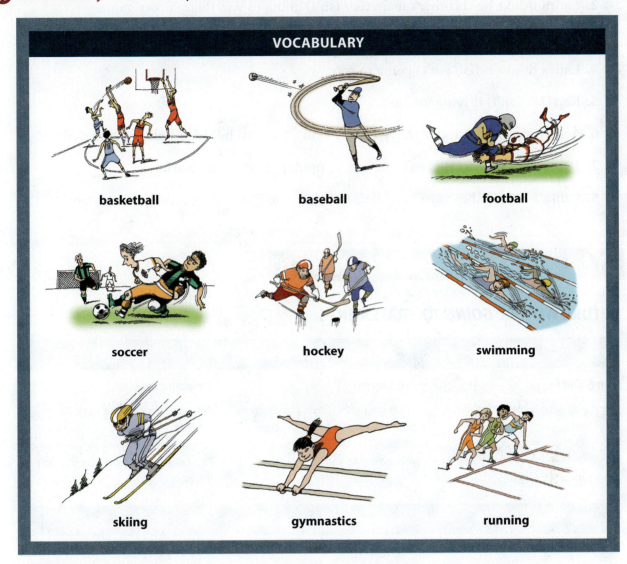

VOCABULARY

basketball

baseball

football

soccer

hockey

swimming

skiing

gymnastics

running

C | Vocabulary *GROUPS: Look at the vocabulary again. Which sport do you like to watch most? Which sport do you like to watch least? Discuss your answers. Rank them 1 (like least) to 9 (like most).*

D | Comprehension *Look again at the opening conversation. Circle the correct answers to complete the sentences.*

1. Ken (**knows /** **doesn't know**) a lot about soccer.

2. Laura thinks her brother's team (**is / isn't**) going to win their soccer game.

3. According to Laura, her brother (**is / isn't**) a good soccer player.

4. Laura thinks it (**is / isn't**) going to rain.

5. Ken (**is / isn't**) driving too fast.

6. According to Laura, you (**have to be / don't have to be**) big to play soccer well.

7. Laura says soccer (**is / isn't**) the most popular sport in the world.

8. Laura is afraid they (**are / are not**) going to make it to the soccer game on time.

STEP 2 GRAMMAR PRESENTATION

FUTURE WITH *BE GOING TO*: STATEMENTS

Affirmative Statements		
am going to	*is going to*	*are going to*
I **am going to have** a party next weekend.	He **is going to graduate** in June. She **is going to be** an Olympic athlete. It **is going to rain** today.	We **are going to see** a movie tonight. You **are going to enjoy** this party. They **are going to bring** pizza to the party.

Negative Statements		
am not going to	*is not going to*	*are not going to*
I **am not going to drive** fast. I'**m not going to drive** fast.	It **is not going to rain**. It'**s not going to rain**. It **isn't going to rain**.	We **are not going to be** late. We'**re not going to be** late. We **aren't going to be** late.

Future Time Expressions		
this afternoon	*tonight*	*tomorrow*
He's going to study **this afternoon**.	He's going to play soccer **tonight**.	He's going to visit his parents **tomorrow**.

GRAMMAR NOTES

1	We can use **be going to** to talk about the **future**.	• We**'re going to be** late. • It**'s going to rain**.
2	To form the future with *be going to*, use **am**, **is**, or **are** + **going to** + the **base form** of the verb.	• They **are going to win**.
3	To make a **negative sentence**, place **not** before **going to**.	• They **are not going to lose**. • It **is not going to snow**.
4	Use **contractions** in conversation and informal writing.	• The game**'s going to start** soon. • It **isn't going to rain**. Don't worry.

REFERENCE NOTE
For **yes / no questions** and **wh- questions** with **be going to**, see Unit 32.

STEP 3 FOCUSED PRACTICE

EXERCISE 1: Discover the Grammar

Underline the examples of **be going to** *+ base form used to make sentences about the future. Then match the questions and answers.*

__e__ **1.** Josh, do I need my heavy coat?

_____ **2.** Dad, what are we going to do tonight?

_____ **3.** Mom, where's Dad going?

_____ **4.** Do you think Mark and Kathy are going to get married?

_____ **5.** What's going to happen next June?

_____ **6.** Does Jason do gymnastics?

a. Yes. Actually, he's going to be in a competition tonight.

b. Probably. They're a great couple.

c. Judy's going to graduate.

d. He and Ben are going to swim for an hour or so at the pool.

e. Yes. It's going to snow. It's a football game, and it's December.

f. We're going to go to the hockey game.

EXERCISE 2: *Be going to*

(Grammar Notes 1–2)

Complete the sentences. Use the correct forms of **be going to** and the verbs in parentheses.

It's Saturday. Annie Olson is on a baseball team. Her team _____*is going to play*_____

                                                1. (play)

this afternoon. The weather _____ warm. Everybody in the

                               2. (be)

family _____ the game. Ben _____ four

      3. (attend)   **4. (invite)**

friends, and Jeremy _____ his girlfriend. Tim and Jessica

                   5. (take)

_____ the game. Mary and Bill Beck _____

      6. (film)   **7. (bring)**

their friends. Everyone thinks Annie's team _____—everyone except

                             8. (win)

Annie. She doesn't think she _____ very well.

                    9. (play)

EXERCISE 3: *Be going to*

(Grammar Notes 1–3)

Look at the pictures. Complete the sentences. Use the correct forms of **be going to** and the verbs in parentheses. Use the affirmative or negative.

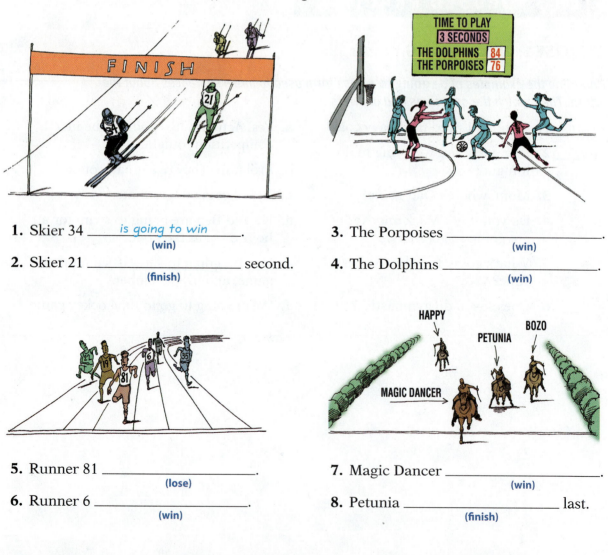

1. Skier 34 _____*is going to win*_____.
            (win)

2. Skier 21 _____ second.
            (finish)

3. The Porpoises _____.
                    (win)

4. The Dolphins _____.
                    (win)

5. Runner 81 _____.
             (lose)

6. Runner 6 _____.
            (win)

7. Magic Dancer _____.
                  (win)

8. Petunia _____ last.
            (finish)

EXERCISE 4: Editing

There are six mistakes in the note. The first mistake is already corrected. Find and correct five more mistakes.

> Dear Kathy,
>
> I hope you're going to be in town Sunday evening. Josh and I are have
> a little party to watch the big game on TV. We are going have pizza and
> dessert. We be going to start the meal about 5:00. I think the game are
> going to start at 6:00. Please come if you can. But can you let us know?
> We going to be out of town until Tuesday. Call after that, OK?
>
> Amanda

STEP 4 COMMUNICATION PRACTICE

EXERCISE 5: Listening

 **A** | *Listen to the conversation. Does Sam's team win or lose their soccer game?*

B | *Read the sentences. Listen to the conversation. Then listen again. Check (✓) T (True), F (False), or NI (No Information).*

	T	F	NI
1. Ken thinks the game is boring.	☐	☑	☐
2. Ken thinks it's going to rain.	☐	☐	☐
3. Laura thinks it's going to rain.	☐	☐	☐
4. The score is 2–1.	☐	☐	☐
5. Laura thinks Sam's team is going to win.	☐	☐	☐
6. Laura has another brother besides Sam.	☐	☐	☐
7. Sam kicks a goal.	☐	☐	☐
8. Ken wants to go to another game sometime.	☐	☐	☐

EXERCISE 6: Pronunciation

A | *Read and listen to the conversations. Circle **going to** when it is pronounced "gonna." Underline **going to** when it is pronounced "going to."*

1. **A:** I think it's going to rain.

   B: I don't think so.

   A: It is going to rain. Believe me!

2. **A:** My team is going to win the game.

   B: No, it isn't.

   A: Yes, it is. It's going to win.

3. **A:** The traffic is terrible. We're not going to make it on time.

   B: Don't worry. We're going to make it. We still have 20 minutes.

4. **A:** I don't think I'm going to pass this course.

   B: Of course you're going to pass it! Stop worrying.

B | *PAIRS: Practice the sentences. Use both pronunciations of **going to**.*

EXERCISE 7: Memory Game: I'm Going to Take . . .

GROUPS: Your group is going to take a trip to the next Olympics. Each person says one thing he or she is going to take on the trip. The next person says what the first speaker is going to take and adds what he or she is going to take. The person who can remember everything is the winner.

> **EXAMPLE:**   **Elena:** I'm going to take my binoculars.
> **Ahmed:** Elena is going to take her binoculars. I'm going to take my camcorder.
> **Anna:** Elena is going to take her binoculars. Ahmed is going to take his camcorder. I'm going to take my camera . . .

EXERCISE 8: Writing

A *Write a paragraph (6 to 10 sentences) about something you are going to do in the future. Choose a topic from the box or choose your own topic.*

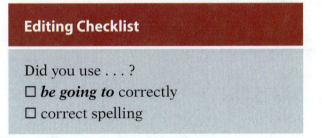

> **attend a sporting event**   **join a sports team   run for 30 minutes every day**
>
> **graduate from high school/college   run a marathon**

> **EXAMPLE:**   My friend and I are going to attend the next Summer Olympics. We're going to fly there from Chicago. Before the Olympics, we're going to spend a week in Chicago. We're going to visit . . .

B *Check your work. Use the Editing Checklist.*

Editing Checklist

Did you use . . . ?
☐ ***be going to*** correctly
☐ correct spelling

Check your answers on page UR-5.

Do you need to review anything?

EXERCISE A

Complete the sentences. Use the correct form of **be going to** *and the verbs in parentheses. Use contractions.*

1. I _____ (not, study) this weekend.

2. I think the Lakers _____ (win).

3. It _____ (snow) tonight.

4. We _____ (not, drive) in the snow.

5. You _____ (love) this restaurant.

EXERCISE B

Put the words in the correct order. Make sentences.

1. _____.
   (are / going to / They / win)

2. _____.
   (We / going to / late / be / are)

3. _____.
   (rain / is / not / It / going to)

4. _____.
   (going to / soon / game / is / The / start)

5. _____.
   (get / there / We / on time / going to / are)

EXERCISE C

Correct Kathy's note. There are five mistakes.

> Dear Amanda,
>
> Thanks for your note! I am going be in town Sunday evening. I'd love to come to your party, but some friends and I are going go out for dinner. Their son going to graduate, and is it probably going to be a long evening. I not am going to get to your house by 5:00. Can I come over at around 9:00? Or is that too late?
>
> Kathy

UNIT 32

Future with *Be going to*: Questions
CAREER PLANS AND GOALS

STEP 1 GRAMMAR IN CONTEXT

Before You Read

PAIRS: Talk about your job goals.

What are you going to do? Where are you going to work? Are you going to help people? Are you going to try to make a lot of money?

Tell the class one of your partner's work goals.

EXAMPLE: Julio loves to fly. He's going to be a pilot.

Read

Read the conversation.

TIM: How was your day?

JESSICA: Actually, I had an interesting call.

TIM: Oh?

JESSICA: You know Dan Evans, the TV producer?

TIM: Sure I do.

JESSICA: Well, he has an idea for a news program.

TIM: Really?

JESSICA: Uh-huh. It's going to be on national TV, and he wants me to be in it.

JEREMY: Awesome! **Are you going to have** a big part?

JESSICA: As a matter of fact, yes. I'm going to be the star.

JEREMY: That's so cool. **When are you going to begin**?

JESSICA: Not for a while.

TIM: **Are you going to travel** a lot?

JESSICA: I think so.

ANNIE: Don't take it, Mom. I don't want you to travel. I want you to stay home.

BEN: Yeah. You always help me with homework. **Who's going to help** me with my homework? **How are you going to take** me to soccer practice?

TIM: Hey, guys. I'm still going to be here.

JESSICA: Anyway, kids, this is all very new. The show isn't going to air for a long time.

Future with *Be going to*: Questions **307**

A | Practice GROUPS OF FIVE: Practice the opening conversation.

B | Vocabulary Listen and repeat the words. Write new words in a notebook.

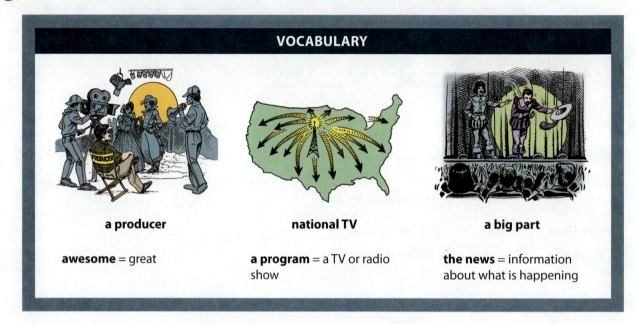

VOCABULARY

a producer

national TV

a big part

awesome = great

a program = a TV or radio show

the news = information about what is happening

C | Vocabulary Complete the sentences. Use the correct vocabulary words.

1. Is _____the news_____ on Channel 2? I want to find out what's happening.

2. George Clooney has _____ in *Oceans 13*.

3. Oprah Winfrey was _____ of the movie *Precious*.

4. You can only see that TV show here. It's not on _____.

5. That movie was _____. Everyone loved it.

6. There's _____ on Channel 4 that's interesting. It's called *How to Find a Great Job*.

D | Comprehension Look again at the opening conversation. Correct the mistakes.

1. Dan Evans is a ~~movie~~ *TV* producer. He has an idea for a new program.

2. It's going to start right away.

3. The producer wants Jessica to have a small part in it.

4. Jeremy is unhappy about Jessica's new job.

5. Tim asks, "Are you going to make a lot of money?"

6. Ben asks, "How are you going to cook for us?"

FUTURE WITH *BE GOING TO*: QUESTIONS

Yes / No Questions	Short Answers	
Am I going to get the job?	Yes, **you are.**	No, **you're not.** OR No, **you aren't.**
Is the program going start soon?	Yes, **it is.**	No, **it's not.** OR No, **it isn't.**
Are we going to move?	Yes, **we are.**	No, **we're not.** OR No, **we aren't.**

Wh- Questions	Short Answers
When are you going to start?	Next Monday.
How are you going to get there?	By bus.
Who is going to help us?	I am.

GRAMMAR NOTES

1	For *yes / no questions* with *be going to*, put *am*, *is*, or *are* **before the subject.**	• **Am I** going to have a part in your show? • **Is he** going to change jobs? • **Are they** going to buy a house?
2	We usually use **contractions** in negative short answers.	**A:** Is he going to change jobs? **B:** No, he**'s not.** OR No, he **isn't.**
3	For a *wh-* question with *be going to*, use the *wh-* **word** + the correct form of *be* + a **subject** + *going to* + the **base form** of the verb.	**A: When is it going to begin**? **B:** Next year.
4	For a *wh-* question about the subject, use *who* or *what* + *is* + *going to* + the **base form** of the verb.	**A: Who is going to be** the producer? **B:** Dan Evans is.

EXERCISE 1: Discover the Grammar

Circle the main verb in each question. Then match the questions and answers.

_____ **1.** What are you going to do?

_____ **2.** When am I going to begin?

_____ **3.** Is she going to travel a lot?

_____ **4.** How are you going to get to work?

a. By bus.

b. I'm going to be the assistant director.

c. You are going to start on May 1.

d. Yes, she is.

EXERCISE 2: *Be going to*

(Grammar Notes 1–2)

Complete the conversations. Use the simple past, the simple present, the present progressive, or **be going to** *for the future. Use the correct forms of the verbs in parentheses.*

1. (rain)

    TIM: It _____*rained*_____ yesterday. It_*'s raining*_____ now.

    _____*Is*_____ it _____*going to rain*_____ tomorrow?

    JESSICA: I'm afraid so. That's what the weather channel says.

2. (work)

    JESSICA: You _____ late now. You _____ late last

    night. _____ you _____ late tomorrow

    night too?

    TIM: Yes, I am. This is always a busy time at work.

3. (have)

    JEREMY: I'm tired of tofu. We _____ tofu last night. We

    _____ tofu now. _____ we

    _____ tofu tomorrow?

    TIM: No, we're not. Tomorrow we _____ veggie burgers.

4. (wear)

    JESSICA: I know you like that sweater, but you always _____ it. You

    _____ it every day last week. You _____ it

    now. _____ you _____ it tomorrow?

    JEREMY: Probably. Michelle likes the color.

    JESSICA: Oh.

5. (watch)

    TIM: You _____ that news program at 5:00. Why

    _____ you _____ it again now?

    JESSICA: It's awesome. I _____ it again tonight at 11:00. I can learn

    from the show.

EXERCISE 3: *Be going to*

(Grammar Notes 1, 3–4)

Write **yes / no** *questions. Use the correct forms of* **be going to** *and the words in parentheses.*

A. Jessica's thoughts about the new job:

1. (I / get the job) *Am I going to get the job* _____ ?

2. (it / mean a lot of work) _____ ?

3. (I / really have a big part) _____ ?

4. (the children / be OK) _____ ?

5. (Tim / spend more time at home) _____ ?

B. Tim's thoughts about the new job:

6. (How often /Jessica / be away from home) _____ ?

7. (When / we / have time together) _____ ?

8. (When / the show/ begin) _____ ?

9. (Who / help when I'm away on business) _____ ?

10. (What / Jessica's new job / do to our marriage) _____ ?

EXERCISE 4: Editing

There are six mistakes in the phone messages. The first mistake is already corrected.
Find and correct five more mistakes.

1. Hi, Jessica. This is Maria. Are you going ~~being~~ *to be* in San Francisco for the conference?

   I need to know. Please call me at 555-8878.

2. Hi, honey. I forgot my date book. Is Fred and Janet going to meet us at 8:00 or 8:30?

   Please call.

3. This message is for Jessica Olson. This is George Selig. When is the conference going

   start?

4. Hi Mom. I'm not going to be home until 9:00. Al and I am going to study together.

5. Hi, Jessica. This is Meg Smith. What time the meeting going to be? Please call me at

   989-555-0007.

6. Hi, Jess. This is Dan. Watch the news tonight at 6:00 on Channel 2. I going to be on it.

EXERCISE 5: Listening

A | *Josh gets a phone call from Amanda. Listen to their conversation. What does Amanda tell Josh? Check (✓) the correct answer.*

_____ **a.** Their parents are going to visit in July.

_____ **b.** They're going to be parents next July.

B | *Now listen to a conversation between Josh and Jason. Circle the correct letter.*

1. Are Josh and Amanda going to move in July?

   a. Yes, they are.   **b.** No, they aren't.

2. When are they going to buy a new house?

   a. In a few years.   **b.** In a couple of months.

3. How long is Amanda going to stay home with the baby?

   a. Three weeks.   **b.** Three months.

4. Who's going to watch the baby when Amanda goes back to work?

   a. Amanda's mother.   **b.** Josh's mother.

C | *Listen again to the conversation between Josh and Jason. What is Josh's question at the end of the conversation?*

Are _____?

EXERCISE 6: Pronunciation

A | *Read and listen to the Pronunciation Note.*

> **Pronunciation Note**
>
> The sounds **/b/** and **/v/** are voiced consonants. You can feel your throat vibrate when you say them.

B | *Listen to each word. Circle the sound of the first letter you hear.*

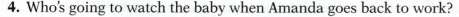

1. (/b/) /p/   **3.** /f/ /v/   **5.** /b/ /p/   **7.** /f/ /v/

2. /b/ /p/   **4.** /f/ /v/   **6.** /b/ /p/   **8.** /f/ /v/

C | Underline the words that begin with the letters **p, b, f,** and **v.** Then listen to the sentences.

1. Is the new <u>program</u> <u>better</u> than the old one?

2. Who is going to be the producer?

3. Are you going to have a big part?

4. Is Tim going to get a part-time job at a bank?

5. Is Jessica going to be very famous?

6. Where is the party going to be?

7. Are they going to buy furniture for the baby?

D | Put your hand on your throat. Repeat each sentence. Notice the voiced sounds.

EXERCISE 7: What Are They Going to Do?

PAIRS: Look at the picture. Write as many questions as you can with **be going to.** *The pair with the most correct questions wins. Ask the class your questions.*

EXERCISE 8: Writing

A | Your friend got a job. Write an email and ask your friend a few questions about the job. Use **be going to** for the future. Underline your examples.

EXAMPLE: Congratulations on getting a job at Goodbuys. When are you going to begin? Are you going to work evenings?

B | Check your work. Use the Editing Checklist.

Editing Checklist
Did you use . . . ?
☐ **be going to** for the future correctly
☐ correct spelling

Check your answers on page UR-5.

Do you need to review anything?

EXERCISE A

Match the questions and answers.

_____ **1.** Is Josh going to be a father?

_____ **2.** Are Josh and Amanda going to move right away?

_____ **3.** Is it going to cost a lot to raise a child?

_____ **4.** Is Amanda's mom going to watch the baby?

_____ **5.** Are you going to help Amanda's mom?

a. Yes, she is.

b. Yes, he is.

c. No, I'm not.

d. No, they're not.

e. Yes, it is.

EXERCISE B

*Complete the questions about a soccer game. Use the correct forms of **be going to** and the verbs in parentheses.*

1. Where _____ the soccer game _____ (be)?

2. When _____ it _____ (start)?

3. How _____ you _____ (get) there?

4. Who _____ you _____ (go) with?

EXERCISE C

Correct the phone messages. There are six mistakes.

1. Hi Karen. This is Pietro. I'm not to going be in the office until 12:00. Bruce and I am going to review the news program.

2. Hi, Debbie. This is Amy. Are you going be in Boston tomorrow? Please call me.

3. This message is for Bill. This is Mark. When the conference is going to start?

4. Hi, Katie. This is Pam. My calendar isn't working. Is John and Oliva going to have a meeting in the conference room or the library? Let me know.

5. Hi, Linda. This is Paula. What time the meeting going to be? Please email me.

FROM GRAMMAR TO WRITING

Write a Description

1 | *Take a photograph or draw a picture of your favorite room in your home. Write about five things. Say something about each thing. Use* **this is /these are** *with singular and plural nouns. Follow the model.*

MODEL

This is an armchair. It's soft. It's my favorite chair. It's in my living room. These are my lamps. They're from my parents. They're beautiful.

2 | *Exchange papers with a partner. Did your partner follow directions and the model? Correct any mistakes in grammar and spelling.*

3 | *Talk to your partner. Discuss the mistakes you made. Then rewrite your own paper and make any necessary changes.*

Write Questions

1 | *Email a friend. Ask your friend four questions about his or her English class. Choose from the question words in the box. Follow the model.*

Are	Is	What	Where	Who

MODEL

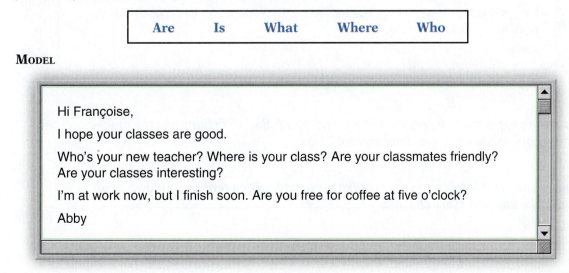

Hi Françoise,

I hope your classes are good.

Who's your new teacher? Where is your class? Are your classmates friendly? Are your classes interesting?

I'm at work now, but I finish soon. Are you free for coffee at five o'clock?

Abby

2 | *Exchange papers with a partner. Did your partner follow directions and the model? Correct any mistakes in grammar and spelling.*

3 | *Talk to your partner. Discuss the mistakes you made. Then rewrite your own paper and make any necessary changes.*

PART III	USING THE PAST OF *Be*: *Wh-* QUESTIONS

Write an Email

1 | *Write an email to a friend about his or her vacation. Choose from the question words in the box. Follow the model.*

How	Was	Were	What	Where	Who

MODEL

To: Sara Pujols
From: Alicia Serrano
Re: Your vacation
Date: July 14

Sara,

How was your vacation in Europe? I hope it was really exciting.

I know you were in Britain, but where were you exactly? How was the weather? It was sunny and hot last summer.

What other countries were you in? How was the flight to Europe?

Let's get together soon. I'm free next week. Are you free for lunch or dinner? I want to hear all about your trip.

Alicia

2 | *Exchange papers with a partner. Did your partner follow directions and the model? Correct any mistakes in grammar and spelling.*

3 | *Talk to your partner. Discuss the mistakes you made. Then rewrite your own paper and make any necessary changes.*

1 Email a friend. Give directions from your school to a party at Bella Vista Restaurant. First, look at the map. Your school is on Pine Street between First and Second Streets. The party is at Bella Vista Restaurant. Bella Vista Restaurant is on Fourth Street between Pine and Maple Streets. Draw a line from your school to the restaurant. Then write your email. Follow the model.

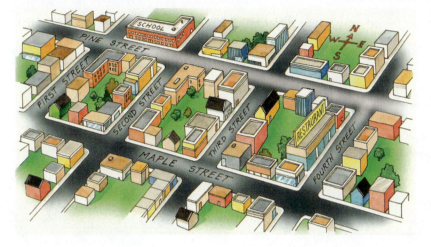

MODEL

Bill's school is on Maple Street between Fourth and Fifth Streets. The party is at Star Restaurant. Star Restaurant is on Maple Street between Fifth and Sixth Streets.

Dear Joe,

I'm glad you can come to my party.

Here are the directions from school.

Walk one block east. The party is at Star Restaurant. It's on Maple Street between Fifth and Sixth Streets.

See you Saturday at eight o'clock.

Bill

2 | *Exchange papers with a partner. Did your partner follow directions and the model? Correct any mistakes in grammar and spelling.*

3 | *Talk to your partner. Discuss the mistakes you made. Then rewrite your own paper and make any necessary changes.*

PART V   USING THE SIMPLE PRESENT: QUESTIONS AND ANSWERS

Write a Letter

1 | *You and a good friend now live in different cities. Answer your friend's letter. Follow the model.*

> Dear _____,
>
>   I often think about you. How is everything in _____?
> Are you busy? What are your days like? What do you do at your job?
> What do you usually do on weekends? Do you ever ski?
>
>   Please write soon.
>
>   _____

MODEL

> Dear Mei-Ling,
>
>   It was great to hear from you.
>   My life here is really different. Sometimes it's busy and exciting. Sometimes it's lonely. It's hard to speak a second language all the time.
>   I enjoy my job. I'm a graphic artist for a small publisher. I love to design CD and book covers, but I don't love to work on very long books.
>   I start work at 9:00 and finish at 5:00. I take the train to work. My co-workers are friendly and helpful, but I don't have any good friends yet.
>   In the evenings I usually watch videos or read. On weekends I go to the movies. I still love movies. I don't ski here. It's too expensive.
>   What about you? Do you still go to the museums? I miss that. I also miss our skiing trips.
>   Please write soon and tell me about yourself. Maybe you can visit me this summer.
>
> Cheers,
> Alfredo

2 | *Exchange papers with a partner. Did your partner follow directions and the model? Correct any mistakes in grammar and spelling.*

3 | *Talk to your partner. Discuss the mistakes you made. Then rewrite your own paper and make any necessary changes.*

Write a Description

1 | *Bring in a photo with four or more people in it. Answer the questions.*

Where are the people? _____

Who are the people? _____

Person A: _____

Person B: _____

Person C: _____

Person D: _____

What are they doing? _____

2 | *Describe the photo. Follow the model.*

MODEL

A Train Station in Italy

    This is a photo of people at a train station in Italy. On the left, a young man is looking up at a sign. It shows train departures. Behind him, several people are standing at a snack bar. In the center of the picture, three young men are waiting for a train. One is wearing a red shirt and shorts. The young man sitting next to him is also wearing shorts. He is looking to the right. Their backpacks are sitting on the station floor. Everyone is enjoying the warm weather.

---

3 | *Exchange papers with a partner. Did your partner follow directions and the model? Correct any mistakes in grammar and spelling.*

4 | *Talk to your partner. Discuss the mistakes you made. Then rewrite your own paper and make any necessary changes.*

1 | *You and a friend are planning to go to a movie. Email your friend and say when you can and can't go and what you want to see. Use* **can, can't, let's,** *and* **the** *in your email. Follow the model.*

Before you write: Fill out the chart.

	Example	**You**
Can't go	Any time on Saturday	
Can go	Sunday afternoon or evening	
Don't want to see	*Twilight*	
Want to see	*Avatar*	
Meet at	3:15 or 6:45	

MODEL

To: Rosa Gonzales
From: Elena Correia
Re: Movie

Rosa,

    Thanks for the movie invitation. Sure, I'd like to go to a movie. I can't go on Saturday, but I can go on Sunday, either in the afternoon or evening. I saw the movie with Penelope Cruz last week, so I don't want to see it again so soon. How about the new Johnny Depp film? Do you want to see that? If you do, let's meet in front of the theater. It starts at 3:30 and 7:00. Let me know which time is good for you.

Elena

2 | *Exchange papers with a partner. Did your partner follow directions and the model? Correct any mistakes in grammar and spelling.*

3 | *Talk to your partner. Discuss the mistakes you made. Then rewrite your own paper and make any necessary changes.*

PART VIII USING THE SIMPLE PAST

Write a Letter

1 | *You are on vacation. Write a letter to your parents or to a friend. Talk about your vacation. Use regular and irregular simple past verb forms in your letter.*

Before you write: Note things that you did in the box.

Example	You
Arrived at 10:00 P.M.	
Took a taxi to the hotel	
Spent the day at the beach	
Swam in the Caribbean	
Got a sunburn	
Went to a folk festival	
Ate at a great restaurant; had delicious seafood	
Went shopping	

MODEL

Dear Mom and Dad,

Greetings from Jamaica! It's beautiful here. The weather is warm and sunny.

Mary and I arrived on Tuesday evening at about 10:00 P.M. It was very late, so we took a taxi to the hotel. Our room is small but comfortable.

On Wednesday we spent the day at the beach. We both swam in the Caribbean. I got a sunburn.

On Wednesday evening we went to a folk festival. It was fun and interesting. There were some good singers.

On Thursday we went shopping in Kingston. I bought you both something nice. In the evening we ate at a restaurant. I had some delicious seafood.

I'll write again soon.

Love,

Amy

2 | Exchange papers with a partner. Did your partner follow directions and the model? Correct any mistakes in grammar and spelling.

3 | Talk to your partner. Discuss the mistakes you made. Then rewrite your own paper and make any necessary changes.

PART IX   USING QUANTITY EXPRESSIONS AND *There is / There are*

Write an Email

1 | You and a friend are preparing for a picnic. Write an email to your friend. Say what you have and don't have. Ask your friend what he or she can bring. Use quantifiers and **there is / there are**. Follow the model.

Before you write: Complete the chart. Say what you have and what you need.

Have	Need

MODEL

To: Skip Kulle
From: Dilvin Ertoglu
Re: Our picnic

Hi, Skip,

    Let's have the picnic at Washington Park. There are a lot of picnic tables. There's a volleyball net. There's also a nice swimming pool, so people can play volleyball or go swimming.

    I have enough hamburgers for 12 people, but I don't have any hot dogs. Can you bring three packages of them? And can you also bring three packages of hot dog buns? I have several quarts of juice, but I don't have any other drinks. Can you bring about four big bottles of soda? Oh, one more thing: I'll bring a large salad. Can you bring something for dessert, maybe some cookies? Or maybe a couple of pies or some fruit?

    Let me know if this is OK. See you soon.
Dilvin

2 | *Exchange papers with a partner. Did your partner follow directions and the model? Correct any mistakes in grammar and spelling.*

3 | *Talk to your partner. Discuss the mistakes you made. Then rewrite your own paper and make any necessary changes.*

| **PART X** | USING COMPARATIVE ADJECTIVES |

Write a Comparison

1 | *Write a comparison of two places you know well. Say how they are similar and how they are different. Follow the model.*

Before you write: Draw two circles like these. In one circle, put the name of one place and write adjectives describing that place. In the other circle, put the name of the other place and write adjectives describing that place. In the middle, write adjectives showing how the two places are similar.

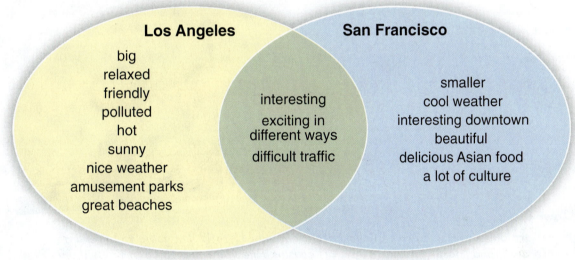

Los Angeles

big
relaxed
friendly
polluted
hot
sunny
nice weather
amusement parks
great beaches

interesting
exciting in
different ways
difficult traffic

San Francisco

smaller
cool weather
interesting downtown
beautiful
delicious Asian food
a lot of culture

MODEL

Los Angeles and San Francisco are two of my favorite cities. They're different in many ways. Los Angeles is a lot bigger than San Francisco, and it's friendlier and more relaxed. It has great amusement parks and beaches. The weather is nicer than the weather in San Francisco. It's hotter and sunnier. But it's also more polluted. San Francisco is cooler. It's more beautiful than Los Angeles. It's more exciting too. It has an interesting downtown and a lot of culture. There's a lot of good food in San Francisco, especially Asian food.

San Francisco and Los Angeles are similar in some ways. They're both very nice, and they're both interesting in their own ways. It's hard to drive in both places because there's so much traffic. But it's worse in Los Angeles.

I like both cities a lot, but I love the weather, the beaches, and the amusement parks in Los Angeles. For me it's a better place.

2 | *Exchange papers with a partner. Did your partner follow directions and the model? Correct any mistakes in grammar and spelling.*

3 | *Talk to your partner. Discuss the mistakes you made. Then rewrite your own paper and make any necessary changes.*

1 | You are going to be in a friend's city next month. Write a note to your friend. Ask if you can get together. Use the future with **be going to** in your note. Follow the model.

Before you write: Complete the chart.

	Example	You
Who	You and your husband	
Where	Toronto, Ontario	
When	July 15 to 19	
Why	Attend a conference; visit cousins	
Free on	Tuesday, July 16, and Thursday, July 18, evenings	

MODEL

Dear Emiko,

   Mark and I are going to be in Toronto from July 15 to 19. I'm going to attend a conference, and Mark is going to visit his cousins. Are you going to be in town then? If you are, can we get together? We're free on Tuesday, July 16, and Thursday, July 18, in the evening. We're going to stay at the Best Eastern Hotel downtown. Is that near you?

   Please let me know. I hope we can get together and see each other.

Cheers,

Gina

2 | Exchange papers with a partner. Did your partner follow directions and the model? Correct any mistakes in grammar and spelling.

3 | Talk to your partner. Discuss the mistakes you made. Then rewrite your own paper and make any necessary changes.

APPENDICES

1 Numbers, Temperature, Days, Months, Seasons, Titles

CARDINAL NUMBERS

1 = one	11 = eleven	21 = twenty-one
2 = two	12 = twelve	30 = thirty
3 = three	13 = thirteen	40 = forty
4 = four	14 = fourteen	50 = fifty
5 = five	15 = fifteen	60 = sixty
6 = six	16 = sixteen	70 = seventy
7 = seven	17 = seventeen	80 = eighty
8 = eight	18 = eighteen	90 = ninety
9 = nine	19 = nineteen	100 = one hundred
10 = ten	20 = twenty	101 = one hundred and one
		200 = two hundred
		1,000 = one thousand
		1,000,000 = one million
		10,000,000 = ten million

EXAMPLES

That book has **eighty-nine** pages.
There are **thirty** days in September.
There are **five** rows in the room.
She is **eleven** years old.
He has **three** children.

ORDINAL NUMBERS

1st = first	11th = eleventh	21st = twenty-first
2nd = second	12th = twelfth	30th = thirtieth
3rd = third	13th = thirteenth	40th = fortieth
4th = fourth	14th = fourteenth	50th = fiftieth
5th = fifth	15th = fifteenth	60th = sixtieth
6th = sixth	16th = sixteenth	70th = seventieth
7th = seventh	17th = seventeenth	80th = eightieth
8th = eighth	18th = eighteenth	90th = ninetieth
9th = ninth	19th = nineteenth	100th = one hundredth
10th = tenth	20th = twentieth	101st = one hundred and first
		200th = two hundredth
		1,000th = one thousandth
		1,000,000th = one millionth
		10,000,000th = ten millionth

EXAMPLES

It's his **fifty-first** birthday.
It's September **thirtieth**.
He's in the **fourth** row.
It's her **eleventh** birthday.
Jeremy is their **first** child.
Annie is their **second** child.
Ben is their **third** child.

TEMPERATURE

We measure the temperature in degrees (°).

Changing from degrees Fahrenheit to degrees Celsius:

$$(°F - 32) \times 5/9 = °C$$

Changing from degrees Celsius to degrees Fahrenheit:

$$(9/5 \times °C) + 32 = °F$$

DAYS OF THE WEEK

Weekdays	Weekend
Monday	Saturday
Tuesday	Sunday
Wednesday	
Thursday	
Friday	

MONTHS OF THE YEAR

MONTH	ABBREVIATION	NUMBER OF DAYS
January	Jan.	31
February	Feb.	28*
March	Mar.	31
April	Apr.	30
May	May	31
June	Jun.	30
July	Jul.	31
August	Aug.	31
September	Sept.	30
October	Oct.	31
November	Nov.	30
December	Dec.	31

*February has 29 days in a leap year, every four years.

(continued on next page)

THE SEASONS	TITLES
NORTHERN HEMISPHERE Spring: March 21–June 20 Summer: June 21–September 20 Autumn or Fall: September 21–December 20 Winter: December 21–March 20 **SOUTHERN HEMISPHERE** Spring: September 21–December 20 Summer: December 21–March 20 Autumn or Fall: March 21–June 20 Winter: June 21–September 20	**Mr. (Mister)** / mɪstər / unmarried or married man **Ms.** / mɪz / unmarried or married woman **Miss** / mɪs / unmarried woman **Mrs.** / mɪsɪz / married woman **Dr. (Doctor)** / dɑktər / doctor (medical doctor or Ph.D.)

2   Time

It's one o'clock.
(It's 1:00.)

It's five after one.
(It's 1:05.)

It's one-ten.
It's ten after one.
(It's 1:10.)

It's one-fifteen.
It's a quarter after one.
(It's 1:15.)

It's one twenty-five.
It's twenty-five after one.
(It's 1:25.)

It's one-thirty.
It's half past one.
(It's 1:30.)

It's one forty-five.
It's a quarter to two.
(It's 1:45.)

It's one-fifty.
It's ten to two.
(It's 1:50.)

TALKING ABOUT TIME

1	You can talk about time this way:	**A:** **What time is it?** **B:** It's one o'clock.
2	A.M. means before noon (the hours between midnight and noon). P.M. means after noon (the hours between noon and midnight). **BE CAREFUL!** When people say 12:00 A.M., they mean midnight. When people say 12:00 P.M., they mean noon.	It's 10:00 A.M. It's 10:00 P.M.
3	We often write time with numbers.	It's one o'clock. = It's **1:00**. It's two-twenty. = It's **2:20**.

3 Plural Nouns: Pronunciation Rules

🎧 PRONUNCIATION RULES

1	The **final sounds** for regular plural nouns are / s /, / z /, and / ɪz /.		
2	The plural is pronounced / s / **after** the **voiceless sounds** / p /, / t /, / k /, / f /, and / θ /.	cups cats books	puffs breaths
3	The plural is pronounced / z / after the **voiced sounds** / b /, / d /, / g /, / v /, / m /, / n /, / ŋ /, / l /, / r /, and / ð /.	cabs cards dogs wives rooms	pans songs balls cars paths
4	The plural is pronounced / z / **after** all **vowel sounds**. Vowels are voiced.	keys tomatoes	movies
5	The plural is pronounced / ɪz / **after** the sounds / s /, / z /, / ʃ /, / ʒ /, / tʃ /, and / dʒ /. (This adds another syllable to the word.)	kisses buzzes dishes	garages matches ages

4 Non-count Nouns and Quantifiers

COMMON NON-COUNT NOUNS*

Food

bread	pasta
broccoli	pepper
butter	pie
cake	pizza
cauliflower	rice
cheese	salsa
chicken	salt
dessert	soup
fish	spaghetti
ice cream	sugar
meat	yogurt

Liquids

coffee	soda
juice	tea
lemonade	water
milk	

Weather

fog	snow
ice	wind
rain	

School Subjects

algebra	history
biology	music
chemistry	psychology
Chinese	science
English	Spanish
geography	

Sports

baseball	soccer
basketball	swimming
football	tennis
gymnastics	volleyball

Abstract Ideas

advice	happiness
beauty	help
energy	noise
existence	stress

Others

furniture	news
homework	paper
information	sleep
mail	time
medicine	work
money	

*Some nouns can be either count or non-count nouns.

Do you want some pizza? (*non-count*)   I don't want salad tonight. (*non-count*)

Let's order a pizza. (*count—an entire pizza*)   Mom is making a salad. (*count*)

QUANTIFIERS

a bottle of (*juice, milk, soda, water*)   a liter of (*juice, milk, soda, water*)

a bowl of (*cereal, soup*)   a loaf of (*bread*)

a can of (*soda, tuna*)   a meter of (*snow, water*)

a cup of (*coffee, hot chocolate, tea*)   a pair of (*gloves, pants, shoes, skis, socks*)

a foot of (*snow, water*)   a piece of (*cake, candy, furniture, meat, paper, pie*)

a gallon of (*gasoline, juice, milk*)   a quart of (*milk, oil*)

a glass of (*juice, milk, water*)   a slice of (*cake, cheese, pie, pizza, toast*)

5　The Simple Present: Pronunciation Rules

PRONUNCIATION RULES FOR THE THIRD-PERSON SINGULAR AFFIRMATIVE

1	The **final sound** for the third-person singular form of the simple present is pronounced / **s** /, / **z** /, or / **ɪz** /. The final sounds of the third-person singular are the same as the final sounds of plural nouns.	/ **s** / walk**s**	/ **z** / ride**s**	/ **ɪz** / danc**es**
2	*Do* and *say* have a change in vowel sound.	I do.　/ **du** / I say.　/ **seɪ** /	She does.　/ **dʌz** / He says.　/ **sɛz** /	

6　The Simple Past: Pronunciation Rules

PRONUNCIATION RULES

1	The **final sounds** for regular verbs in the simple past are / **t** /, / **d** /, and / **ɪd** /.			
2	The final sound is pronounced / **t** / **after** the **voiceless sounds** / **f** /, / **k** /, / **p** /, / **s** /, / **ʃ** /, and /**tʃ**/.	laug**hed** li**ked**	develo**ped** cros**sed**	wa**shed** wat**ched**
3	The final sound is pronounced / **d** / **after** the **voiced sounds** / **b** /, / **g** /, / **dʒ** /, / **l** /, / **m** /, / **n** /, / **r** /, / **ŋ** /, / **ð** /, / **ʒ** /, / **v** /, and / **z** /.	ru**bbed** hu**gged** ju**dged** ca**lled**	hu**mmed** hi**red** ba**nged** ba**thed**	massa**ged** mo**ved** u**sed**
4	The final sound is pronounced / **d** / **after vowel sounds**.	sta**yed** agr**eed**	d**ied** arg**ued**	sn**owed**
5	The final sound is pronounced / **ɪd** / after / **t** / and / **d** /.　/ **ɪd** / adds a syllable.	act end	ac**ted** en**ded**	

7 Base Forms and Past Forms of Common Irregular Verbs

Base Form	Past Form		Base Form	Past Form		Base Form	Past Form
be	was, were		give	gave		say	said
begin	began		go	went		see	saw
break	broke		grow	grew		sing	sang
bring	brought		have	had		sit	sat
build	built		hear	heard		sleep	slept
buy	bought		hit	hit		speak	spoke
come	came		know	knew		spend	spent
do	did		leave	left		stand	stood
drink	drank		lose	lost		swim	swam
drive	drove		make	made		take	took
eat	ate		mean	meant		tell	told
fall	fell		meet	met		think	thought
find	found		put	put		understand	understood
fly	flew		read /rid/	read /rɛd/		wake	woke
forget	forgot		ride	rode		win	won
get	got		run	ran		write	wrote

8 Pronunciation Table

These are the pronunciation symbols used in this text. Listen to the pronunciation of the key words.

VOWELS		CONSONANTS			
Symbol	Key Word	Symbol	Key Word	Symbol	Key Word
i	beat, feed	p	pack, happy	ʃ	ship, machine, station, special, discussion
ɪ	bit, did	b	back, rubber		
eɪ	date, paid	t	tie	ʒ	measure, vision
ɛ	bet, bed	d	die	h	hot, who
æ	bat, bad	k	came, key, quick	m	men, some
ɑ	box, odd, father	g	game, guest	n	sun, know, pneumonia
ɔ	bought, dog	tʃ	church, nature, watch	ŋ	sung, ringing
oʊ	boat, road	dʒ	judge, general, major	w	wet, white
ʊ	book, good	f	fan, photograph	l	light, long
u	boot, food, student	v	van	r	right, wrong
ʌ	but, mud, mother	θ	thing, breath	y	yes, use, music
ə	banana, among	ð	then, breathe	t	butter, bottle
ɚ	shirt, murder	s	sip, city, psychology		
aɪ	bite, cry, buy, eye	z	zip, please, goes		
aʊ	about, how				
ɔɪ	voice, boy				
ɪr	beer				
ɛr	bare				
ɑr	bar				
ɔr	door				
ʊr	tour				

GLOSSARY OF GRAMMAR TERMS

action verb   A verb that describes an action.
- *Jeremy and Yoshio **are studying** at the library.*
- *Tim **drives** to work every day.*

adjective   A word that describes a noun or pronoun.
- *Redmond is a **small peaceful** city.*

adverb   A word that describes an action verb, an adverb, an adjective, or a sentence.
- *We're leaving on vacation **tomorrow**.*

adverb of frequency   A word that tells how often something happens.
- *We **usually** eat lunch at noon.*

affirmative statement   A sentence that does not use a negative verb form (*not*).
- ***I have two brothers.***

apostrophe   A punctuation mark (') used to show possession and to write a contraction.
- *He's in my father's car.*

base form   The simple form of a verb without any ending, such as -*ing*, -*ed*, or -*s*.
- *Arnold is going to **come** at 8:00. We can **eat** then.*

be going to future   A verb form used to make predictions, express general facts in the future, or to talk about definite plans that were made before now.
- *Amanda says it**'s going to be** cold, so she**'s going to take** a coat.*

capital letter   The large form of a letter of the alphabet. Sentences start with a capital letter.
- ***A**, **B**, **C**, etc.*

comma   A punctuation mark (,) used to separate items in a list or parts of a sentence.
- *We went to a restaurant**,** and we ate chicken**,** potatoes**,** and broccoli.*

common noun   A noun for a person, place, or thing. It is not capitalized.
- *The **man** got a **book** at the **library**.*

comparative form   An adjective or adverb ending in -*er* or following *more*. It is used in comparing two things or people.
- *My sister is **older** and **more intelligent** than my brother.*

consonants   The letters ***b**, **c**, **d**, **f**, **g**, **h**, **j**, **k**, **l**, **m**, **n**, **p**, **q**, **r**, **s**, **t**, **v**, **x**, **z*** , and sometimes ***w*** and ***y***.

contraction   A short form of two words. An apostrophe (') replaces the missing letter(s).
- ***it's*** = *it is*
- ***I'm*** = *I am*
- ***can't*** = *cannot*

count noun   A noun you can count. It usually has a singular and a plural form.
- *The **man** has one big **dog** and two small **dogs**.*

definite article *the*   It makes a noun specific.
- *We saw a movie. **The** movie starred Jackie Chan.*

exclamation point   An end punctuation mark (**!**). It shows strong emotion.
- *Help**!** Call the police**!***

formal language   Language we usually use for business settings, academic settings, or with people we don't know.
- ***Good morning, ladies** and **gentlemen. May** we begin?*

imperative   A sentence used to give instructions, directions, commands, and suggestions. It uses the base form of the verb. The subject (*you*) is not a part of the sentence.
- ***Turn** right at the corner. **Drive** to the end of the street. **Stop!***

indefinite article *a* or *an*   Words used before singular non-count nouns.
- *Josh brought **a** sandwich and **an** apple for lunch.*

informal language   The language we usually use with family and friends, in email messages, and in other informal settings.
- ***Hey**, Jeremy, **what's up**?*

irregular verb   A verb that does not form the simple past by adding -*d* or -*ed*.

- They **ate** a fancy meal last night. Jessica's boss **came** to dinner.

negative statement   A statement with a negative verb form (*not*).

- **Ben didn't study. He wasn't ready for the test.**

non-action (stative) verb   A verb that does not describe an action. It can describe an emotion, a state, a sense, or a thought. We usually don't use non-action verbs in the progressive.

- I **like** that actor. He **is** very famous, and I **believe** he won an award.

non-count noun   A noun we usually do not count. We don't put *a*, *an*, or a number before a non-count noun.

- All we need is **rice**, **water**, **salt**, and **butter**.

noun   A word that refers to a person, animal, place, thing, or idea.

- **Annie** has a **friend** at the **library**. She gave her a **book** about **birds**.

noun modifier   A noun that describes another noun.

- Samantha is a **chemistry** professor. She loves **spy** movies.

object   A noun or pronoun that receives the action of the verb.

- Jason sold a **car**. Mark bought **it**.

object pronoun   A pronoun following a verb or a preposition.

- We asked **him** to show the photos to **them**.

ordinal number   The form of a number that shows the order or sequence of something.

- The team scored 21 points in the **first** quarter and 33 in the **fourth** quarter.

period   A punctuation mark (**.**) used at the end of a statement or to show an abbreviation.

- Mr**.** Mendoza, please call on Saturday**.**

plural   The form that means more than one.

- **We** sat in **our chairs** reading **our books**.

possessive   An adjective, noun, or pronoun that shows belonging.

- **Her** book is in **John's** car. **Mine** is at the office.

preposition   A word that goes before a noun or pronoun object. A preposition often shows time or place.

- Maria saw it **on** the table **at** two o'clock.

present progressive   A verb form that shows an action happening now or planned for the future.

- I**'m working** hard now, but I**'m taking** a vacation soon.

pronoun   A word that replaces a noun or a noun phrase.

- **He** is a friend. I know **him** well.

proper noun   The actual name of a person, place, or thing. A proper noun begins with a capital letter.

- **Helen** is living in **St. Louis**. She is studying **Spanish** at **Washington University**.

quantifier   A word or phrase that comes before a noun and expresses an amount or number of that noun.

- Jeannette used **a little** sugar, **some** flour, **four** eggs, and **a quart of** milk.

question mark   A punctuation mark (**?**) used at the end of a question.

- Where are you going**?** How long are you going to be out**?**

regular verb   A verb that forms the simple past by adding -*d* or -*ed*.

- We **lived** in Kenya. My mother **visited** us there.

sentence   A group of words with a subject and a verb. It can stand alone.

- **We opened the window.**
- **Did they paint the house?**

simple past   A verb form used to show a completed action or idea in the past.

- The plane **landed** at 9:00. We **took** a bus to the hotel.

simple present   A verb form used to show habitual actions or states, general facts, or conditions that are true now.

- Yoshio **loves** to ski, and it **snows** a lot in his area, so he**'s** very happy.

singular   The form that means only one.

- **I** put on **my hat** and **coat** and closed the **door**.

small letter   The small form of a letter of the alphabet. We use small letters for most words except for proper nouns and the first word of a sentence.

- *a*, *b*, *c*, etc.

subject   The person, place, or thing that a sentence is about.

- **The children** ate at the mall.

subject pronoun   A pronoun used to replace a subject noun.

- Kathy works hard. **She** loves her work.

syllable   A group of letters with one vowel sound. Words are made up of one or more syllables.

- One syllable—**win**
- Two syllables—**ta ble**
- Three syllables—**im por tant**

third-person singular   The verb form used with *he*, *she*, and *it*.

- Jessica **is** a reporter. She **works** for a TV station.

verb   A word used to describe an action, a fact, or a state.

- Ken **drives** to work now. He **has** a new car, and he **is** a careful driver.

vowels   The letters *a*, *e*, *i*, *o*, *u*, and sometimes *w* and *y*.

wh- question   A question that asks for information. It begins with *how, what, when, where, why, which, who,* or *whose.*

- **What's** your name?
- **Where** are you from?
- **How** do you feel?

yes / no question   A question that has a *yes* or a *no* answer.

- **Did you arrive on time?** Yes, I did.
- **Are you from Uruguay?** No, I'm not.
- **Can you swim well?** Yes, I can.

PUZZLES, GAMES, AND INFORMATION GAP
ANSWER KEY

UNIT 4

After You Read

    E. the Space Needle

UNIT 10

8. True or False?

    1. Antonio Banderas comes from Spain. / True

    2. Most people in China eat with chopsticks. / True

    3. People in Japan drive on the right. / False: People in Japan drive on the left.

    4. People in Great Britain drive on the right. / False: People in Great Britain drive on the left.

    5. People live at the North Pole. / False: People don't live at the North Pole.

    6. Penguins live in deserts. / False: Penguins live in Antarctica.

    7. It snows in Chile in July. / True.

UNIT 12

8. Information Gap

Student A's Answers

    2. relatives: your parents, brothers, sisters, grandparents, and so on

    3. opposite: totally different

    4. smart: intelligent

    5. cousins: the children of your aunt or uncle

    6. cute: good-looking

    7. single: not married

    8. second: between first and third

Student B's Answers

    2. boring: not interesting   **6.** unhappy: sad

    3. noon: 12 P.M.   **7.** terrible: very bad

    4. midnight: 12 A.M.   **8.** nice: good

    5. super: great

UNIT 13

2. Who Am I?

Wolfgang Amadeus Mozart

UNIT 19

8. Writing

    A. a salad

UNIT REVIEW ANSWER KEY

Note: In this answer key, where a short or contracted form is given, the full or long form is also correct (unless the purpose of the exercise is to practice the short or contracted forms).

UNIT 1

A 1. This is 3. This is 5. These are
  2. These are 4. This is

B 1. She 3. It 5. We
  2. He 4. They

C 1. These are 3. We're 5. I'm
  2. Is this 4. Are

UNIT 2

A 1. spoons 3. forks 5. pots
  2. glasses 4. knives

B 1. a chicken 3. apples 5. a notebook
  2. bananas 4. an umbrella

C 1. These are good ~~muffin~~. *muffins*

  2. I have ~~a~~ idea. *an*

  3. My sister has two ~~child~~. *children*

  4. My roommate is from ~~canada~~. *Canada*

  5. I need ‸ fork. *a*

UNIT 3

A 1. It is 3. She is 5. We are
  2. He is 4. They are

B 1. It's expensive.

  2. They're not on vacation. OR They aren't on vacation.

  3. I'm not a chef.

  4. He's not in Australia. OR He isn't in Australia.

  5. We're in the class.

C 1. **A:** The hotels ~~is~~ cheap here. *are*
  B: ~~You~~ right. ~~They~~ great. *You're* *They're*

  2. **A:** ~~Machiko~~ from Seattle. She's a student. *Machiko's*
  B: No, ~~she~~ not. She's a chef. *she's*

UNIT 4

A 1. That 3. that 5. Those
  2. those 4. That

B 1. He 3. your 5. It's
  2. Her 4. They

C **A:** Is that ~~you~~ family in the photo? *your*

  B: Yes. That's ~~me~~ brother and sister. *my*

  A: What are ~~they're~~ names? *their*

  B: ~~He's~~ name is Robert, and her name is Tammy. *His*

  A: And is that ~~you're~~ dog? *your*

  B: Yes. Its name is "Spot."

UNIT 5

A 1. d 3. e 5. b
  2. c 4. a

B 1. Who 3. who 5. who
  2. What 4. What

C 1. **A:** Is he a dentist?
  B: No, he's not. ~~He~~ a writer. *He's*

  2. **A:** Is your sister single?
  B: No, ~~she~~ not. *she's*

  3. **A:** Is your mother a travel agent?
  B: No, she ~~no is~~. *isn't*

  4. **A:** ~~Is~~ you from Brazil? *Are*
  B: Yes, ~~I'm~~. *I am*

UNIT 6

A 1. in 3. at 5. on the
  2. in 4. between

B 1. on 4. next to
  2. between 5. on the corner of
  3. across from

C 1. **A:** Is your apartment ~~in~~ the second floor? *on*
  B: No, it's on the ~~three~~ floor. *third*

  2. **A:** ~~Where~~ the bookstore? *Where's*
  B: It's ‸ First Avenue. *on*
  A: Is it next ‸ the museum? *to*
  B: Yes, it is.

UNIT 7

A 1. Were   3. were   5. wasn't
    2. weren't   4. Was   6. was

B 1. he wasn't. He was at the library.
    2. they weren't. They were sick.

C Kathy,

Sorry I ~~weren't~~ *wasn't* at the basketball game on Tuesday afternoon. I ~~were~~ *was* sick at home. It ~~be~~ *was* really boring.

~~Are~~ *Were* you at the gym yesterday? ~~Was~~ *Were* Amanda and Josh there?

Mark

UNIT 8

A **A:** Where were you last night?
    B: I was at the movies.
    A: How was the movie?
    B: It was funny.
    A: Who were you with?
    B: I was with Jane and Andrew.

B 1. Where   3. Who   5. When
    2. How   4. How long

C **A:** Hi. How ~~were~~ *was* your vacation?
    B: It ^*was* great.
    A: Where ~~was~~ *were* you?
    B: In London.
    A: In London? How *was* the weather ~~was~~?
    B: It was rainy.

UNIT 9

A 1. don't open   3. Don't eat   5. Turn
    2. Read   4. Don't worry

B ~~Do not~~ *Don't* start Unit ~~9~~ *10*.
Don't start Unit 10.

C 1. Please ~~to~~ stop at the corner.
    2. ~~You not~~ *Don't* make a U-turn.
    3. ~~Turns~~ *Turn* right, please.
    4. ~~Don't please~~ *Please don't* park here.
    5. Don't ~~to~~ turn left.

UNIT 10

A 1. likes . . . doesn't like
    2. don't want . . . wants . . . want

B 1. live   2. likes . . . like   3. has . . . have

C 1. Look at this photo.
    2. This is my cousin Juan. He ~~don't~~ *doesn't* look like me!
    3. Juan and his wife, Alicia, ~~lives~~ *live* in Spain.
    4. Alicia ~~is stay~~ *stays* at home with the children, and Juan ~~work~~ *works* in an office.
    5. They both ~~speaks~~ *speak* Spanish very well.

UNIT 11

A 1. b   3. c
    2. a   4. d

B 1. **A:** Does Steve's radio work?
      B: No, it doesn't.
    2. **A:** Does the store have radios?
      B: Yes, it does.
    3. **A:** Do Tim and Jeremy work at Goodbuys?
      B: No, they don't.

C **A:** ~~Does~~ *Do* you want to go to the park today?
    B: Sorry. I need to get a gift for my sister. Do you ~~has~~ *have* any ideas?
    A: Sure. Does she ~~likes~~ *like* music? CDs are a good gift.
    B: No, she ~~don't~~ *doesn't*.
    A: Well, does she like books?
    B: Yes, she ~~is~~ *does*. Thanks. That's a great idea!

UNIT 12

A 1. What time   3. Why
    2. Who OR What   4. What

B 1. Where do your cousins live?
    2. When does your father start work?
    3. What does he do?
    4. How does he like his job?
    5. Why do you and your sister walk to school?
    6. What time does your cat wake up?

C **A:** I have a new job.
    B: Really? Where ~~you do~~ *do you* work?
    A: At GoodBuys.
    B: What ~~does~~ *do* you do?
    A: I'm an *electronic technician*.
    B: What ~~means~~ *does* *electronic technician* *mean*^?
    A: An electronic technician fixes electronic devices.
    B: How ~~are~~ *do* you like the work?
    A: I like it a lot.

B: What time ~~do~~ you start?
 (do inserted)

A: At 9:00 in the morning.

UNIT 13

A **1.** e   **3.** b   **5.** d
   2. a   **4.** c

B **1.** is   **3.** has   **5.** are
   2. does . . . have   **4.** Does . . . have

C **A:** Could you please meet my friend Maria at the bus stop?

B: OK. What does she look like?

A: ~~She~~ *She's* thin, and she ~~have~~ *has* brown hair and brown eyes.

B: ~~Has~~ *Is* she tall or short?

A: She ~~has~~ *is* average height.

B: ~~Is~~ *Does* she have short hair?

A: No, it's long.

UNIT 14

A **1.** c   **3.** a
   2. d   **4.** b

B **1. A:** How often do you skip lunch?

   B: I sometimes skip lunch.

   2. A: What do you usually do on the weekends?

   B: I often go to the movies.

   3. A: Do you ever eat donuts for breakfast?

   B: No, I never do.

C **A:** Do you always ~~be~~ eat healthy food?

B: Oh, yes. I ~~am~~ usually eat a lot of fruit and vegetables.

A: Do you ~~have ever~~ *ever have* fast food?

B: Rarely—and only on the weekend.

A: And I hear you ~~have always~~ *always have* breakfast.

B: Yes, I *never* skip breakfast ~~never~~. Breakfast is very important!

UNIT 15

A **1.** 'm talking   **4.** 's watching
   2. 'm not doing   **5.** aren't feeling
   3. isn't doing   **6.** 're playing

B **1.** Jessica and her family are living in Redmond.

   2. Jessica is standing between her parents.

   3. Jessica's mother and father are not working.

   4. Tim and Steve are watching a game on TV.

C **1.** He not standing. *(He isn't OR He's not)*

   2. ~~She~~ *She's* wearing glasses.

   3. It isn't ~~snow~~ *snowing* today.

   4. They're ~~listen~~ *listening* to a CD.

   5. ~~We not~~ *We're not OR We aren't* playing cards.

UNIT 16

A **1.** e   **3.** d   **5.** a
   2. b   **4.** c

B **1. A:** Is Rob going to the movies?

   B: he isn't OR he's not

   2. A: Are John and Eleanor celebrating an anniversary?

   B: they're not OR they aren't

C **1. A:** Is *it* snowing?

   B: Yes, ~~it's~~ *it is*.

   2. A: Are you ~~make~~ *making* a mess?

   B: No, I *I'm* not.

   3. A: Are the children ~~be~~ doing their homework?

   B: No, ~~they not~~ *they're not OR they aren't*. They're watching TV.

UNIT 17

A **1.** c   **3.** b   **5.** a
   2. e   **4.** d

B **1.** What is Steve watching on TV?

   2. Why are you calling me now?

   3. How are you enjoying the class?

   4. Who is taking the bus to work?

   5. Where are you going with that book?

C **1. A:** ~~Who~~ *Who's* teaching the class?

   B: ~~Mark's~~ *Mark is*.

   2. A: Why ~~you are~~ *are you* smiling?

   B: I'm ~~watch~~ *watching* a funny movie.

   3. A: What is your sister ~~wear~~ *wearing*?

   B: A blue sweatshirt and jeans.

UNIT 18

A **1.** this   **3.** those   **5.** That's
   2. that   **4.** these

B **1.** Mark's   **3.** Smiths' . . . Mr. Bryant's
   2. children's

C **1. A:** Is that a new dress?

   B: No, it's my ~~sisters'~~ *sister's* dress.

2. A: Do you like ~~this~~ *these* glasses on me?

B: Yes, I really like ~~that~~ *those* glasses. They make you look smart.

3. A: Why are you wearing your ~~mom~~ *mom's* slacks?

B: Because my jeans don't fit. ~~That~~ *That's* why.

4. A: Where are my keys?

B: They're on ~~this~~ *that* counter over there.

UNIT 19

A 1. chips   3. pizza   5. milk
    2. cereal   4. water

B 1. an   3. a   5. cup of
    2. any   4. Ø

C 1. I always drink two ~~cup~~ *cups* of coffee for breakfast.

    2. Usually I have ~~an~~ eggs and ∧ *a* slice of toast.

    3. Sometimes I have fruit, like ∧ bananas.

    4. I also like ~~any~~ *some* milk and cereal.

UNIT 20

A 1. d   3. a
    2. c   4. b

B 1. **A:** one

    B: one

    2. **A:** an umbrella in general

    B: a specific umbrella

    3. **A:** one library

    B: a book in general

C 1. Bozo's suit is a very bright ~~ones~~ *one*.

    2. Each shoe is ~~the~~ *a* different color.

    3. He's wearing ~~a~~ *an* orange shoe and ~~an~~ *a* yellow one.

    4. He's wearing ~~the~~ *a* funny hat too.

    5. He looks like a clown!

UNIT 21

A 1. can't   3. can't
    2. Can   4. Can

B 1. **A:** Can . . . explain   **B:** can't read

    A: can help

    2. **B:** can't watch   **A:** can . . . do

    B: can go

C **A:** Pietro can't ~~speaks~~ *speak* Chinese. He can ~~to~~ speak Italian.

    B: Can he ~~speaking~~ *speak* Spanish?

    A: No, he ~~not can~~ *can't*, but I ~~can't~~ *can*.

UNIT 22

A 1. checked in . . . didn't check out

    2. studied . . . didn't watch TV

    3. started . . . didn't finish

B 1. graduated   3. didn't work   5. ended up
    2. started   4. failed

C 1. We didn't ~~stayed~~ *stay* with our friends.
    2. The guests ~~are~~ arrived at the hotel.
    3. I ~~call~~ *called* you this morning.
    4. She ~~was enjoy~~ *enjoyed* her trip.

UNIT 23

A 1. went   3. ate   5. drank
    2. made   4. saw   6. fell

B 1. Did . . . play   3. Did . . . snow
    2. Did . . . stay up   4. Did . . . take

C 1. **A:** ~~You moved~~ *Did you move* to this city in 2009?

    B: No, I ~~don't~~ *didn't*. I moved here in 2010.

    2. **A:** Did Katharine ~~took~~ *take* her keys?

    B: No, she didn't.

    3. **A:** ~~Do~~ *Did* your parents go out of town?

    B: Yes, they ~~are~~ went on vacation.

UNIT 24

A 1. c   3. e   5. b
    2. d   4. a

B 1. When did the accident happen?

    2. How did the accident happen?

    3. Why did Rob drive to the supermarket?

    4. Who did Rob drive there with?

    5. Where did Rob take the car?

C **A:** Where did the accident ~~happened~~ *happen*?

    B: It ~~did happen~~ *happened* in front of the library.

    A: When ~~it was~~ *did it* occur?

    B: It occurred at 10:00 this morning.

    A: How ~~it happened~~ *did it happen*?

    B: A car hit another car.

    A: How long did it ~~takes~~ *take* the police to come?

    B: It took 20 minutes.

A **1. A.** him   **B.** He
   2. A. they   **B.** them . . . We

B **1.** her   **3.** them   **5.** them
   2. him   **4.** her

C Dear Doris and Jim,

   Thank you for inviting ~~we~~ _us_ to the party on June

10. ~~Us~~ _We_ will bring some cookies for dessert. ~~It~~ _They_ are

really good, and we hope you like ~~they~~ _them_. I don't have

your address. Could you please email ~~its~~ _it_ to us?

See you on Saturday!
Sarah and Stan

A **1.** many   **3.** much   **5.** much
   2. many   **4.** many

B **1.** A lot   **3.** a little   **5.** Not much
   2. Not many   **4.** A lot

C **1. A:** How much time do you spend on the phone
      each week?
      B: Not ~~many~~ _much_ time. Only a couple of hours.
   2. A: How many movies do you see each year?
      B: Not ~~much~~ _many_. Only two or three.
   3. A: How ~~much~~ _many_ email messages do you send
      each day?
      B: Each day? Only one or two. But I send a
      ~~little~~ _lot_ of text messages—maybe 20 or 30.
   4. A: How much time do you spend surfing the
      Internet?
      B: I spend ~~many~~ _a lot of_ time. Maybe six hours a day!

A **1.** Is there   **3.** are there   **5.** there are
   2. there is   **4.** there's

B **1.** there   **3.** They   **5.** There
   2. there   **4.** they

C **A:** What is the West Edmonton Mall?
   B: ~~There's~~ _It's_ a gigantic shopping center in
      Edmonton, Canada.
   A: What is ~~they~~ _there_ to see in the mall?
   B: Well, ~~there~~ _it_ is probably the biggest mall in
      North America. ~~There~~ _It_ has 800 stores, and it is
      even a skating rink.

A **1.** personal   **3.** artistic   **5.** honest
   2. spy   **4.** fun-loving

B **1.** new running shoes
   2. big chicken sandwiches
   3. an expensive wool suit
   4. a popular pizza restaurant
   5. a brick apartment building

C I'm ~~an~~ _a_ smart, lively 35-year-old woman. I like to

cook, and I enjoy ~~longs~~ _long_ walks on the beach. I'm

not a ~~tennis-great~~ _great tennis_ player, but I love to play tennis!

I'm looking for ~~a~~ _an_ educated, ~~man sensitive~~ _sensitive man_. Do you
have similar interests? Let's get together!

A **1.** faster   **3.** healthier   **5.** worse
   2. more expensive   **4.** better

B **1. A:** Is Miami hotter than Los Angeles?
      B: I think Miami is hotter.
   2. A: Are amusement parks more interesting than
      museums?
      B: I think amusement parks are more
      interesting.
   3. A: Are you older than your sister?
      B: Yes, but she's taller.

C I met two interesting men through the personal

ads—Ken and John. Ken is smarter and ~~funny~~ _funnier_
than John. But John is ~~more~~ richer and more

handsome. Ken is ~~more nice~~ _nicer_, so I think Ken is
much ~~good~~ _better_.

A **1.** in   **3.** at   **5.** on
   2. on   **4.** in

B **1. A:** What do your children do in the afternoon?
      B: They often watch TV in the afternoon.
   2. A: What time is breakfast?
      B: Breakfast is usually at 8:00.
   3. A: Where do you go on holidays?
      B: We usually go to the beach on holidays.

C On weekdays, my life is a little boring. I usually

leave the house at 6:00 _in_ the morning. I start

work at 8:00, and I go home at 6:00 P.M. ~~On~~ _At_
dinnertime, I surf the Internet. Then I make

phone calls ~~at~~ _in_ the evening. I go to bed at 11:00 at
~~the~~ night.

UNIT 31

A 1. 'm not going to study 4. 're not going to drive
2. are going to win 5. 're going to love
3. 's going to snow

B 1. They are going to win.
2. We are going to be late.
3. It is not going to rain.
4. The game is going to start soon.
5. We are going to get there on time.

C Dear Amanda,

Thanks for your note! I am going *to* be in town Sunday evening. I'd love to come to your party, but some friends and I are going *to* go out for dinner. Their son *is* going to graduate, and ~~is it~~ *it is* probably going to be a long evening. I ~~not am~~ *am not* going to get to your house by 5:00. Can I come over at around 9:00? Or is that too late?

Kathy

UNIT 32

A 1. b 3. e 5. c
2. d 4. a

B 1. is . . . going to be 3. are . . . going to get
2. is . . . going to start 4. are . . . going to go

C 1. Hi Karen. This is Pietro. I'm not ~~to going~~ *going to* be in the office until 12:00. Bruce and I ~~am~~ *are* going to review the news program.

2. Hi, Debbie. This is Amy. Are you going *to* be in Boston tomorrow? Please call me.

3. This message is for Bill. This is Mark. When ~~the conference is~~ *is the conference* going to start?

4. Hi, Katie. This is Pam. My calendar isn't working. ~~Is~~ *Are* John and Oliva going to have a meeting in the conference room or the library? Let me know.

5. Hi, Linda. This is Paula. What time *is* the meeting going to be? Please email me.

CREDITS

INDEX